THE BLOOMSBURY POCKET ENCYCLOPEDIA OF THE WORLD

Bloomsbury Books
London

CONTENTS

ls

Motorway/Highway

Other Main Road

t scales smaller than 1:3 million

Principal Road: Motorway/Highway

Other Main Road

Main Railway

ns & Cities – Population

> 5,000,000

1-5,000,000

500,000 -1,000,000

< 500,000

aris National Capital

Airport

International Boundary

International Boundary – not defined or in dispute

Internal Boundary

River

Canal

Marsh or Swamp

Relief

Note –

The 0-100 contour layer appears only at scales larger than 1:3 million

▲ 1510 Peak (in metres)

5000 metres

4000

3000

2000

1000

500

200

100

0

Land below sea level

Alaska
(U.S.A.)
CANADA
Greenland
(Den.)
ICELAND
NORWAY
SWEDEN
DENMARK
IRELAND
U.K.
GERMANY
NETH.
BELG.
FRANCE
SW.
AUST.
SLO.
CRO.
ITALY
UNITED STATES
OF AMERICA
Açores
PORTUGAL
SPAIN
TUNISIA
MOROCCO
Canary Is.
MEXICO
THE BAHAMAS
Western
Sahara
ALGERIA
LIBYA
CUBA
JAMAICA
DOM. REP.
BELIZE
HAITI
MAURITANIA
MALI
NIGER
GUATEMALA
HONDURAS
EL SALVADOR
NICARAGUA
CAPE VERDE
IS.
SENEGAL
THE GAMBIA
CHAD
COSTA RICA
TRIN. &
TOBAGO
BURKINA
FASO
GUINEA-BISSAU
GUINEA
VENEZUELA
NIGERIA
PANAMA
GUYANA
SIERRA LEONE
SURINAM
LIBERIA
C.A.R.
COLOMBIA
FR. GUIANA
CÔTE
D'IVOIRE
GHANA
TOGO
BENIN
CAM.
EQ.
GUINEA
ECUADOR
GABON
CONGO
ZAIRE
BRAZIL
PERU
ANGOLA
BOLIVIA
NAMIBIA
PARAGUAY
ARGENTINA
URUGUAY
CHILE
Falkland Is.
S. Georgia

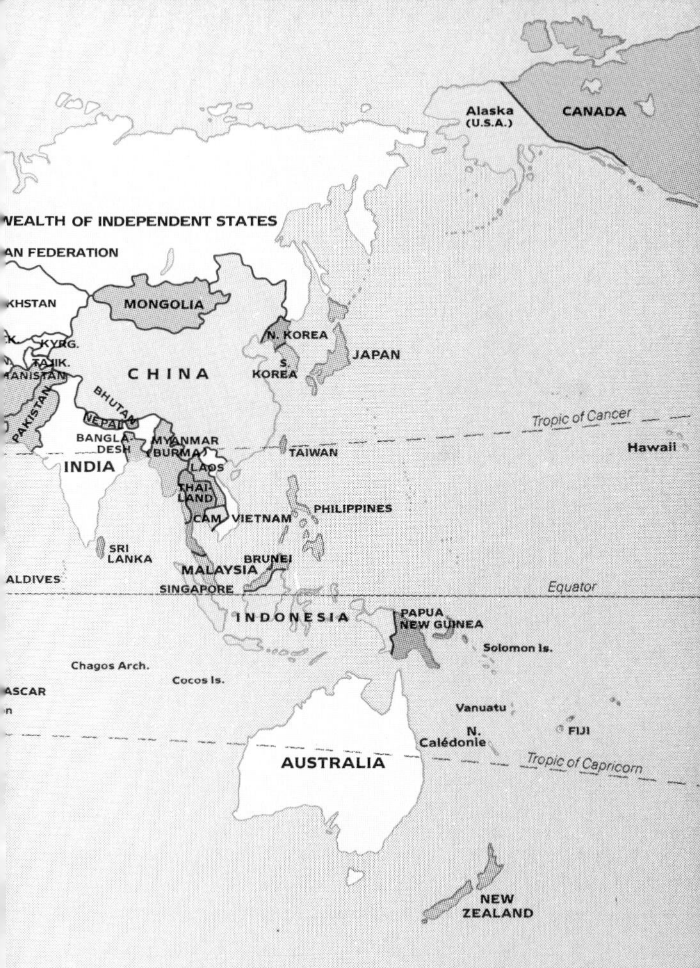

Alaska
(U.S.A.)
CANADA
WEALTH OF INDEPENDENT STATES
AN FEDERATION
KHSTAN
MONGOLIA
KYRG.
TAJIK.
ANISTAN
PAKISTAN
CHINA
N. KOREA
S. KOREA
JAPAN
BHUTAN
NEPAL
BANGLA-
DESH
MYANMAR
(BURMA)
INDIA
LAOS
THAI-
LAND
CAM
VIETNAM
TAIWAN
PHILIPPINES
Tropic of Cancer
Hawaii
SRI
LANKA
BRUNEI
MALAYSIA
ALDIVES
SINGAPORE
Equator
INDONESIA
PAPUA
NEW GUINEA
Solomon Is.
Chagos Arch.
Cocos Is.
ASCAR
Vanuatu
N.
Calédonie
FIJI
AUSTRALIA
Tropic of Capricorn
NEW
ZEALAND

NORTH & CENTRAL AMERICA

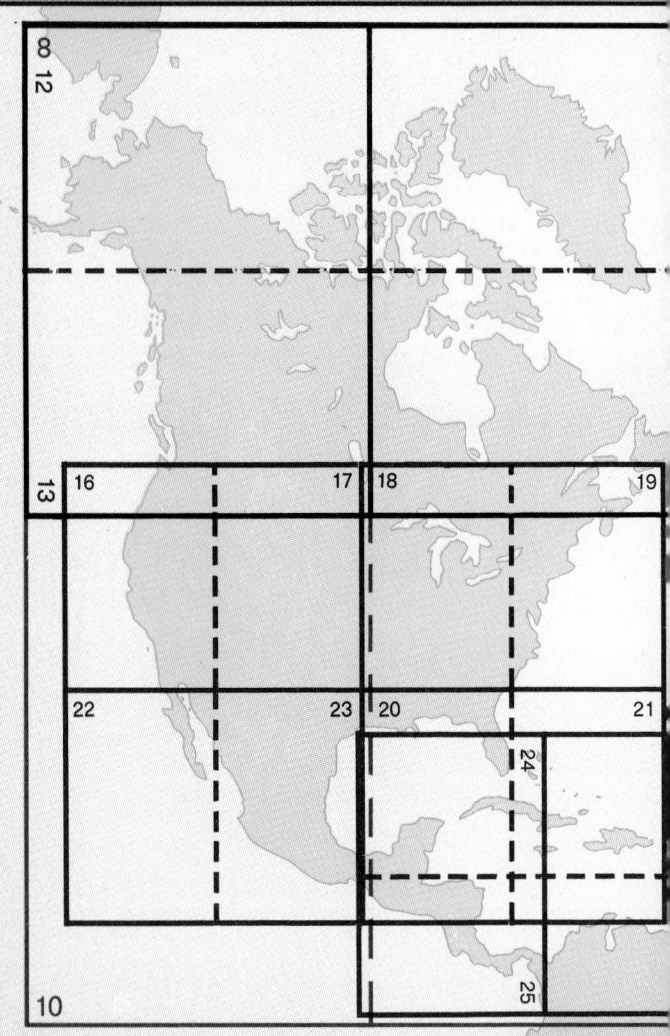

NORTH AMERICA POLITICAL (N)

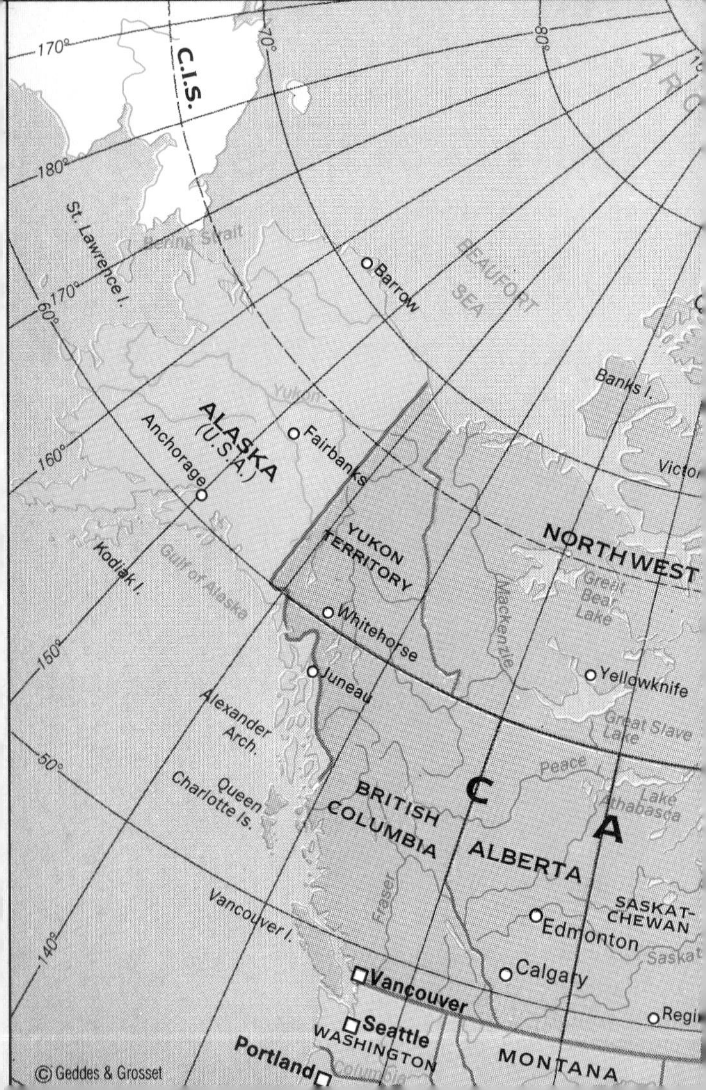

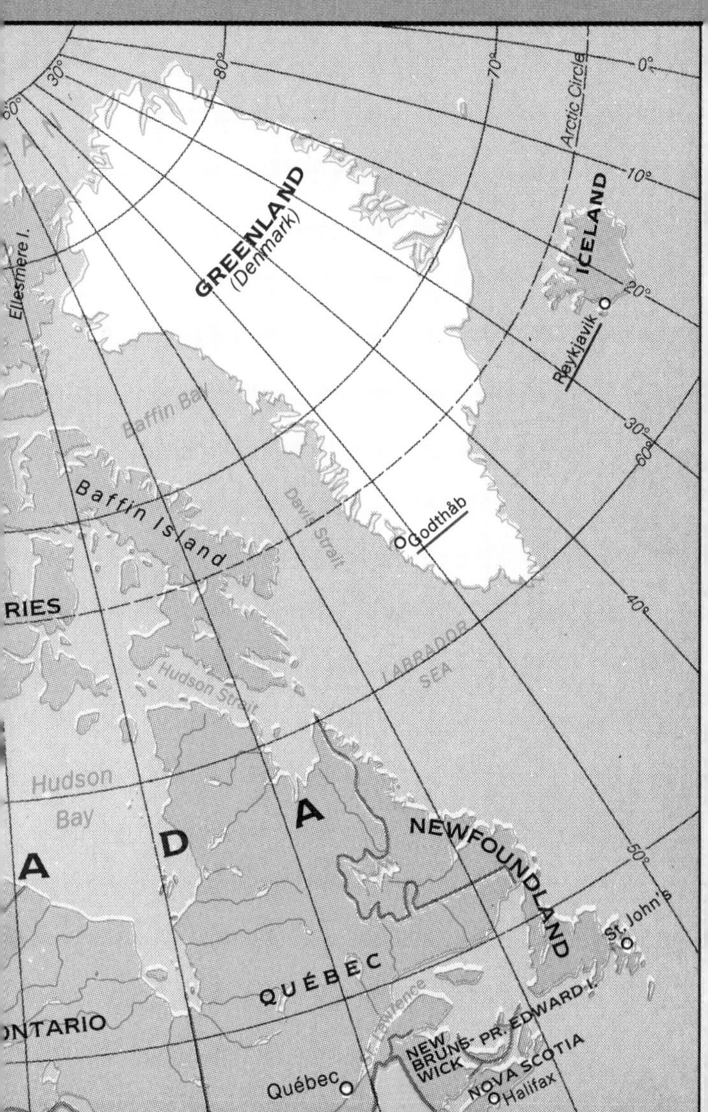

GREENLAND
(Denmark)
ICELAND
Reykjavik
Godthåb
Arctic Circle
Ellesmere I.
Baffin Bay
Baffin Island
Davis Strait
LABRADOR
SEA
Hudson Strait
Hudson
Bay
RIES
A
D
A
NEWFOUNDLAND
St. John's
QUÉBEC
ONTARIO
PR. EDWARD I.
NEW
BRUNS-
WICK
NOVA SCOTIA
Halifax
Québec
0°
10°
20°
30°
40°
50°
60°
70°
80°

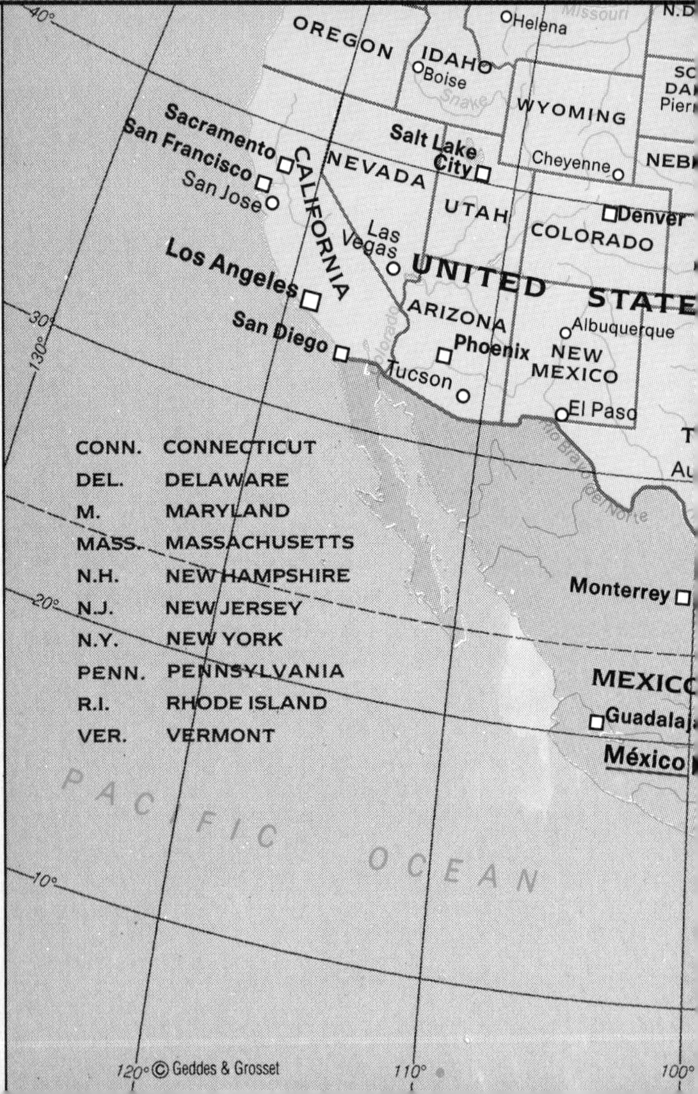

NORTH AMERICA POLITICAL (S)

CONN.	CONNECTICUT
DEL.	DELAWARE
M.	MARYLAND
MASS.	MASSACHUSETTS
N.H.	NEW HAMPSHIRE
N.J.	NEW JERSEY
N.Y.	NEW YORK
PENN.	PENNSYLVANIA
R.I.	RHODE ISLAND
VER.	VERMONT

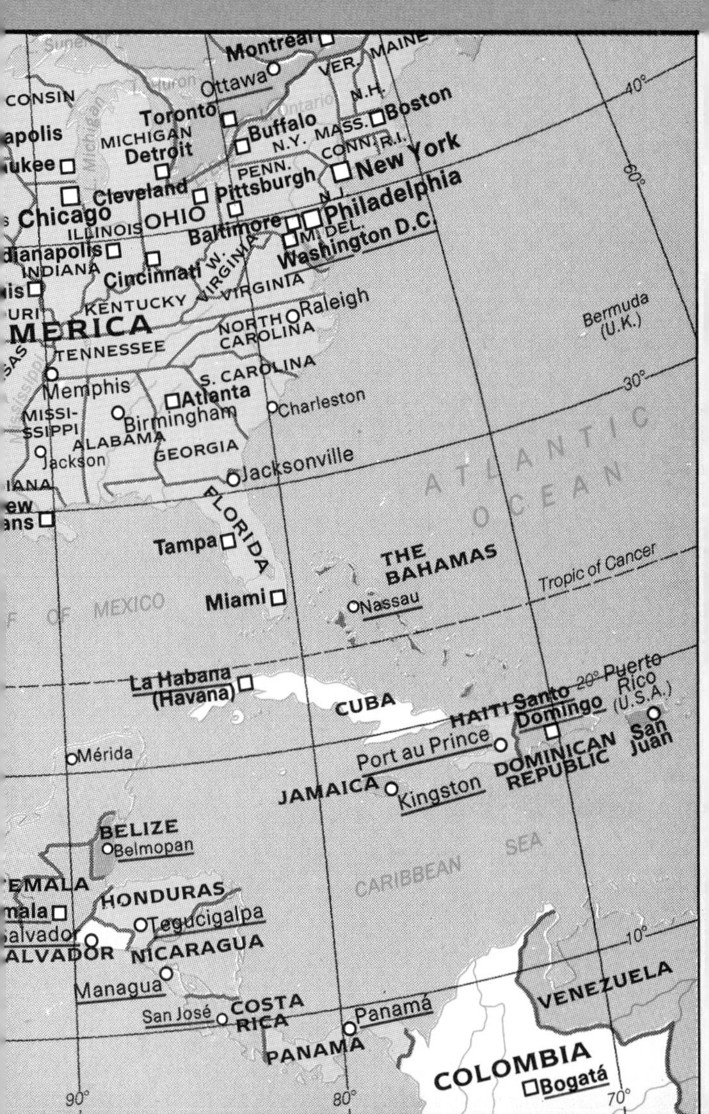
Montreal
Ottawa
VER.
MAINE
N.H.
Toronto
Buffalo
MASS.
Boston
MICHIGAN
Detroit
N.Y.
CONN.
R.I.
PENN.
New York
Pittsburgh
Cleveland
Chicago
ILLINOIS
OHIO
Philadelphia
Baltimore
MD.
DEL.
Washington D.C.
INDIANA
Cincinnati
W. VIRGINIA
VIRGINIA
KENTUCKY
NORTH CAROLINA
Raleigh
TENNESSEE
Memphis
S. CAROLINA
Atlanta
Charleston
MISSISSIPPI
Birmingham
ALABAMA
GEORGIA
Jackson
Jacksonville
FLORIDA
Tampa
Miami
ATLANTIC OCEAN
Bermuda (U.K.)
THE BAHAMAS
Nassau
Tropic of Cancer
MEXICO
La Habana (Havana)
CUBA
HAITI
Santo Domingo
Puerto Rico (U.S.A.)
San Juan
Port au Prince
DOMINICAN REPUBLIC
Mérida
JAMAICA
Kingston
BELIZE
Belmopan
CARIBBEAN SEA
HONDURAS
Tegucigalpa
NICARAGUA
Managua
San José
COSTA RICA
Panamá
PANAMA
VENEZUELA
COLOMBIA
Bogatá
40°
30°
20°
10°
60°
90°
80°
70°

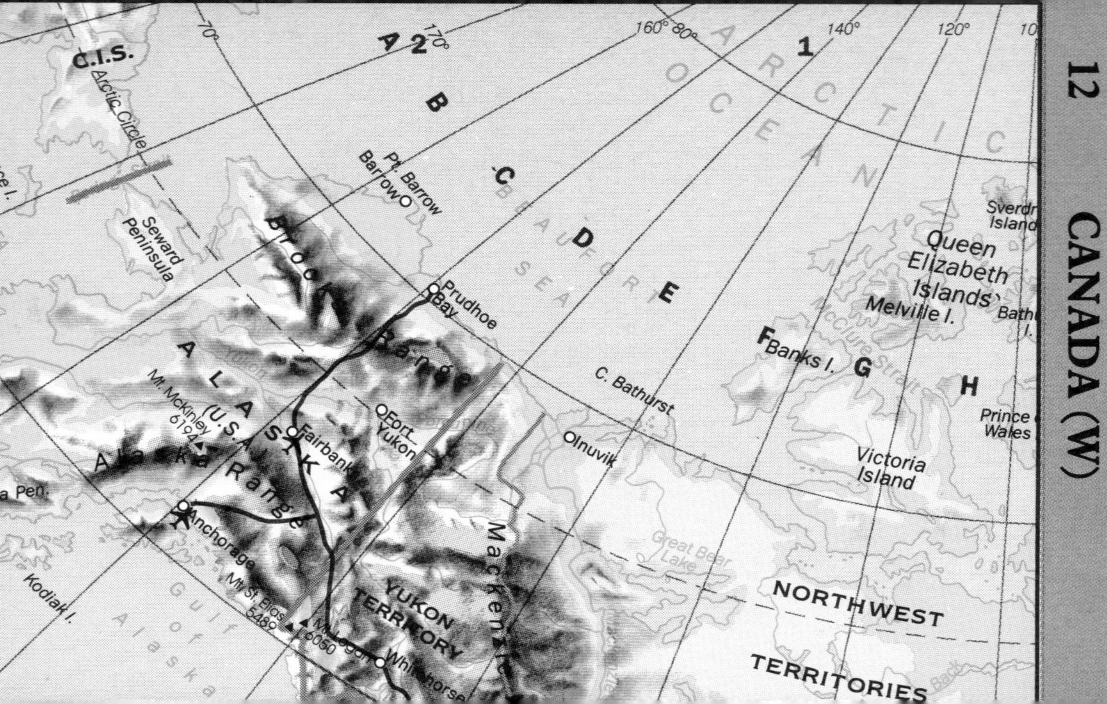
ARCTIC OCEAN
Queen Elizabeth Islands
Melville I.
McClure Strait
Victoria Island
Banks I.
NORTHWEST TERRITORIES
Great Bear Lake
C. Bathurst
Inuvik
BEAUFORT SEA
Mackenzie
Prudhoe Bay
Pt. Barrow
Barrow
Fort Yukon
YUKON TERRITORY
Brooks Range
ALASKA (U.S.A.)
Fairbanks
Alaska Range
Anchorage
Mt. McKinley 6194
Mt. St. Elias 5489
Gulf of Alaska
Seward Peninsula
Arctic Circle
C.I.S.
St. Lawrence I.
BERING SEA
Nunivak I.
Alaska Pen.
Kodiak I.

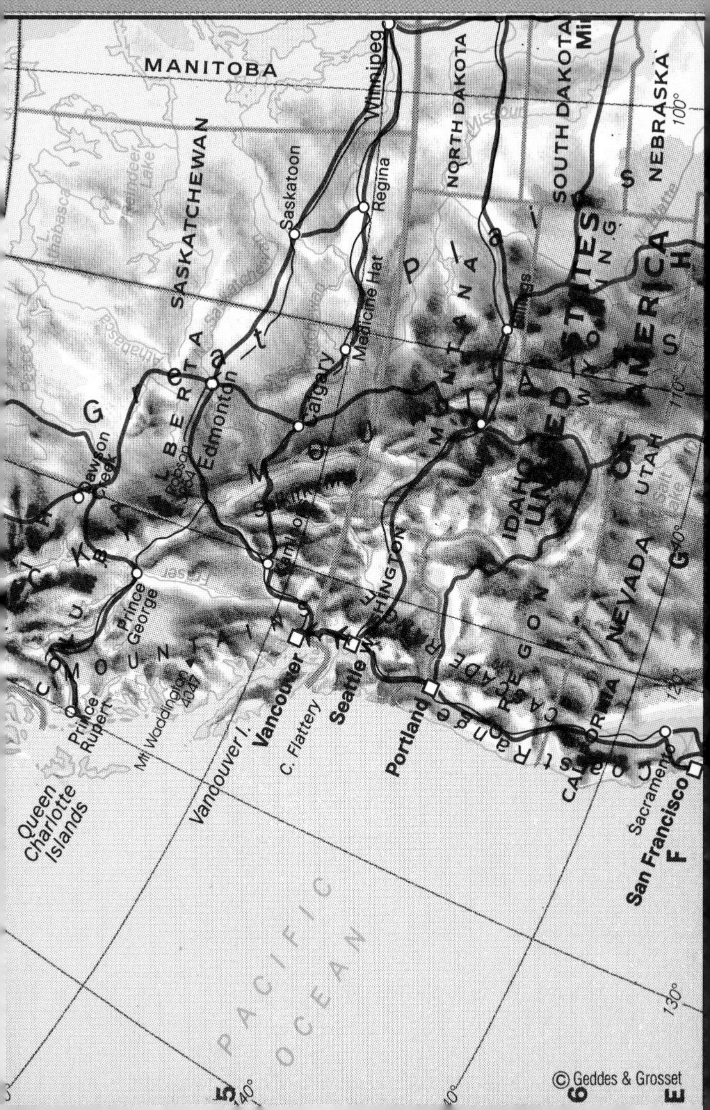
MANITOBA
SASKATCHEWAN
ALBERTA
NORTH DAKOTA
SOUTH DAKOTA
NEBRASKA
MONTANA
WASHINGTON
IDAHO
OREGON
NEVADA
UTAH
CALIFORNIA
UNITED STATES OF AMERICA
Winnipeg
Saskatoon
Regina
Medicine Hat
Calgary
Edmonton
Dawson Creek
Prince George
Prince Rupert
Mt Waddington
Billings
Vancouver
Vancouver I.
C. Flattery
Seattle
Portland
Sacramento
San Francisco
Queen Charlotte Islands
PACIFIC OCEAN
100°
110°
120°
130°
140°

GREENLAND
(Denmark.)
ICELAND
Reykjavik
Arctic Circle
Denmark Strait
Kap Farvel
Julianehåb
(Qaqortoq)
Frederikshåb
(Paamiut)
Godthåb
(Nuuk)
Gunnbjørn Fjeld
3700
Mt. Forel
3360
Davis Strait
Disko
Cumberland Sound
Resolution I.
Thule
Baffin Bay
Baffin Island
Bylot I.
Melville Peninsula
NORTH WEST
TERRITORIES
Ellesmere I.
Axel Heiberg I.
Queen Elizabeth Islands
Devon I.
Somerset I.
Boothia Pen.
© Geddes & Grosset

Churchill
Bay
Churchill
Nelson
Belcher Is.
James Bay
Eastmain
Lake Winnipeg
ONTARIO
Kenora
Thunder Bay
Lake Superior
MINNESOTA
Fargo
UNITED STATES OF AMERICA
St. Paul
Minneapolis
WISCONSIN
Mississippi
IOWA
Sault Ste Marie
Lake Michigan
MICHIGAN
Milwaukee
Chicago
INDIANA
Detroit
Lake Huron
Sudbury
North Bay
Ottawa
Montréal
Toronto
Hamilton
Niagra
Buffalo
Ontario
Erie
Cleveland
OHIO
PENNSYLVANIA
NEW JERSEY
Philadelphia
New York
NEW YORK
VERMONT
NEW HAMPSHIRE
MASS.
CONN.
R.I.
Boston
C. Cod.
MAINE
Québec
Arvida
Laurentian Plateau
QUEBEC
Labrador
NEWFOUNDLAND
Island of Newfoundland
St. Lawrence
Gulf of St. Lawrence
Anticosti I.
NEW BRUNSWICK
Charlottetown
St. John
Prince Edward Island
NOVA SCOTIA
Halifax
C. Sable
Cape Breton I.
Channel-Port-aux-Basques
St. John's
C. Race
CONN. CONNECTICUT
MASS. MASSACHUSETTS
R.I. RHODE ISLAND
ATLANTIC OCEAN
5
6
J
K
L
M
40°
50°
60°
70°
80°
90°

1
2
130°
40°
30°
120°
C. Flattery
BRITISH
Vancouver
WASHINGTON
Seattle
Olympia
Spokane
Portland
Salem
OREGON
Great Sandy Desert
COAST
CASCADE RANGE
Winnemucca
Sacramento
San Francisco
San Jose
Reno
Carson City
NEVADA
Great Basin
Stockton
CALIFORNIA
Sierra Nevada
Fresno
Death Valley
Las Vegas
PACIFIC OCEAN
Los Angeles
Pasadena
Channel Islands
San Diego
Tijuana
Mexicali
Desert
Sono

C
D
110°
100°
Calgary
ALBERTA
SASKATCHEWAN
Regina
MANITOBA
Medicine Hat
CANADA
Winnipeg
MONTANA
Helena
NORTH DAKOTA
Bismarck
Fargo
MINNESOTA
Yellowstone
Billings
Buffalo
SOUTH DAKOTA
Rapid City
Pierre
WYOMING
Casper
Sioux Falls
Missouri
UNITED STATES OF AMERICA
Ogden
NEBRASKA
Omaha
Cheyenne
Platte
Lincoln
Denver
COLORADO
San Juan Mts
Colorado Springs
KANSAS
Topeka
Arkansas
Wichita
Santa Fe
Tulsa
OKLAHOMA
Albuquerque
Amarillo
Oklahoma City
NEW MEXICO
3532
Lubbock
Red

D
E
F
90°
80°
CANADA
ONTARIO
MINNESOTA
Kenora
Thunder Bay
Lake Superior
Duluth
Sault Ste. Marie
Sudbury
North Bay
Ottawa
MICHIGAN
Lake Huron
Minneapolis
St. Paul
WISCONSIN
Rochester
Lake Michigan
Toronto
Hamilton
Niagara
Grand Rapids
Milwaukee
Madison
Lansing
Detroit
Lake Erie
Cleveland
IOWA
Rockford
Chicago
Toledo
Akron
Des Moines
Ft. Wayne
OHIO
INDIANA
ILLINOIS
Colombus
Indianapolis
Dayton
Springfield
Cincinnati
WEST VIRGINIA
UNITED STATES OF AMERICA
Kansas City
Frankfort
Charleston
Jefferson City
St. Louis
Louisville
Evansville
MISSOURI
KENTUCKY
Ozark Plateau
Springfield
Greensboro
Nashville
Knoxville
NORTH
TENNESSEE
Chattanooga
ARKANSAS
Memphis
Huntsville
Little Rock
Atlanta
Augusta
Birmingham

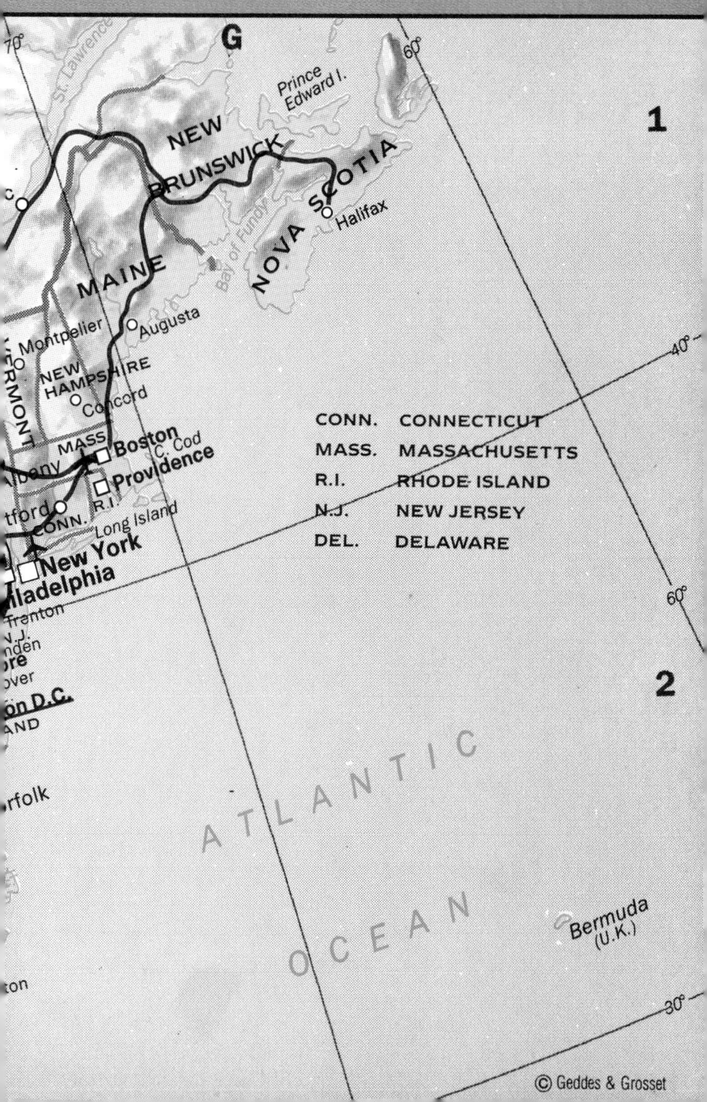
G
Prince Edward I.
1
NEW BRUNSWICK
NOVA SCOTIA
Halifax
Bay of Fundy
MAINE
Augusta
Montpelier
VERMONT
NEW HAMPSHIRE
Concord
MASS.
Boston
C. Cod
Providence
R.I.
CONN.
Long Island
New York
Philadelphia
Trenton
N.J.
2
CONN. CONNECTICUT
MASS. MASSACHUSETTS
R.I. RHODE ISLAND
N.J. NEW JERSEY
DEL. DELAWARE
ATLANTIC
OCEAN
Bermuda (U.K.)

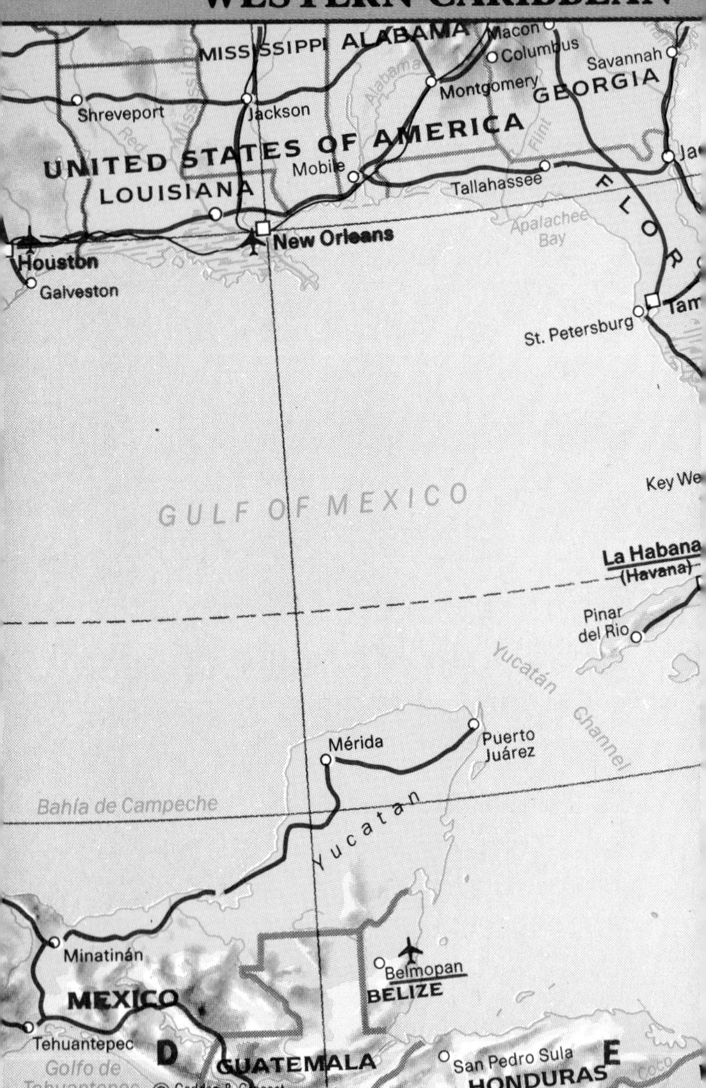
MISSISSIPPI
ALABAMA
Macon
Columbus
Savannah
GEORGIA
Montgomery
Alabama
Shreveport
Jackson
Mississippi
Red
Flint
UNITED STATES OF AMERICA
Mobile
Tallahassee
LOUISIANA
FLOR
Apalachee Bay
New Orleans
Houston
Galveston
St. Petersburg
GULF OF MEXICO
La Habana
(Havana)
Pinar del Rio
Yucatán Channel
Mérida
Puerto Juárez
Bahía de Campeche
Yucatan
Minatinán
Belmopan
BELIZE
MEXICO
Tehuantepec
D
GUATEMALA
San Pedro Sula
E
HONDURAS
Golfo de Tehuantepec
© Geddes & Grosset
90°

3
Great Abaco I.
erdale
Eleuthera I.
THE BAHAMAS
Cat I.
Nassau
dros I.
Long I.
WEST INDIES
Tropic of Cancer
Acklins I.
20°
DOMINICAN REPUBLIC
Great Inagua I.
Camaguey
A
Guantánamo
HAITI
Santo Domingo
Santiago de Cuba
Port au Prince
ls.
4
Kingston
JAMAICA
SEA
CARIBBEAN
Aruba (Neth.)
Curaçao (Neth.)
F
COLOMBIA
VENEZUELA
80°

U.S.A. (S.W.), MEXICO, ALASKA & HAWAIIAN I

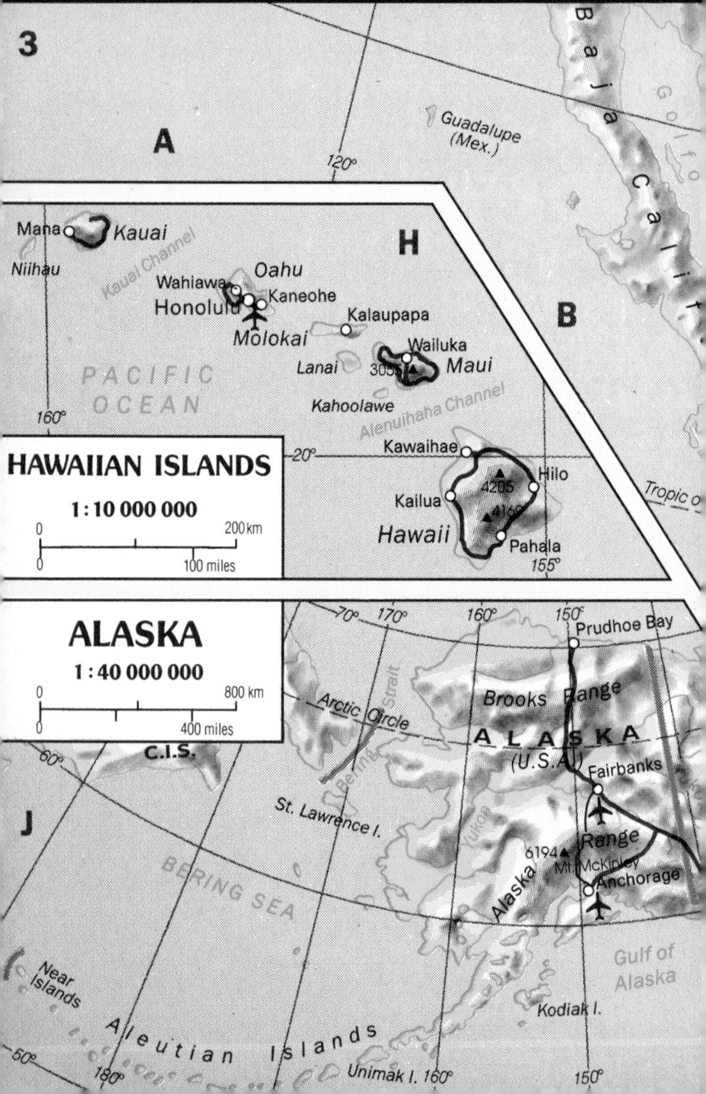

3

A

Guadalupe (Mex.)

120°

Baja Calif

Golfo

H

B

Mana
Kauai
Niihau
Kauai Channel
Oahu
Wahiawa
Kaneohe
Honolulu
Molokai
Kalaupapa
Wailuka
Maui
Lanai
3055
Kahoolawe
Alenuihaha Channel
PACIFIC OCEAN
160°
20°
Kawaihae
Hilo
4205
Kailua
4169
Hawaii
Pahala
155°
Tropic o

HAWAIIAN ISLANDS

1:10 000 000

0 200 km

0 100 miles

ALASKA

1:40 000 000

0 800 km

0 400 miles

70° 170° 160° 150°
Prudhoe Bay
Brooks Range
Arctic Circle
Bering Strait
ALASKA (U.S.A.)
C.I.S.
60°
Fairbanks
J
St. Lawrence I.
Yukon
Range
6194
Mt.McKinley
Anchorage
Alaska
BERING SEA
Gulf of Alaska
Near Islands
Kodiak I.
Aleutian Islands
50°
180°
Unimak I. 160°
150°

UNITED STATES OF AMERICA
TEXAS
Dallas
Fort Worth
El Paso
Ciudad Juárez
Odessa
Colorado
Austin
San Antonio
Chihuahua
Rio Bravo del Norte
Rio Grande
Laredo
Corpus Christi
Sierra Madre Occidental
Sierra Madre Oriental
Los Mochis
Culiacán
Torreón
Monterrey
Saltillo
Brownsville
Matamoros
Mazatlán
MEXICO
Aguascalientes
San Luis Potosí
Tampico
Guadalajara
León
México
Veracruz
5699
Citlaltépetl
Puebla
Sierra Madre del Sur
Acapulco
4
C
D
100°

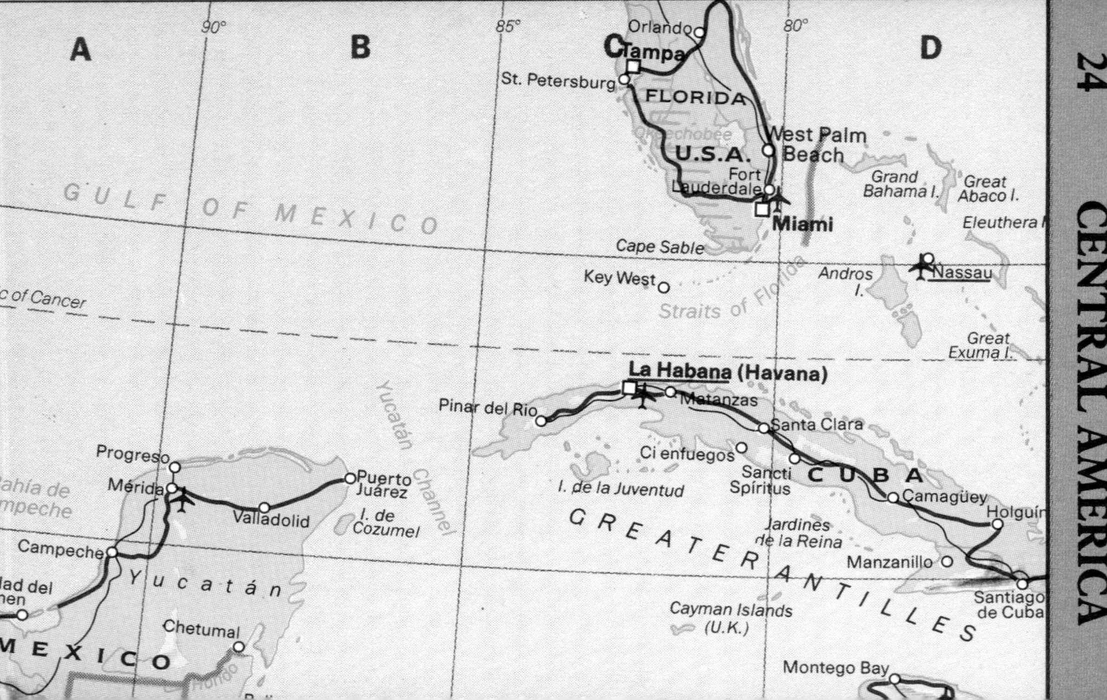

A
B
C
D
1
2
90°
85°
80°
25°
20°
GULF OF MEXICO
Tropic of Cancer
Orlando
Tampa
St. Petersburg
FLORIDA
Okeechobee
U.S.A.
West Palm Beach
Fort Lauderdale
Miami
Cape Sable
Key West
Straits of Florida
Grand Bahama I.
Great Abaco I.
Eleuthera I.
Andros I.
Nassau
Great Exuma I.
La Habana (Havana)
Matanzas
Pinar del Rio
Santa Clara
Ci enfuegos
Sancti Spíritus
CUBA
I. de la Juventud
Camagüey
Holguín
Jardines de la Reina
Manzanillo
Santiago de Cuba
GREATER ANTILLES
Cayman Islands (U.K.)
Montego Bay
Yucatán Channel
Progreso
Mérida
Puerto Juárez
Valladolid
I. de Cozumel
Bahía de Campeche
Campeche
Yucatán
Cuidad del Carmen
Chetumal
MEXICO

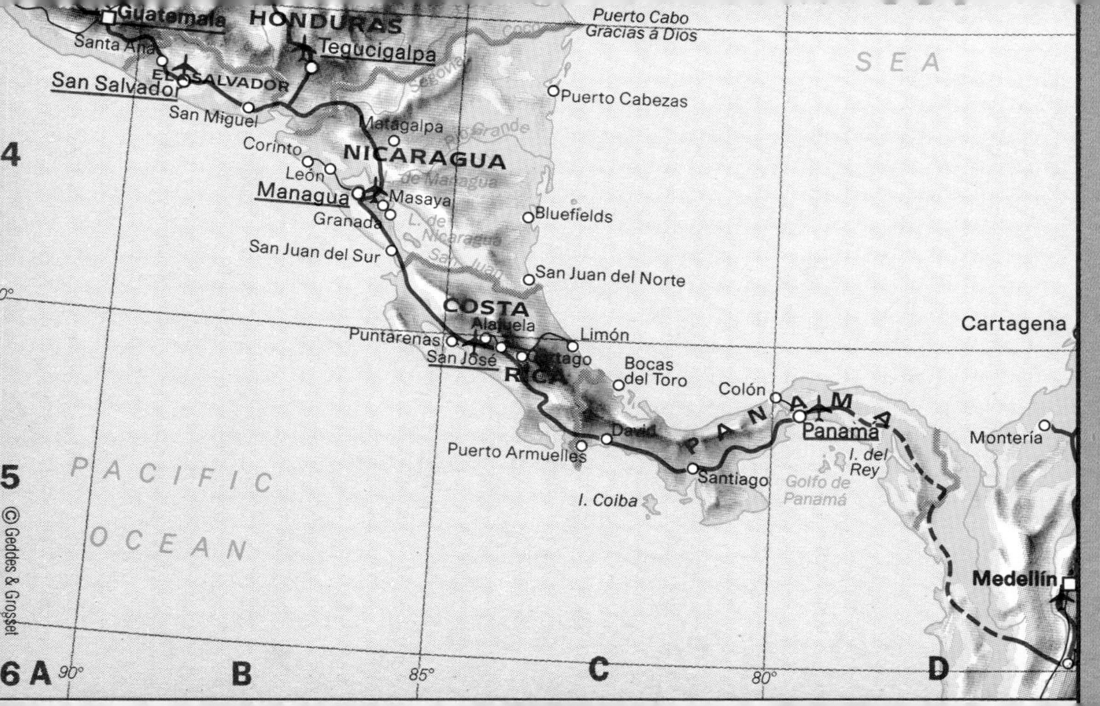
Guatemala
HONDURAS
Puerto Cabo
Gracias á Dios
Santa Ana
Tegucigalpa
SEA
EL SALVADOR
San Salvador
Puerto Cabezas
San Miguel
Matagalpa
Corinto
NICARAGUA
León
Managua
Masaya
Granada
L. de Nicaragua
Bluefields
San Juan del Sur
San Juan del Norte
10°
COSTA RICA
Alajuela
Cartagena
Puntarenas
Limón
San José
Cartago
Bocas del Toro
Colón
PANAMA
Panamá
Montería
David
Puerto Armuelles
I. del Rey
Santiago
Golfo de Panamá
I. Coiba
PACIFIC
OCEAN
Medellín
4
5
6
A
B
C
D
90°
85°
80°

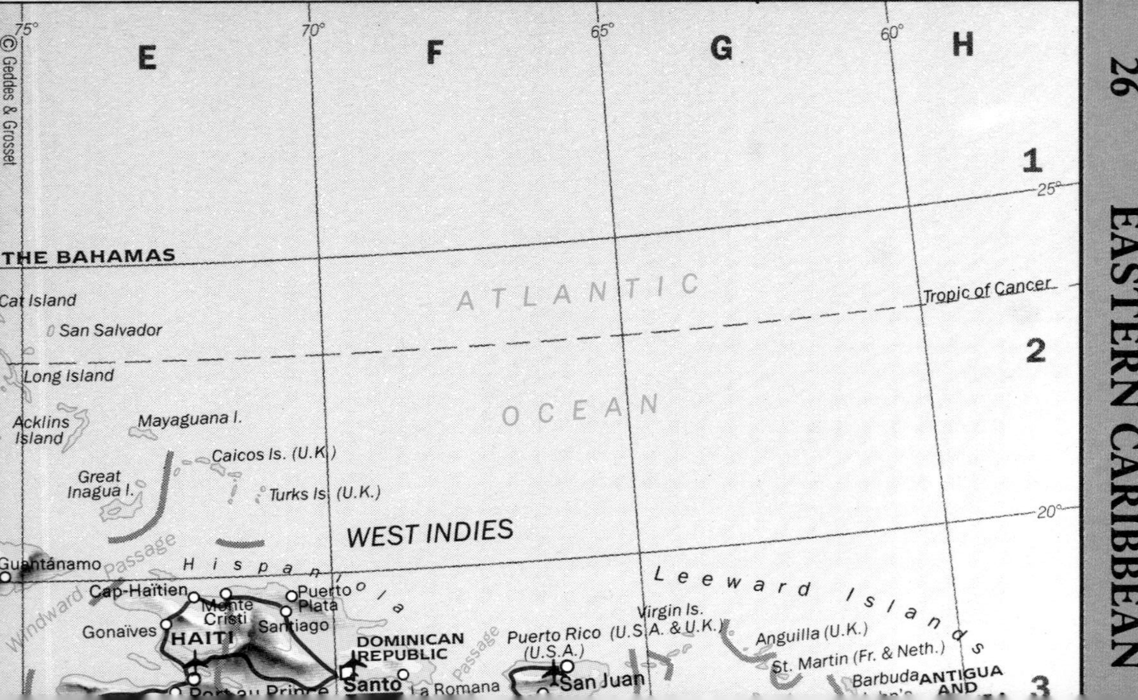
75°
70°
65°
60°
E
F
G
H
1
2
3
25°
20°
THE BAHAMAS
ATLANTIC
OCEAN
Tropic of Cancer
Cat Island
San Salvador
Long Island
Acklins Island
Mayaguana I.
Caicos Is. (U.K.)
Great Inagua I.
Turks Is. (U.K.)
WEST INDIES
Guantánamo
Windward Passage
Hispaniola
Leeward Islands
Cap-Haïtien
Monte Cristi
Puerto Plata
Santiago
Gonaïves
HAITI
DOMINICAN REPUBLIC
Santo
La Romana
Passage
Puerto Rico (U.S.A.)
San Juan
Virgin Is. (U.S.A. & U.K.)
Anguilla (U.K.)
St. Martin (Fr. & Neth.)
Barbuda
ANTIGUA AND
© Geddes & Grosset

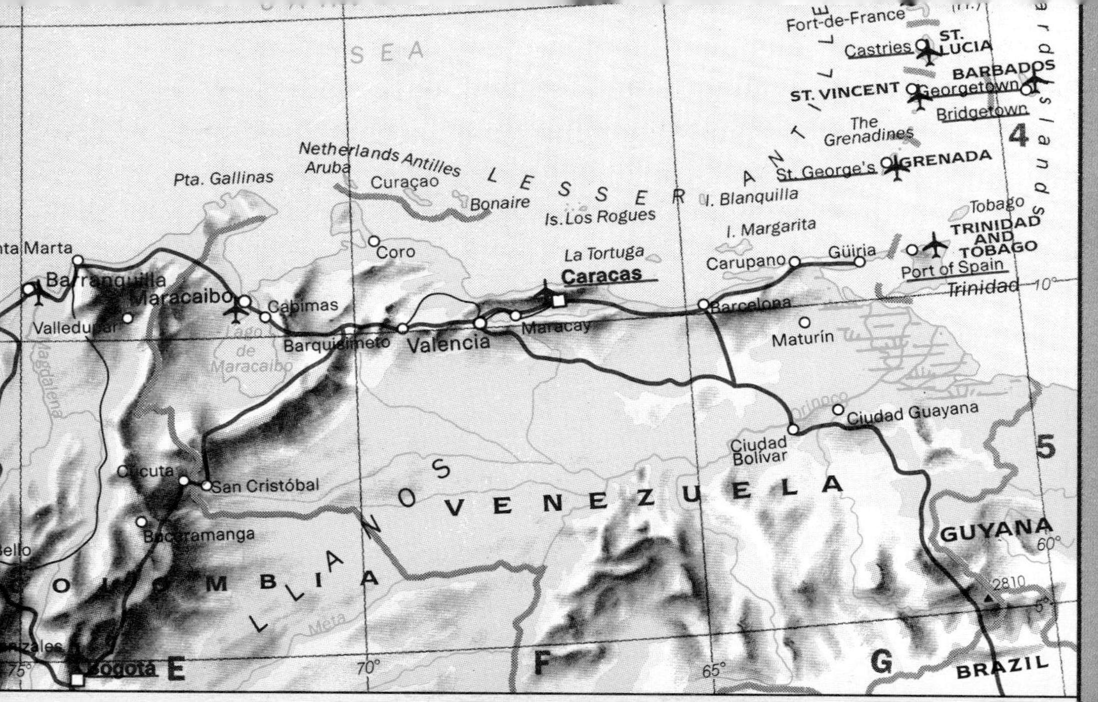
SEA
Fort-de-France
Castries
ST. LUCIA
BARBADOS
ST. VINCENT
Georgetown
Bridgetown
The Grenadines
4
St. George's
GRENADA
LESSER ANTILLE
Netherlands Antilles
Aruba
Curaçao
Bonaire
Pta. Gallinas
Is. Los Rogues
I. Blanquilla
I. Margarita
Tobago
TRINIDAD AND TOBAGO
Port of Spain
Trinidad
10°
Coro
La Tortuga
Caracas
Carupano
Güiria
Barranquilla
Maracaibo
Cabimas
Valledupar
Lago de Maracaibo
Magdalena
Barquisimeto
Valencia
Maracay
Barcelona
Maturín
Orinoco
Ciudad Guayana
Ciudad Bolívar
5
Cúcuta
San Cristóbal
LLANOS
VENEZUELA
Bucaramanga
Bello
COLOMBIA
Meta
GUYANA
60°
2810
BRAZIL
Bogotá
E
F
G
75°
70°
65°

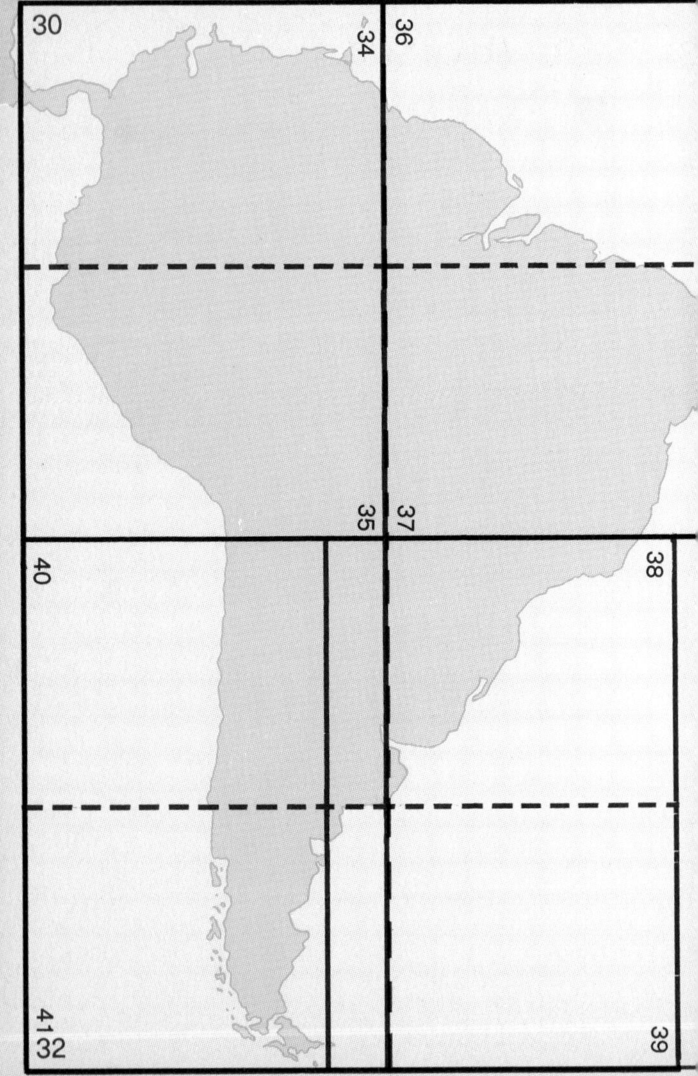
30
34
36
35
37
40
38
41
32
39

SOUTH AMERICA POLITICAL (N)

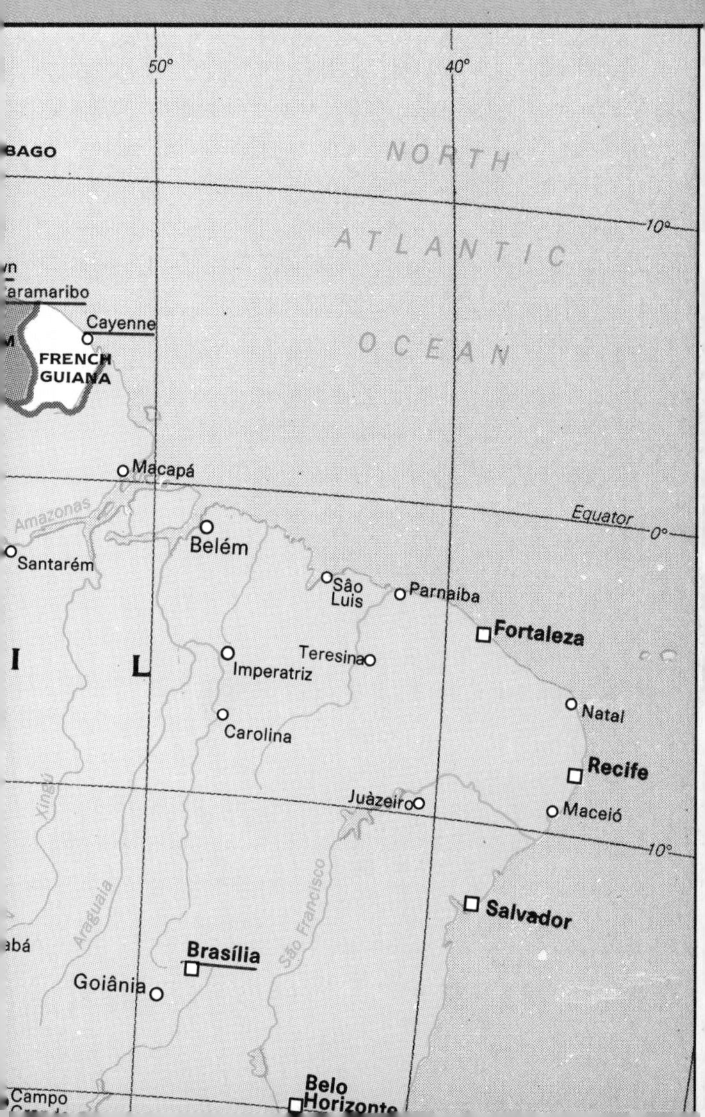

50°
40°
BAGO
NORTH
ATLANTIC
OCEAN
10°
Paramaribo
Cayenne
FRENCH
GUIANA
Macapá
Amazonas
Equator
0°
Belém
Santarém
São
Luis
Parnaiba
Fortaleza
Teresina
Imperatriz
Carolina
Natal
Recife
Juàzeiro
Maceió
10°
Xingu
Araguaia
São Francisco
Salvador
Brasília
Goiânia
Belo
Horizonte
Campo

SOUTH AMERICA POLITICAL (S)

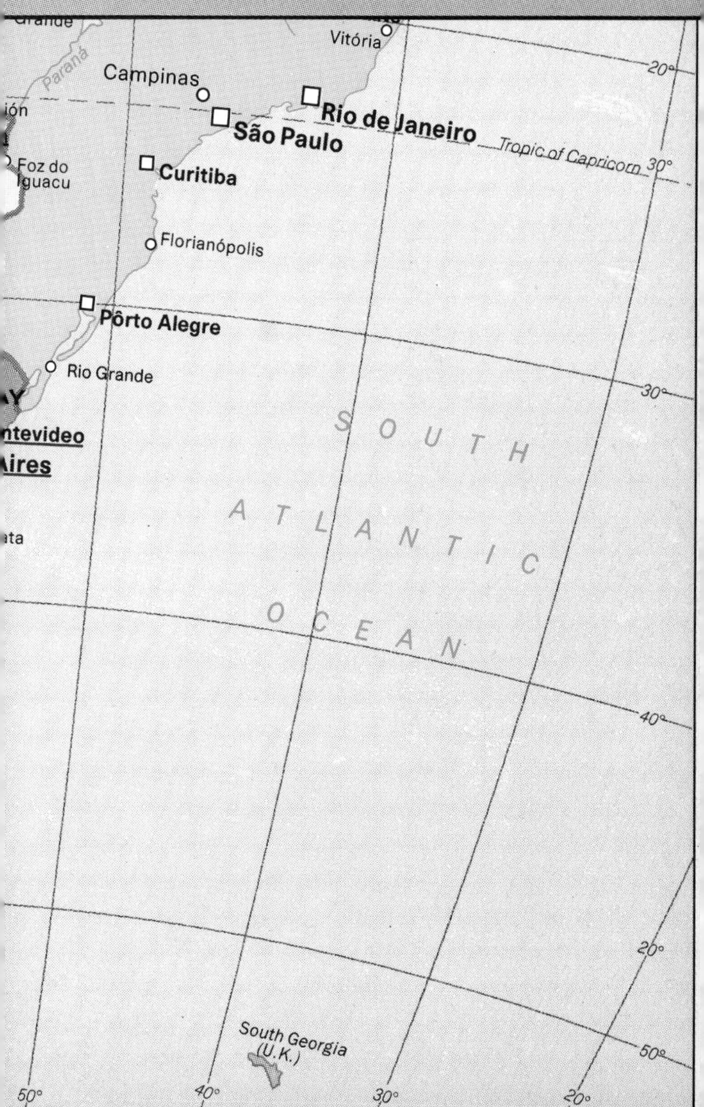

Paraná
Vitória
Campinas
Rio de Janeiro
São Paulo
Foz do Iguacu
Curitiba
Florianópolis
Pôrto Alegre
Rio Grande
ntevideo
Aires
Tropic of Capricorn
SOUTH ATLANTIC OCEAN
South Georgia (U.K.)
20°
30°
30°
40°
20°
50°
50°
40°
30°
20°

A
B
C
D
1
2
80°
70°
60°
10°
CARIBBEAN SEA
Guadeloupe (Fr.)
DOMINICA
Martinique (Fr.
ST. LUCIA
ST. VINCENT
BARBADOS
GRENADA
Lesser Antilles
Netherlands Antilles
Curaçao
Pta. Gallinas
Coro
Port of Spain
TRINIDAD AND TOBAGO
Güiria
Caracas
Santa Marta
Barranquilla
Cartagena
Valledupar
Maracaibo
Cabimas
Barquisimeto
Valencia
Barcelona
Panamá
PANAMA
Montería
Cúcuta
San Cristóbal
Bucaramanga
LLANOS
VENEZUELA
Orinoco
Ciudad Bolivar
Ciudad Guayana
El Dorado
GUYANA
2810
Bello
Medellín
Manizales
Pereira
Bogotá
Meta
Puerto Ayacucho
Buenaventura
Malpelo (Col.)
Cali
COLOMBIA
5750
Neiva
Cordillera Occidental
Pasto
Cucuí
Pico da Neblina 3014
Boa Vista
RORAIMA
Caracaraí
Branco

SELVAS
BRAZIL
Madeira
Lábrea
Humaitá
Pôrto Velho
Cruzeiro do Sul
Purus
ACRE
Rio Branco
RONDÔNIA
Serra dos Parecis
MA
Loja
3
Piura
Chiclayo
Trujillo
Chimbote
Pucallpa
Huascarán
6768
CORDILLERA DE LOS ANDES
10°
PERU
Callao
Lima
Huancayo
Cuzco
Iça
Ancohuma
6388
BOLIVIA
La Paz
Cochabamba
Santa Cruz
Oruro
Altiplano
Sucre
Potosí
6542
Arequipa
Mollendo
Arica
Iquique
4
PACIFIC
OCEAN

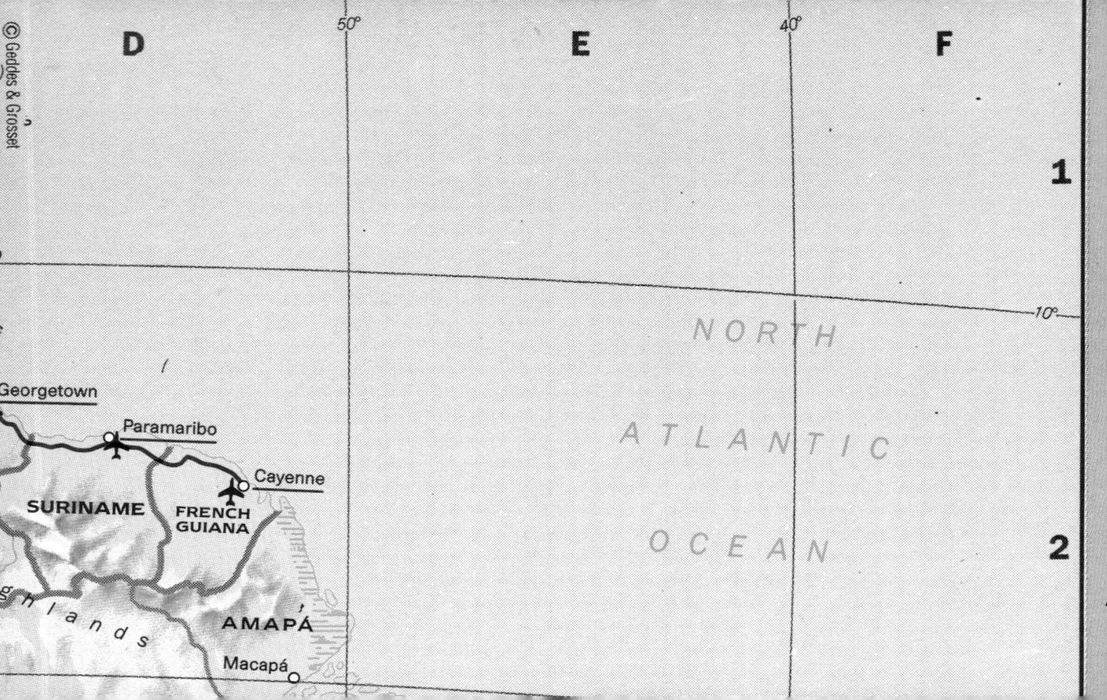
D
E
F
50°
40°
10°
1
2
NORTH
ATLANTIC
OCEAN
Georgetown
Paramaribo
Cayenne
SURINAME
FRENCH GUIANA
AMAPÁ
Macapá
© Geddes & Grosset

Codó
Fortaleza
MARANHÃO
Imperatriz
Teresina
C E A R Á
Mossoró
C. de São Roque
RIO GRANDE DO NORTE
Natal
3
Serra do Cachimbo
Xingu
Carolina
B R A Z I L
P I A U Í
PARAÍBA
João Pessoa
PERNAMBUCO
Recife
Juàzeiro
ALAGOAS
Maceió
Barragem de Sobradinho
SERGIPE
Aracaju
10°
Brazilian Highlands
B A H I A
Alagoinhas
Salvador
T O G R O S S O
Planalto do Mato Grosso
G O I Á S
Jequié
Cuiabá
Brasília
DIST.FED.
Itabuna
Anápolis
Goiânia
Montes Claros
Serra da Espinhaço
4
Teófilo Otoni
Corumbá
MATO GROSSO DO SUL
Uberaba
MINAS GERAIS
Campo Grande
Franca
Belo Horizonte
ESPÍRITO SANTO

5
Campo Grande
Horizonte
Vitória
SÃO PAULO
Dourados
Marília
São Carlos
Campos
RIO DE JANEIRO
Campinas
Sorocaba
São Paulo
Rio de Janeiro
PARAGUAY
Concepción
FORMOSA
GRAN CHACO
Pilcomayo
Paraguay
Asunción
PARANA
Foz do Iguacu
Curitiba
CHACO
Encarnación
MISIONES
SANTA CATARINA
Resistencia
Corrientes
Florianópolis
Passo Fundo
Lajes
CORRIENTES
RIO GRANDE DO SUL
SANTA FÉ
Pôrto Alegre
Concordia
Santa Fé
Salto
Bagé
ENTRE RÍOS
Paraná
Melo
Rio Grande
Rosario
URUGUAY
Buenos Aires
Montevideo
Río de la Plata
La Plata
BUENOS AIRES
© Geddes & Grosset

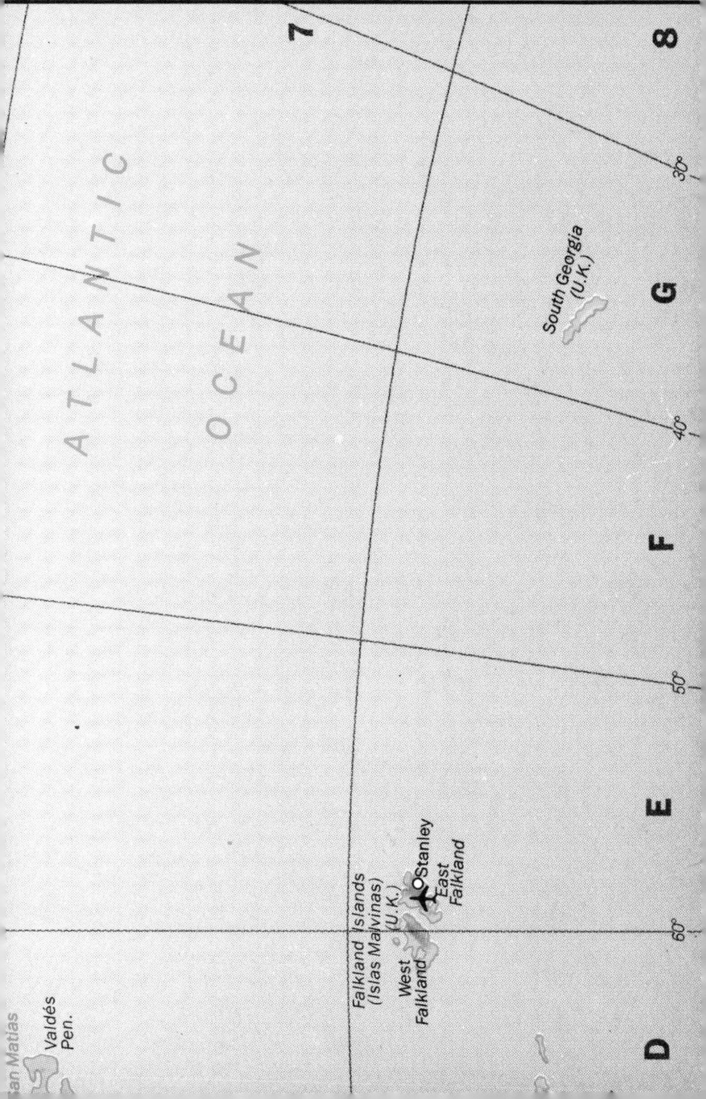

ATLANTIC
OCEAN
South Georgia
(U.K.)
Falkland Islands
(Islas Malvinas)
(U.K.)
Stanley
East
Falkland
West
Falkland
Valdés
Pen.
an Matías
7
8
D
E
F
G
30°
40°
50°
60°

PARAGUAY
Pilcomayo
FORMOSA
GRAN CHACO
CHACO
Resistencia
Corrientes
CORRI
SANTA FÉ
Santa Fé
Concordia
ENTRE RÍOS
Paraná
Rosario
Buenos Aires
BUENOS AIRES
La
SANTIAGO DEL ESTERO
CORDOBA
Córdoba
Mercedes
SAN LUIS
Salado
Santa Rosa
PAMPA
ARGENTINA
MENDOZA
Mendoza
SAN JUAN
San Juan
LA RIOJA
CATAMARCA
6908
San Miguel de Tucumán
TUCUMÁN
SALTA
Salta
JUJUY
LOS ANDES
Calama
Desierto de Atacama
Aconcagua 6960
Santiago
CHILE
Antofagasta
Chañaral
La Serena
Viña del Mar
Valparaíso
Rancagua
Talca
Talcahuano
Islas Juan Fernández (Chile)
Islas de Los Desventurados (Chile)
Tropic of Capricorn
20°
30°
5
6

OCEAN
Puerto Montt
I. de Chiloé
CHUBUT
2400
Arch.
de Los
Chonos
Golfo de
Comodoro Rivadavia
San Jorge
San Matías
Valdés
Pen.
4058
S. Valentín
SANTA CRUZ
PATAGONIA
San Julián
3600
Falkland Islands
(Islas Malvinas)
(U.K.)
West
Falkland
East
Falkland
Bahía Grande
Río Gallegos
Estrecho
de Magallanes
Tierra del Fuego
TIERRA
DEL
FUEGO
Punta Arenas
I. Santa Inés
C. de Hornos
(Cape Horn)
40°
50°
60°
70°
80°
90°
7
8
A
B
C

48
87
89
83
93
95
86
88
82
85
91
77
92
94
76
84
90
70
71
74
75
72
73
68
69
46

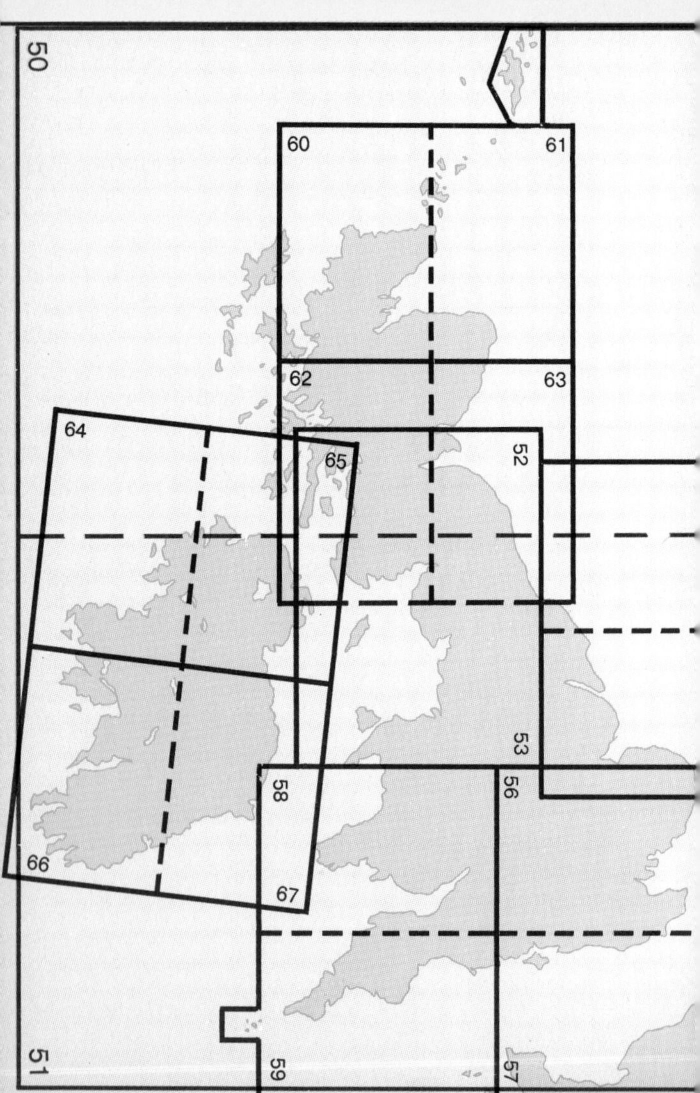
50
60
61
62
63
64
65
52
53
58
56
66
67
51
59
57

EUROPE POLITICAL (W

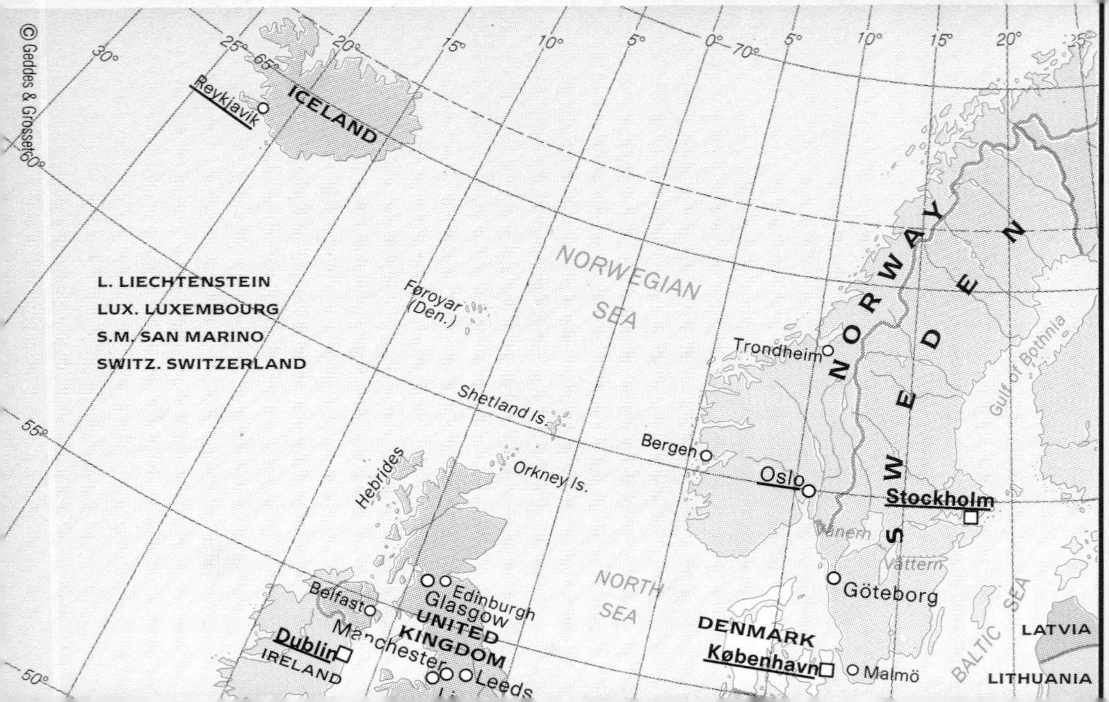

Luxembourg
Lux.
Bonn
Frankfurt
Dresden
Wrocław
Kraków
Paris
GERMANY
Praha
THE CZECH LANDS
Stuttgart
München
Danube
SLOVAKIA
Bratislava
Nantes
Loire
Bay of Biscay
FRANCE
Zürich
SWITZ.
Bern
L.
Wien
AUSTRIA
Miskolc
Bordeaux
Graz
Budapest
HUNGARY
Lyon
Milano
Torino
SLOVENIA
Ljubljana
Zagreb
Porto
Bilbao
Toulouse
Rhône
Po
Venezia
CROATIA
Tim
Genova
BOSNIA
Duero
Ebro
Nice
Bologna
Beograd
PORTUGAL
ANDORRA
Marseille
MONACO
Firenze
HERZEGOVINA
YUGOSLAVIA
Zaragoza
S.M.
Sarajevo
Lisboa
Tajo
Madrid
Barcelona
Corse
ADRIATIC SEA
SPAIN
Valencia
ITALY
Roma
CRO.
Skopje
Islas Baleares
Sardegna
Napoli
Tiranë
Sevilla
Bari
ALBANIA
TYRRHENIAN SEA
Malaga
Gibraltar (U.K.)
GREECE
IONIAN SEA
Palermo
Alger
Oran
Sicilia
Rabat
Casablanca
Tunis
MOROCCO
ALGERIA
TUNISIA
MALTA
MEDITERRANEAN SEA
45°
40°
35°
5°
0°
5°
10°
20°

RUSSIAN FEDERATION
DEPENDENT STATES
FINLAND
ESTONIA
LATVIA
LITHUANIA
BARENTS SEA
Arctic Circle
Murmansk
Arkhangel'sk
Sev. Dvina
Ozero Onezhskoye
Ladozhskoye Ozero
Tampere
Helsingfors
St Petersburg
Tallinn
Riga
Moskva
Gor'kiy
Kazan
Perm
Yeketerinburg
Chelyabinsk
Ufa
Kuybyshev
Ob
Irtysh
Tobol
Oka
© Geddes & Grosset

Kiyev
Khar'kov
Dnepr
L'vov
UKRAINE
Dnepropetrovsk
Donetsk
Rostov-na-Donu
Astrakhan
MOLDAVIA
Odessa
Cluj-Napoca
Kishinev
ROMANIA
CASPIAN
București
Constanța
BLACK SEA
Danube
Sofiya
BULGARIA
Plovdiv
GEORGIA
Tbilisi
AZERBAIJAN
Baku
SEA
ARMENIA
Yerevan
AZER.
Erzurum
Samsun
TURKEY
Istanbul
Tabríz
Thessaloníki
Bursa
Ankara
Kayseri
Tehrān
IRAN
Al Mawşil
AEGEAN SEA
Athínai
Izmir
Adana
IRAQ
SYRIA
Baghdād
Tigris
Euphrates
CYPRUS
Ródhos
Kríti
Nicosia
LEBANON
Dimashq
25°
30°
35°
40°
45°
50°

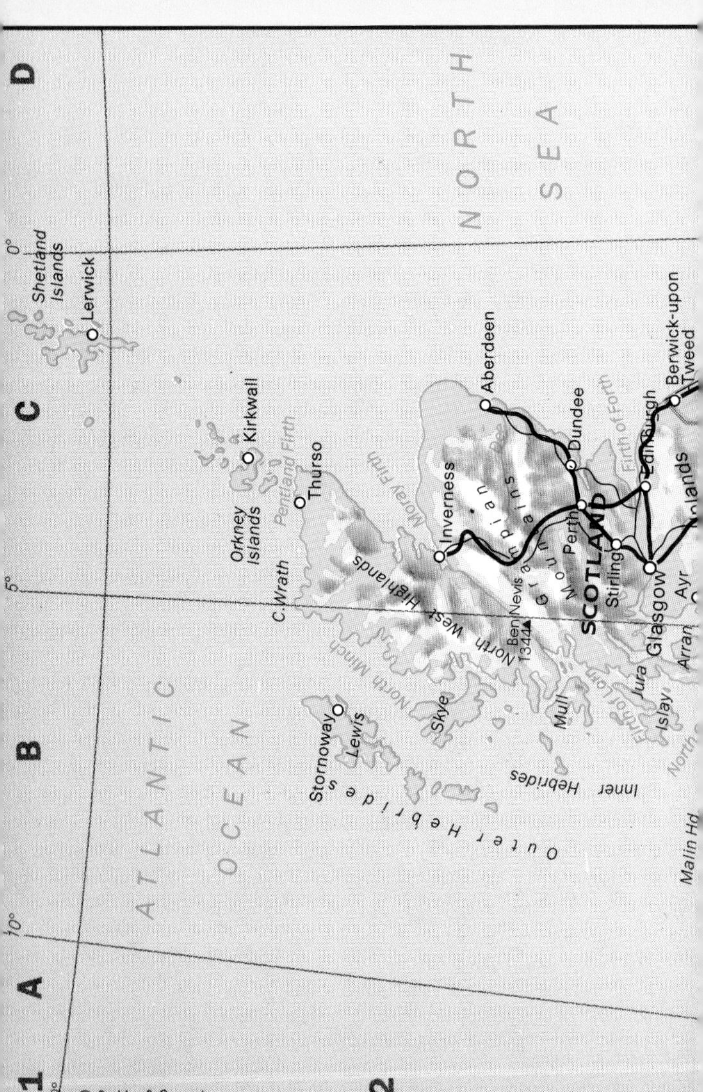
A
B
C
D
1
2
0°
5°
10°
60°
NORTH SEA
ATLANTIC OCEAN
Shetland Islands
Lerwick
Orkney Islands
Kirkwall
Pentland Firth
Thurso
C.Wrath
Moray Firth
Inverness
Aberdeen
Dee
Dundee
Firth of Forth
Edinburgh
Berwick-upon Tweed
Perth
Stirling
Glasgow
Ayr
Arran
SCOTLAND
Grampian Mountains
Ben Nevis 1344
North West Highlands
North Minch
Skye
Lewis
Stornoway
Outer Hebrides
Inner Hebrides
Mull
Jura
Islay
Firth of Lorn
Malin Hd
© Geddes & Grosset

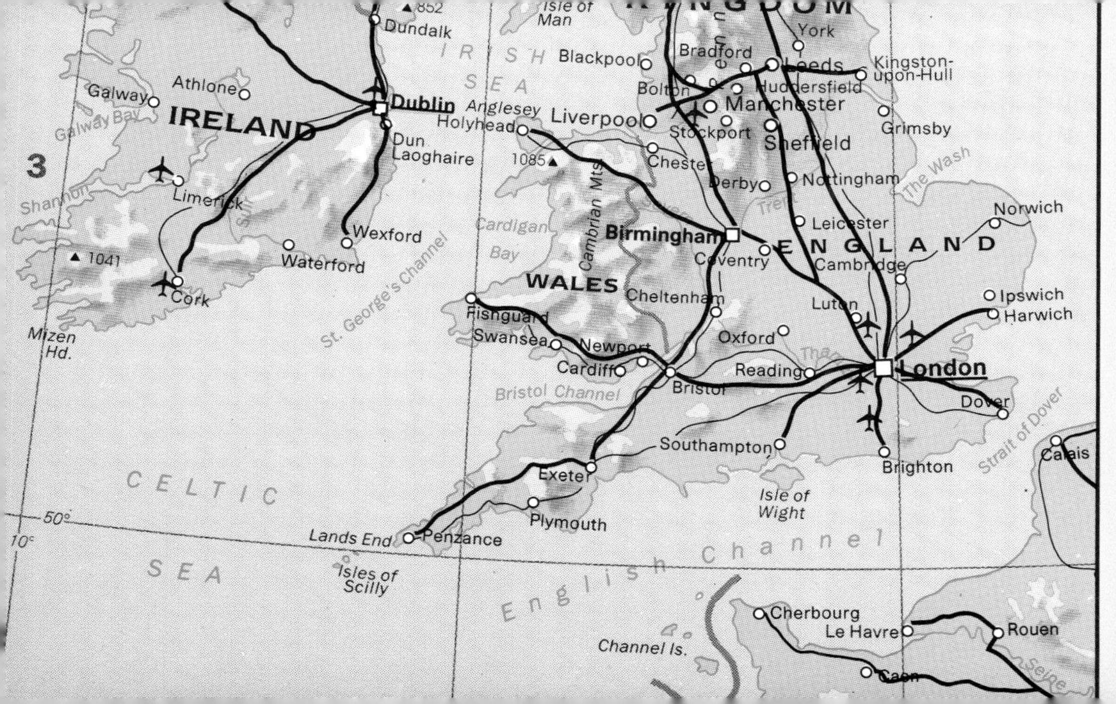
852
Dundalk
Isle of Man
IRISH SEA
Blackpool
Bradford
York
Leeds
Kingston-upon-Hull
Bolton
Huddersfield
Manchester
Galway
Athlone
Dublin
Anglesey
Holyhead
Liverpool
Stockport
Sheffield
Grimsby
Galway Bay
IRELAND
Dun Laoghaire
Chester
3
1085
Derby
Nottingham
The Wash
Shannon
Limerick
Cambrian Mts
Leicester
Norwich
Wexford
Cardigan Bay
Birmingham
ENGLAND
1041
Waterford
Coventry
Cambridge
WALES
St. George's Channel
Cork
Cheltenham
Ipswich
Luton
Harwich
Fishguard
Mizen Hd.
Swansea
Newport
Oxford
Cardiff
Reading
London
Bristol
Bristol Channel
Dover
Southampton
Strait of Dover
Calais
Brighton
Exeter
CELTIC SEA
Isle of Wight
50°
Plymouth
10°
Lands End
Penzance
English Channel
Isles of Scilly
Cherbourg
Le Havre
Rouen
Channel Is.
Caen
Seine

A
B
C
D
E
1
2
6°
5°
4°
3°
56°
55°
Perth
TAYSIDE
FIFE
Inveraray
CENTRAL
Stirling
Dunfermline
Firth of Forth
STRATHCLYDE
Greenock
Falkirk
Edinburgh
Dunbar
Jura
Tarbert
Glasgow
LOTHIAN
Paisley
Islay
Galashiels
Kintyre
Arran
Firth of Clyde
BORDERS
Southern Uplands
816
Ayr
Campbeltown
SCOTLAND
Cheviot Hills
NORTHUMBERLAND
DUMFRIES AND GALLOWAY
Dumfries
North Channel
Ballymena
ANTRIM
Larne
Stranraer
Carlisle
Hexham
© Geddes & Grosset

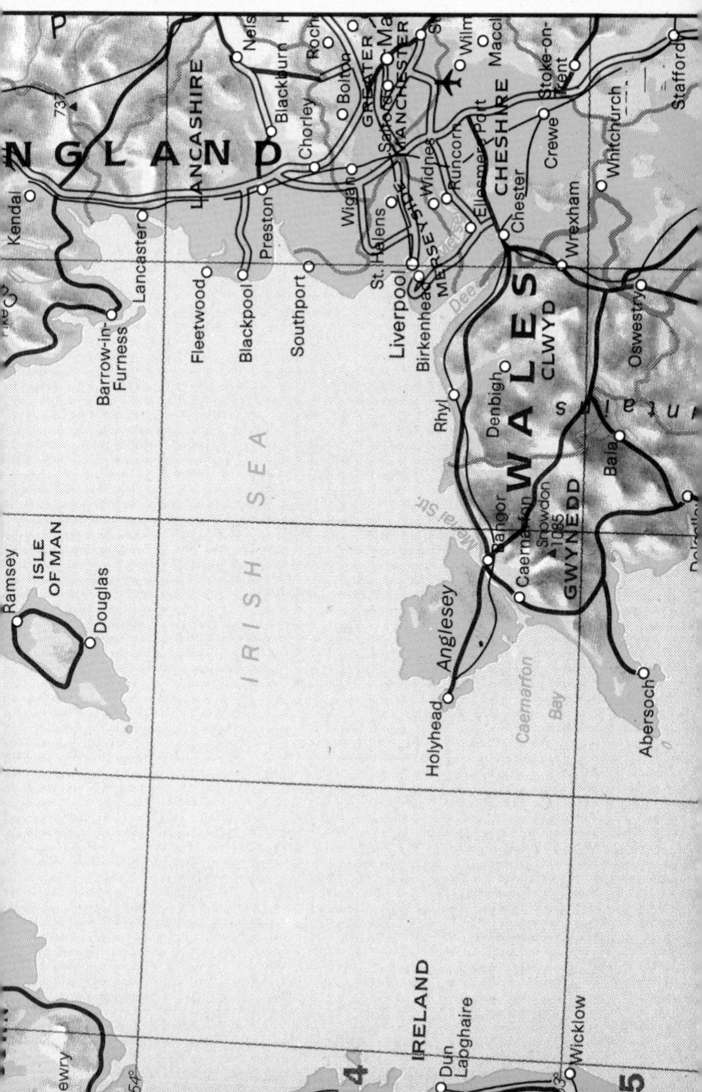
ENGLAND
LANCASHIRE
GREATER MANCHESTER
MERSEYSIDE
CHESHIRE
WALES
CLWYD
GWYNEDD
ISLE OF MAN
IRELAND
IRISH SEA
Kendal
Lancaster
Barrow-in-Furness
Fleetwood
Blackpool
Preston
Southport
Blackburn
Chorley
Bolton
Wigan
St. Helens
Liverpool
Birkenhead
Widnes
Runcorn
Ellesmere Port
Chester
Crewe
Stoke-on-Trent
Whitchurch
Stafford
Wrexham
Oswestry
Denbigh
Rhyl
Bala
Bangor
Caernarfon
Snowdon
1085
Menai St.
Anglesey
Holyhead
Caernarfon Bay
Abersoch
Ramsey
Douglas
Dun Laoghaire
Wicklow
Dee
737
54°
4
5

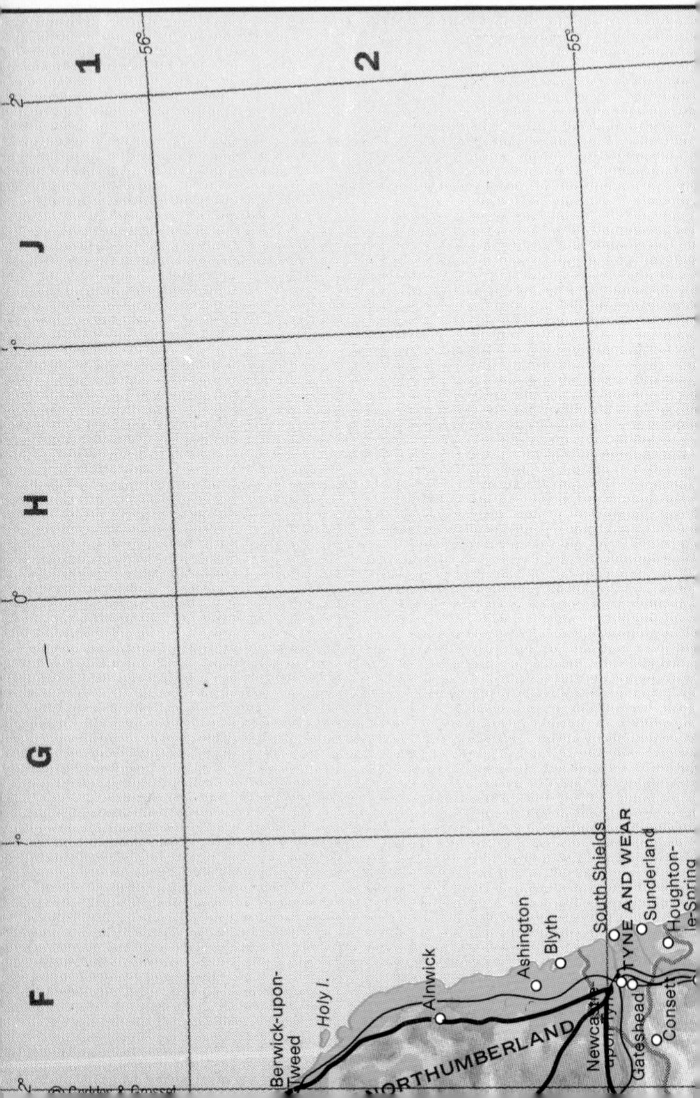

1
2
56°
55°
J
H
G
F
Berwick-upon-Tweed
Holy I.
Alnwick
Ashington
Blyth
South Shields
TYNE AND WEAR
Sunderland
Houghton-le-Spring
Newcastle upon Tyne
Gateshead
Consett
NORTHUMBERLAND

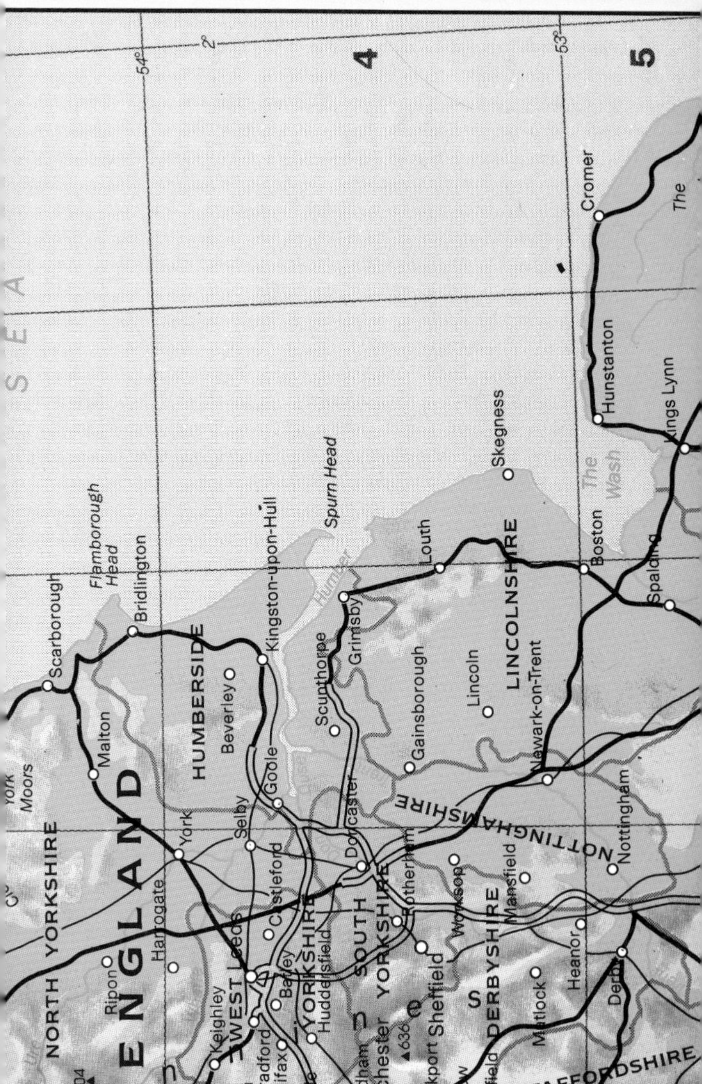

S E A
4
5
54°
53°
2°
NORTH YORKSHIRE
York Moors
ENGLAND
HUMBERSIDE
LINCOLNSHIRE
NOTTINGHAMSHIRE
DERBYSHIRE
STAFFORDSHIRE
WEST YORKSHIRE
SOUTH YORKSHIRE
Scarborough
Flamborough Head
Bridlington
Kingston-upon-Hull
Spurn Head
Humber
Grimsby
Scunthorpe
Louth
Skegness
The Wash
Boston
Spalding
Kings Lynn
Hunstanton
Cromer
The
Malton
Beverley
Goole
Gainsborough
Lincoln
Newark-on-Trent
York
Selby
Doncaster
Rotherham
Worksop
Mansfield
Nottingham
Heanor
Derby
Matlock
Sheffield
Castleford
Harrogate
Ripon
Leeds
Batley
Huddersfield
Keighley
Bradford
Halifax
Oldham
Stockport
636
704

5
6
52°
LEICESTERSHIRE
Leicester
Walsall
West Bromwich
Birmingham
Hinckley
WEST MIDLANDS
Coventry
Rugby
Corby
Peterborough
The Fens
NORFOLK
Broads
Norwich
Great Yarmouth
Ely
Thetford
CAMBRIDGESHIRE
NORTHAMPTONSHIRE
Warwick
WARWICKSHIRE
Stratford-on-Avon
Northampton
Bedford
BEDFORDSHIRE
Cambridge
Bury St. Edmunds
SUFFOLK
Saxmundham
Ipswich
Felixstowe
Harwich
Colchester
ESSEX
Clacton-on-Sea
Banbury
BUCKINGHAMSHIRE
Milton Keynes
Buckingham
HERTFORDSHIRE
Cheltenham
GLOUCESTERSHIRE
Luton
Aylesbury
St. Albans
Harlow
Oxford
Chesham
Chelmsford
OXFORDSHIRE
Chiltern Hills
Watford
Didcot
Basildon
GREATER LONDON
London
Southend-on-Sea
Swindon
Thames
Reading
Windsor
Chippenham
Kennet
BERKSHIRE
Rochester
Margate
Canterbury
Trowbridge
WILTSHIRE
Basingstoke
SURREY
North Downs
Maidstone
Warminster
Aldershot
Guildford
Tonbridge
KENT
Dover
Royal Tunbridge
Ashford
Channel Tunnel
HAMPSHIRE
Crawley

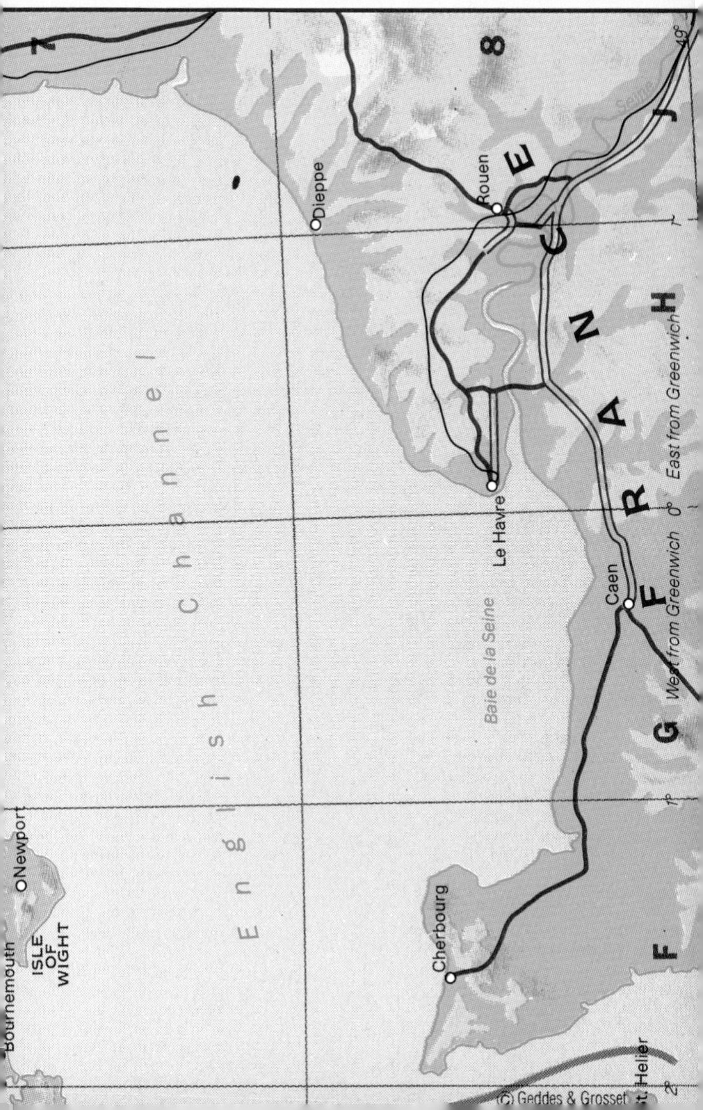
English Channel
Baie de la Seine
Bournemouth
ISLE OF WIGHT
Newport
Dieppe
Rouen
Le Havre
Caen
Cherbourg
Seine
FRANCE
F
G
H
J
7
8
49°
1°
0°
East from Greenwich
West from Greenwich
(C) Geddes & Grosset

Telford
Wolverhampton
Dudley
SHROPSHIRE
Church Stretton
Shrewsbury
HEREFORD AND WORCESTER
Hereford
Gloucester
GLOUCESTER -SHIRE
Stroud
Cotswold Hills
Kingswood
Bath
AVON
Bristol
Weston-super-Mare
Severn
Newport
Cwmbran
GWENT
Abergavenny
Cardiff
SOUTH GLAMORGAN
Barry
Bridgwater
Exmoor
MID GLAMORGAN
Merthyr Tydfil
Breacon Beacons
886
Llandrindod Wells
Builth Wells
POWYS
WALES
Welshpool
Cambrian Mountains
Dolgellau
892
Aberystwyth
DYFED
Carmarthen
WEST GLAMORGAN
Port Talbot
Swansea
Bristol Channel
Ilfracombe
Lundy
Carmarthen Bay
Cardigan Bay
Cardigan
Fishguard
St. Davids
Milford Haven
Pembroke
St. George's Channel
52°
5
6

Scale 1:1 900 000

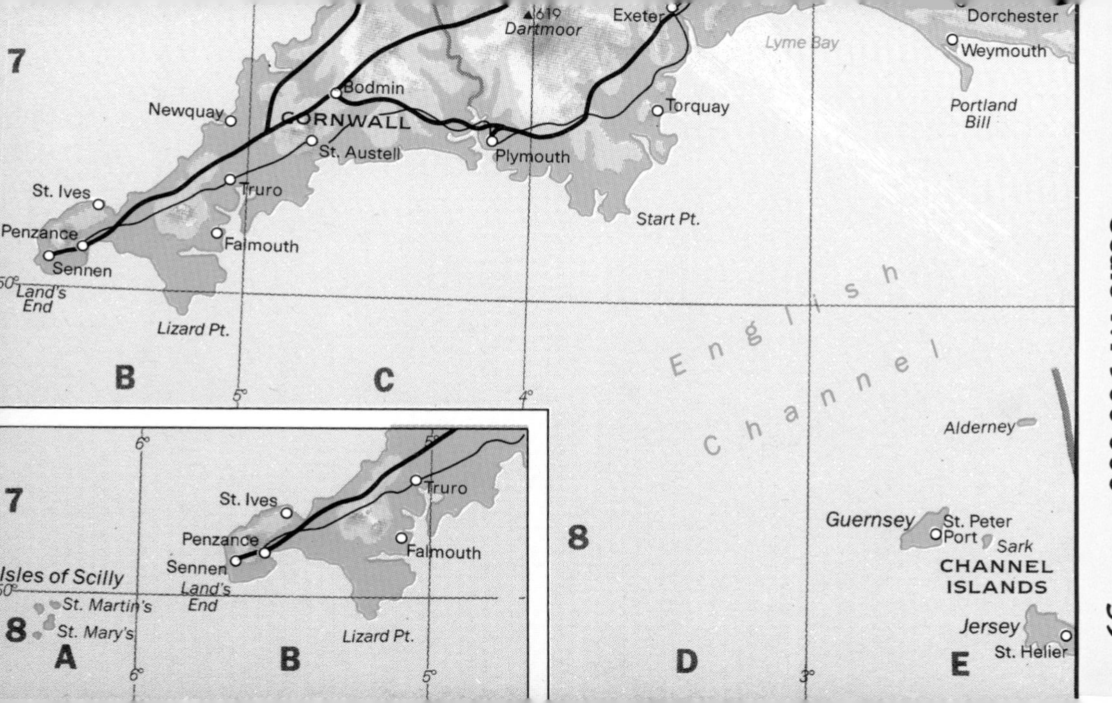

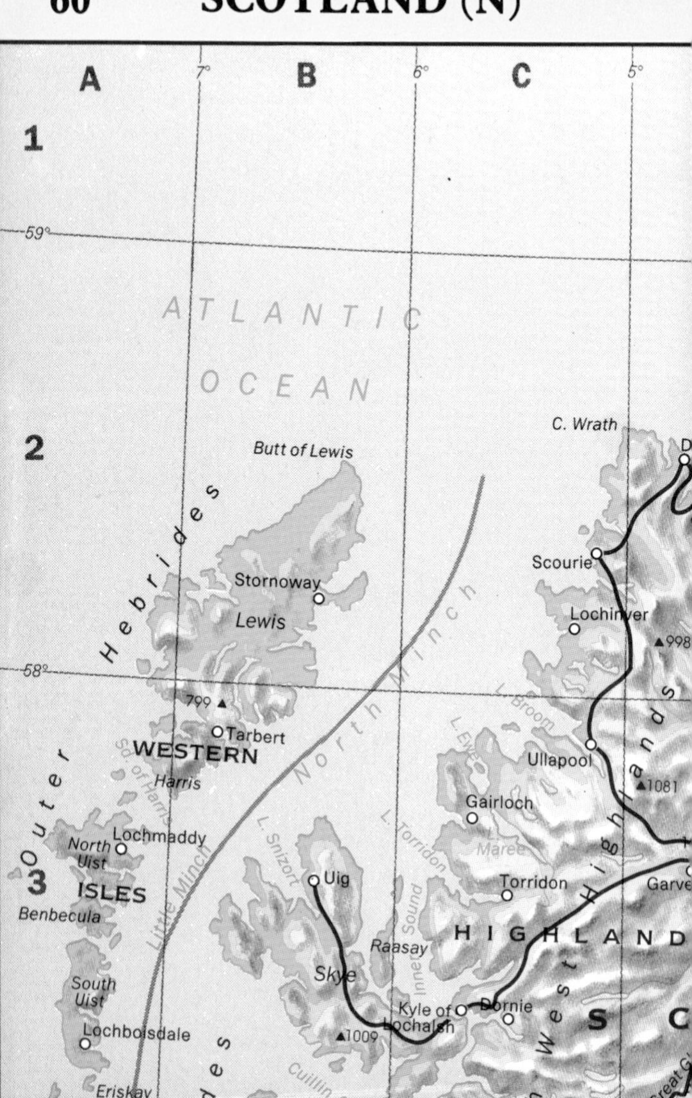

A
B
C
7°
6°
5°
1
2
3
59°
58°
57°
ATLANTIC
OCEAN
C. Wrath
Butt of Lewis
Outer Hebrides
Stornoway
Lewis
Scourie
Lochinver
998
799
Tarbert
WESTERN
Harris
Sd. of Harris
L. Broom
L. Ewe
Ullapool
1081
North Minch
Gairloch
L. Maree
L. Torridon
Lochmaddy
North Uist
Little Minch
L. Snizort
Uig
Torridon
Garve
ISLES
Benbecula
Inner Sound
HIGHLAND
Raasay
Skye
South Uist
Kyle of Lochalsh
Dornie
Lochboisdale
1009
West Highlands
Cuillin Sd.
Eriskay
Barra
Mallaig
© Geddes & Grosset

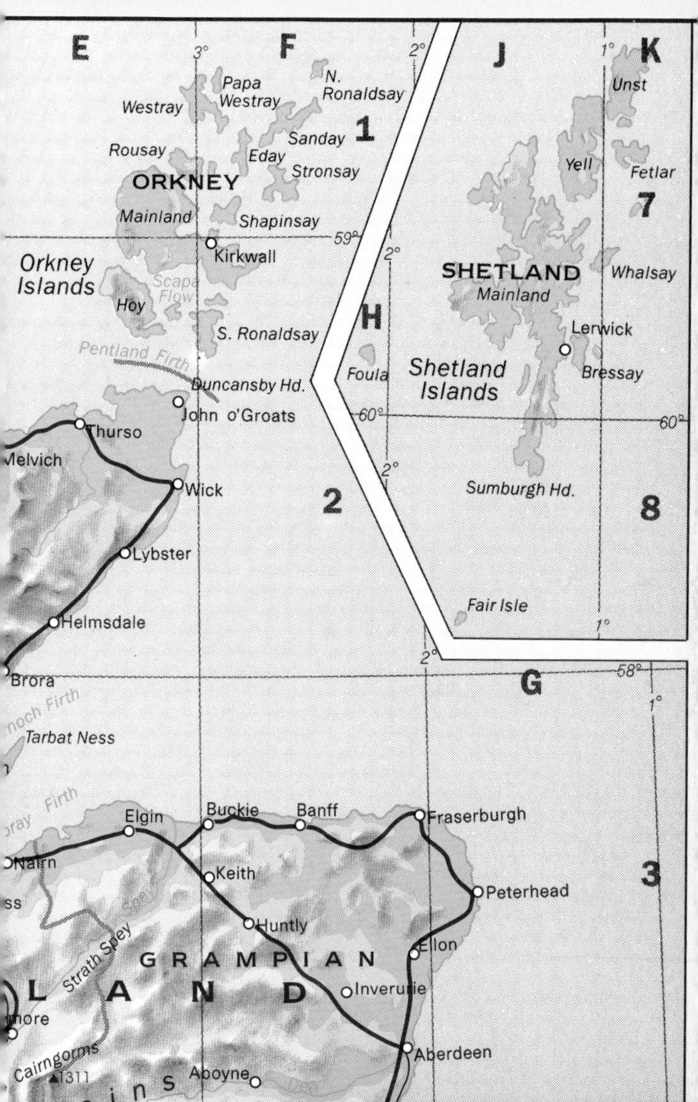
E
F
J
K
3°
2°
1°
Papa Westray
N. Ronaldsay
Westray
Unst
Sanday
1
Rousay
Eday
Stronsay
Yell
Fetlar
ORKNEY
7
Mainland
Shapinsay
59°
Kirkwall
2°
Orkney Islands
SHETLAND
Whalsay
Scapa Flow
Mainland
Hoy
H
S. Ronaldsay
Lerwick
Pentland Firth
Shetland Islands
Bressay
Duncansby Hd.
Foula
John o'Groats
60°
Thurso
Melvich
Wick
2
Sumburgh Hd.
8
Lybster
Fair Isle
Helmsdale
Brora
G
58°
Tarbat Ness
Elgin
Buckie
Banff
Fraserburgh
Nairn
Keith
3
Peterhead
Spey
Huntly
Strath Spey
GRAMPIAN
Ellon
L A N D
Inverurie
Aberdeen
Cairngorms
1311
Aboyne

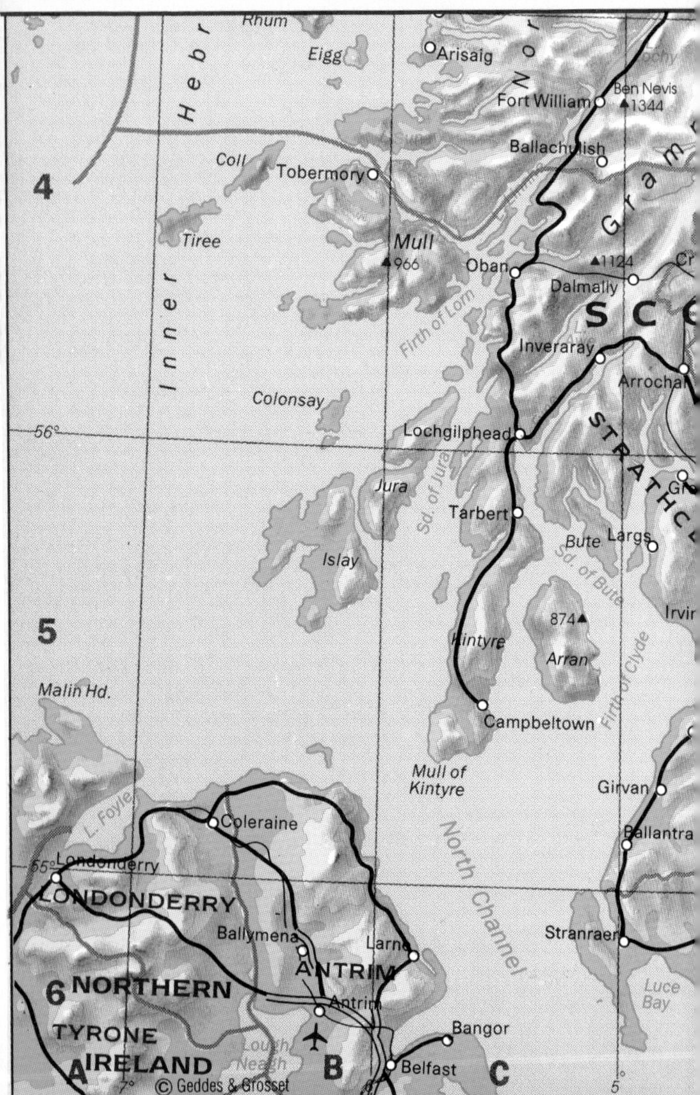

Rhum
Eigg
Arisaig
Fort William
Ben Nevis
1344
Ballachulish
Coll
Tobermory
4
Inner Hebr
Tiree
Mull
966
Oban
1124
Dalmally
Firth of Lorn
S C
Inveraray
Arrochar
Colonsay
56°
Lochgilphead
STRATHC
Jura
Sd. of Jura
Tarbert
Bute
Largs
Islay
Sd. of Bute
874
5
Kintyre
Arran
Firth of Clyde
Malin Hd.
Campbeltown
Mull of Kintyre
Girvan
L. Foyle
Coleraine
North Channel
Ballantra
55°
Londonderry
LONDONDERRY
Ballymena
Larne
Stranraer
ANTRIM
6 NORTHERN
Antrim
Luce Bay
TYRONE
Bangor
IRELAND
Lough Neagh
A
B
Belfast
C
7°
6°
5°

Braemar
1155
Stonehaven
Laurencekirk
Blair Atholl
Pitlochry
Montrose
AYSIDE
Forfar
Dunkeld
Arbroath
4
Dundee
Firth of Tay
Perth
St. Andrews
Cupar
Ochil Hills
FIFE
Fife Ness
NORTH
SEA
Glenrothes
Stirling
Kirkcaldy
Dunfermline
Firth of Forth
Falkirk
Dunbar
56°
Edinburgh
Musselburgh
St. Abb's Hd.
Livingston
LOTHIAN
Berwick-upon
-Tweed
Lanark
Peebles
Uplands
Galashiels
5
Jedburgh
BORDERS
816
Hawick
Cheviot Hills
Alnwick
Moffat
Teviothead
NORTHUMBERLAND
Tyne
Dumfries
Gretna
TYNE AND
55°
Newcastle
upon Tyne
WEAR
South
Shields
Carlisle
ENGLAND
Solway Firth
Durham
6
CUMBRIA
DURHAM
Penrith
E
F
G
3°
2°

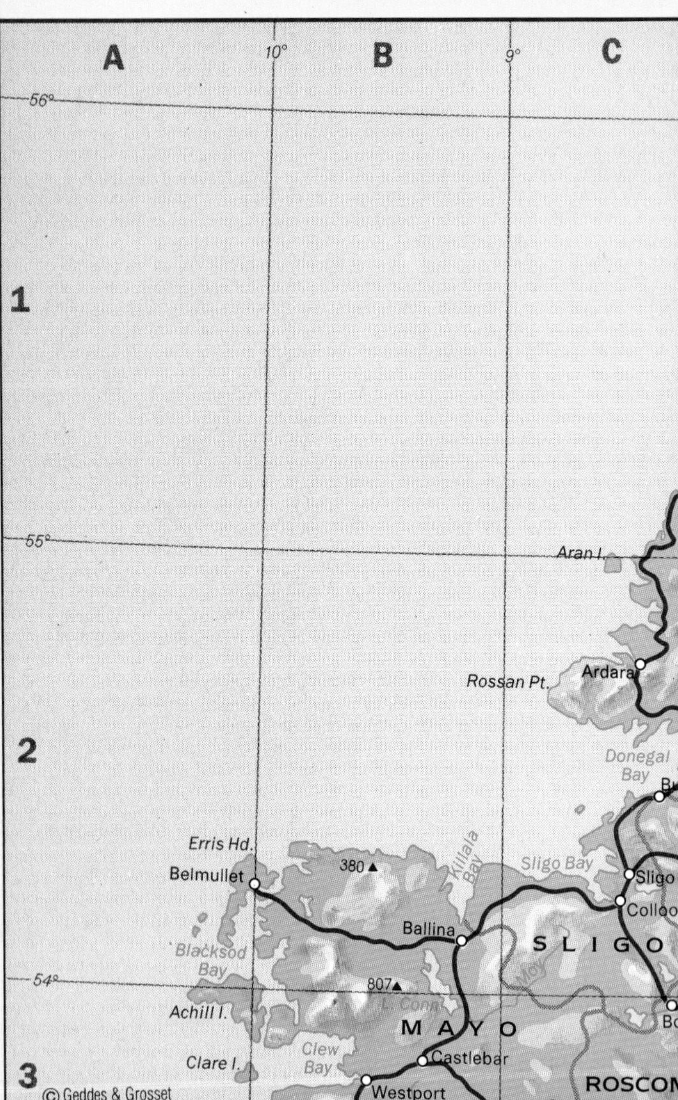
A
10°
B
9°
C
56°
1
55°
Aran I.
Ardara
Rossan Pt.
2
Donegal
Bay
Erris Hd.
380
Killala
Bay
Sligo Bay
Belmullet
Sligo
Collooney
Ballina
SLIGO
Blacksod
Bay
Moy
54°
807
L. Conn
Achill I.
MAYO
Clew
Bay
Clare I.
Castlebar
3
Westport
ROSCOM

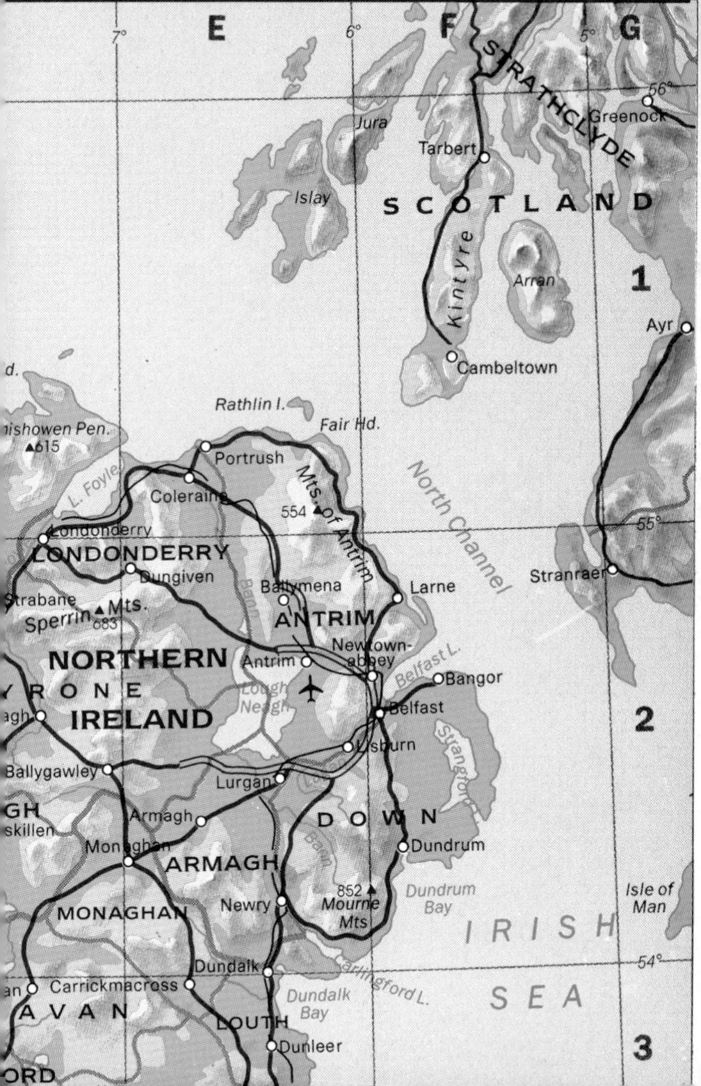
E
F
G
7°
6°
5°
56°
55°
54°
1
2
3
STRATHCLYDE
Greenock
Jura
Tarbert
Islay
SCOTLAND
Kintyre
Arran
Ayr
Cambeltown
Rathlin I.
Fair Hd.
Inishowen Pen.
615
Portrush
L. Foyle
Coleraine
Mts. of Antrim
554
North Channel
Londonderry
LONDONDERRY
Dungiven
Bann
Ballymena
Larne
Stranraer
Strabane
Sperrin Mts.
683
ANTRIM
Newtownabbey
NORTHERN
Antrim
Belfast L.
Bangor
TYRONE
Lough Neagh
Belfast
IRELAND
Lisburn
Strangford L.
Ballygawley
Lurgan
DOWN
Armagh
Monaghan
Dundrum
ARMAGH
852
Mourne Mts
Dundrum Bay
Isle of Man
MONAGHAN
Newry
IRISH
Dundalk
Carrickmacross
Carlingford L.
Dundalk Bay
SEA
LOUTH
Dunleer

Killary Harbour
Claremorris
Roscom
L. Mask
3
Clifden
Slyne Hd.
L. Corrib
GALWAY
Ballinasloe
Galway
Athenry
Kilkieran Bay
Galway Bay
Kinvarra
Aran Is.
Gort
53°
IR
Hags Hd.
Ennistymon
CLARE
Ennis
Kilrush
Limerick
4
Loop Hd.
Tarbert
LIMERICK
Shannon Estuary
Tipperary
Tralee Bay
Feale
Ráth Luirc
Tralee
Sybil Pt.
953
KERRY
Dingle
Mallow
Blackwater
Dingle Bay
Carrauntoohil
1041
Killarney
52°
CORK
774
Kenmare
Cork
Bandon
Bantry
5
Dursey Hd.
Bantry Bay
Old Head of Kinsale
Mizen Hd.
A
B
C
10°
9°

Kells
Drogheda
geworthstown
An Uaimh (Navan)
MEATH
Balbriggan
Mullingar
EATH
Kinnegad
DUBLIN
Howth Hd.
Dublin Bay
IRISH
Tullamore
Liffey
Dublin
Dun Laoghaire
ALY
KILDARE
Bog of Allen
Naas
Bray
Kildare
850
Wicklow Mts
Port Laoise
SEA
AND
WICKLOW
Wicklow
53°
OIS
926
Wicklow Hd.
Wicklow
Carlow
Arklow
CARLOW
Kilkenny
KILKENNY
4
WEXFORD
Enniscorthy
Channel
Wexford Bay
New Ross
Wexford
Rosslare
Waterford
RFORD
Carnsore Pt.
garvan
Waterford Harbour
52°
Fishguard
St. George's
WALES
5
D
E
F
7°
6°
5°
3

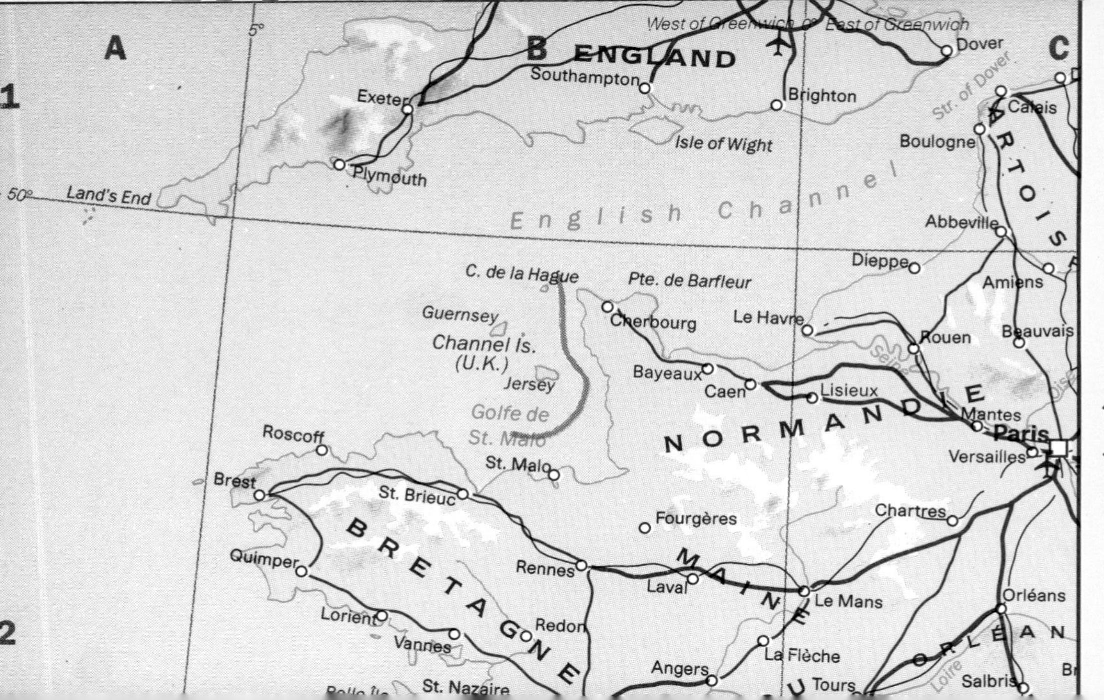
A
B
C
1
2
ENGLAND
West of Greenwich
East of Greenwich
Dover
Southampton
Brighton
Exeter
Plymouth
Isle of Wight
Str. of Dover
Calais
Boulogne
ARTOIS
Land's End
50°
5°
English Channel
Abbeville
Dieppe
Amiens
C. de la Hague
Pte. de Barfleur
Guernsey
Cherbourg
Le Havre
Rouen
Beauvais
Channel Is.
(U.K.)
Jersey
Golfe de
St. Malo
Bayeaux
Caen
Lisieux
Seine
NORMANDIE
Mantes
Paris
Versailles
Roscoff
St. Malo
Brest
St. Brieuc
Fourgères
Chartres
BRETAGNE
Quimper
Rennes
MAINE
Laval
Le Mans
Orléans
Lorient
Redon
Vannes
La Flèche
ORLÉAN
Angers
Loire
Salbris
St. Nazaire
Tours

Île de Ré
La Rochelle
Bay of Biscay
Île d'Oléron
Saintes
Gironde
Ruffec
Angoulême
Limoges
LIMOUSIN
Creuse
Thiviers
Périgueux
Brive-la-Gaillarde
Souillac
Bordeaux
Dordogne
GUYENNE
Arcachon
Cahors
Agen
Montauban
Les Landes
Golfe de Gascogne
Dax
Garonne
Toulouse
3
Oviedo
Santander
Bayonne
GASCOGNE
Bilbao
San Sebastián
Pau
Tarbes
St. Gaudens
Carcassonne
Cordillera Cantabrica
Léon
Vitoria
PYRÉNÉES
3298
SPAIN
Burgos
Ebro
ROUSSILL
ANDORRA
Andorra la Vella
45°
5°
A
B
C
Grosset

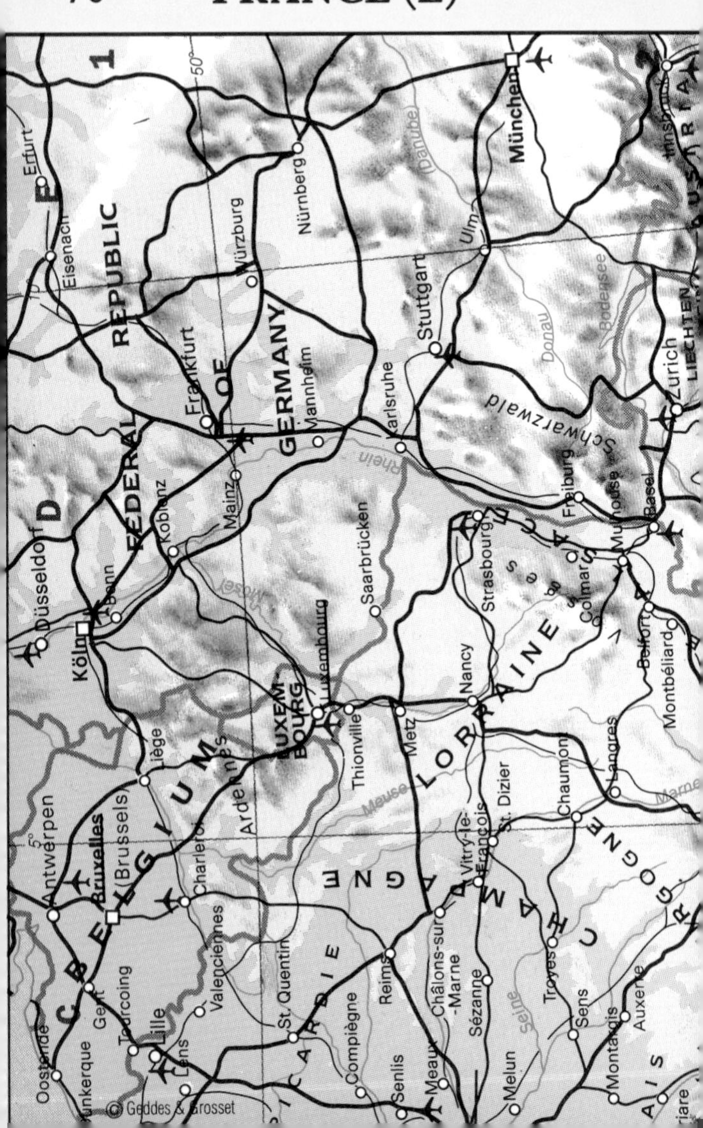
1
50°
Erfurt
Eisenach
Nürnberg
Würzburg
München
Ulm
Stuttgart
Frankfurt
Mannheim
Karlsruhe
Mainz
Koblenz
Bonn
Köln
Düsseldorf
FEDERAL REPUBLIC OF GERMANY
D
(Danube)
Donau
Bodensee
Schwarzwald
Rhein
Mosel
Saarbrücken
Luxembourg
LUXEMBOURG
Thionville
Metz
Nancy
Strasbourg
Colmar
Freiburg
Mulhouse
Basel
Zurich
Belfort
Montbéliard
LORRAINE
Langres
Chaumont
St. Dizier
Vitry-le-François
Châlons-sur-Marne
Reims
St. Quentin
Compiègne
Senlis
Meaux
Sézanne
Melun
Troyes
Sens
Montargis
Auxerre
Marne
Meuse
Seine
Liège
Ardennes
Charleroi
Valenciennes
Lille
Lens
Tourcoing
Gent
Oostende
Antwerpen
5°
Bruxelles (Brussels)
BELGIUM
© Geddes & Grosset

Mâcon
Bourg-en-Bresse
Genève
Trento
Roanne
Annecy
Matterhorn
4477
Mt. Blanc
4807
Aosta
Garda
Clermont-Ferrand
Lyon
Loire
Chambéry
4061
Novara
Milano
Brescia
Verona
1886
St. Étienne
AUVERGNE
SAVOIE
ITALY
Piacenza
45°
Massif Central
Grenoble
Torino
Valence
Briançon
Modena
Rhône
DAUPHINÉ
3841
Po
Genova
Mende
LANGUEDOC
G. di Genova
Millau
Orange
Avignon
Durance
San Remo
LIGURIAN SEA
Pisa
Nîmes
Nice
MONACO
Monaco
Livorno
Arles
PROVENCE
3
Montpellier
Cannes
Côte d'Azur
Béziers
Marseille
St. Tropez
Cap Corse
Golfe du Lion
Toulon
Narbonne
Îles d'Hyères
Bastia
Elba
Perpignan
MEDITERRANEAN SEA
Corse (Fr.)
C
D
E
5°
10°

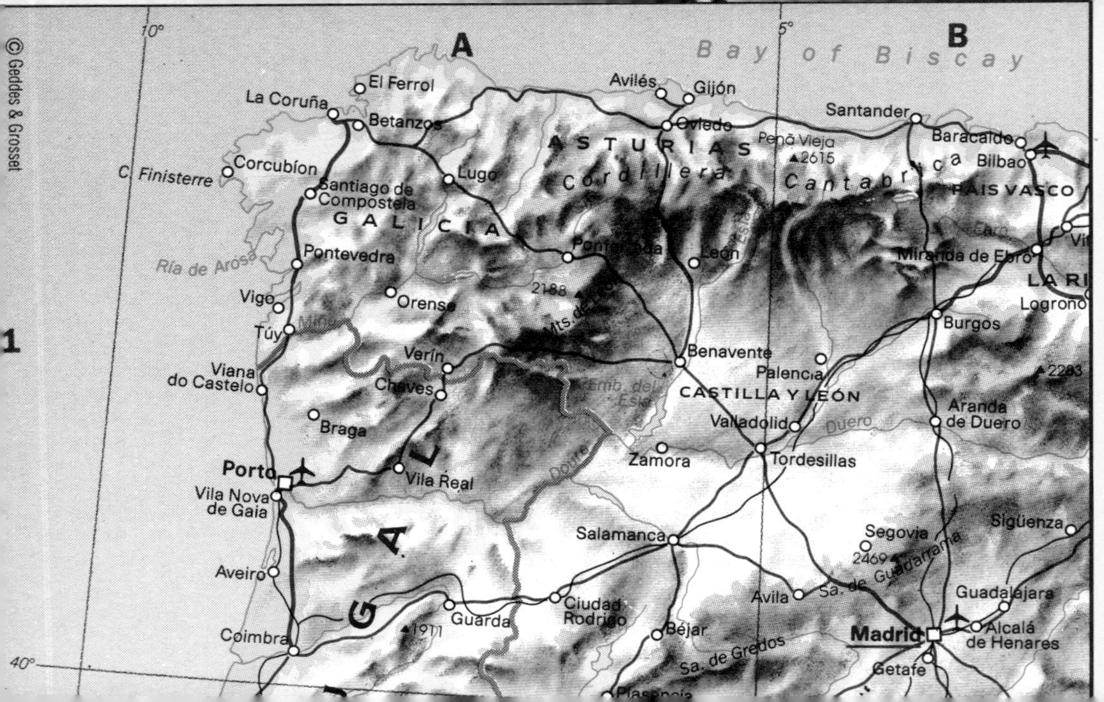
10°
5°
40°
A
B
1
Bay of Biscay
El Ferrol
La Coruña
Betanzos
Avilés
Gijón
Oviedo
Santander
Baracaldo
Bilbao
C. Finisterre
Corcubíon
Lugo
ASTURIAS
Cordillera Cantabrica
Peña Vieja
2615
PAIS VASCO
Santiago de Compostela
GALICIA
Ponferrada
León
Miranda de Ebro
LA RI
Logroño
Ría de Arosa
Pontevedra
Vigo
Orense
2188
Túy
Burgos
Verín
Benavente
Palencia
2283
Viana do Castelo
Chaves
CASTILLA Y LEÓN
Emb. del Esla
Braga
Valladolid
Duero
Aranda de Duero
Porto
Vila Real
Zamora
Tordesillas
Douro
Vila Nova de Gaia
Salamanca
Segovia
Sigüenza
2469
Sa. de Guadarrama
Aveiro
Avila
Guadalajara
Guarda
Ciudad Rodrigo
1911
Coimbra
Béjar
Madrid
Alcalá de Henares
Sa. de Gredos
Getafe

Lisboa
(Lisbon)
Almada
Setúbal
C. Espichel
Estremoz
Badajoz
Mérida
Ciudad Real
Manzanares
Valdepeñas
Puertollano
Zafra
Guadiana
Grandola
Beja
Sierra Morena
Linares
Sa. de Segura
Aracena
Córdoba
Jaén
Odemira
Guadalquivir
Ecija
Baza
ANDALUCIA
Sevilla
Huelva
Tavira
Lagos
Faro
C. de São Vicente
Golfo de Cádiz
Loja
Granada
3482
Antequera
Sa. Nevada
Jerez de la Frontera
Ronda
Malaga
Motril
Cádiz
Costa de la Luz
Marbella
Costa del Sol
ATLANTIC OCEAN
Algeciras
Gibraltar (U.K.)
Str. of Gibraltar
Tanger
Ceuta (Sp.)
Tetouan
MOROCCO
Melilla (Sp.)
2
10°
35°
A
B

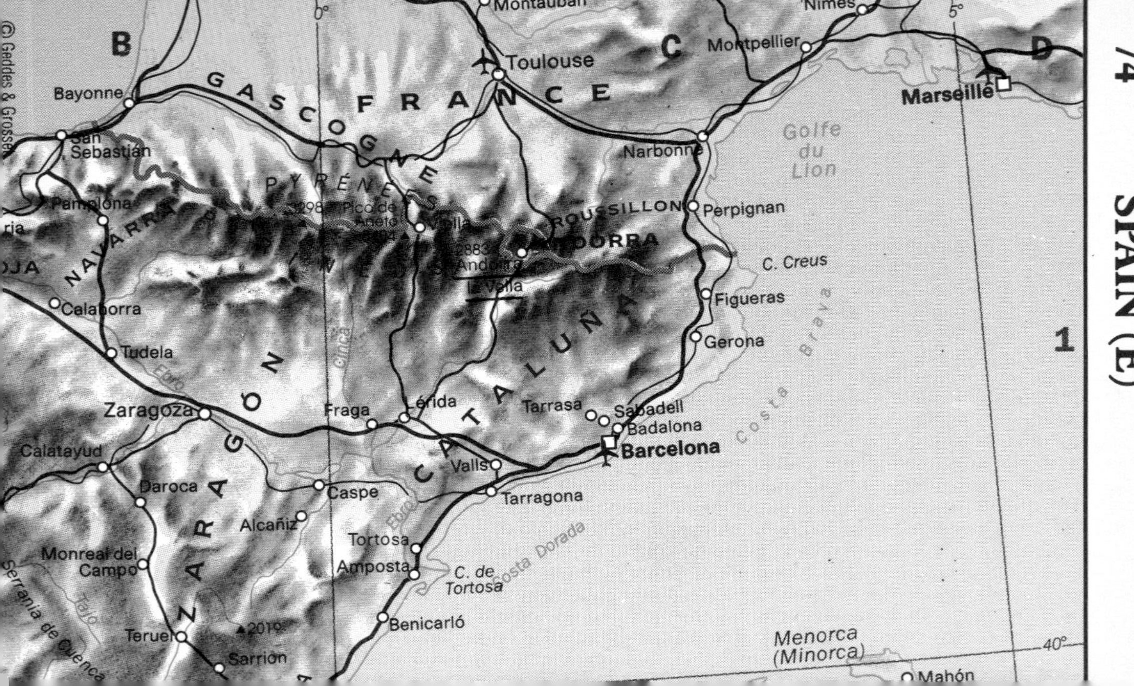

B
C
D
1
Montauban
Nîmes
Montpellier
Toulouse
Marseille
Bayonne
FRANCE
GASCOGNE
San Sebastián
Narbonne
Golfe du Lion
PYRÉNÉES
Pamplona
NAVARRA
3298 Pico de Aneto
Viella
ROUSSILLON
Perpignan
2883
ANDORRA
Andorra La Vella
C. Creus
Figueras
Calahorra
Gerona
Costa Brava
Tudela
Ebro
Cinca
CATALUÑA
Zaragoza
Fraga
Lérida
Tarrasa
Sabadell
Badalona
Barcelona
Calatayud
Valls
Daroca
Caspe
Tarragona
ARAGÓN
Alcañiz
Tortosa
Costa Dorada
Monreal del Campo
Amposta
C. de Tortosa
Serranía de Cuenca
Tajo
Benicarló
2019
Teruel
Sarrión
Menorca (Minorca)
Mahón
0°
5°
40°

Ibiza
(Sp.)
Formentera
Alcoy
Benidorm
Hellín
M U R C I A
Alicante
Cieza
Elche
MEDITTERRANEAN
Costa Blanca
Murcia
SEA
2
Lorca
Cartagena
5°
Costa Calida
Bejaia
Almería
Alger
(Algiers)
Blida
Dahra
Mostaganem
A L G E R I A
Oran
Sidi Bel Abbès
35°
B
West of Greenwich 0° East of Greenwich
C

Dijon
A
B
FRANCHE-COMTE
Jura
Biel
Zurich
LIECHTENSTEIN
Luzern
Bern
Vadu
SWITZERLAND
Mâcon
Lausanne
Genève
SAVOIE
Lyon
Mt. Blanc
4807
4477
Matterhorn
Domodossola
Aosta
Como
4061
Monza
Berg
FRANCE
Novara
Milano
Bres
45°
Grenoble
Valence
DAUPHINE
Torino
Po
Alessandria
Rhône
Mondovi
Cuneo
Genova
Avignon
Savona
Durance
G. di Genova
PROVENCE
Nice
San Remo
Monaco
MONACO
Massa
LIGURIAN SEA
Marseille
Cannes
Toulon
St. Tropez
C. Corse
Piomb
Bastia
2
Calvi
Mt. Cinto
2710
Ajaccio
Cateraggio
CORSE
(Fr.)
Porto Vecchio

Salzburg
15°
Bruck an der Mur
AUSTRIA
Brenner P.
3798
Grossglockner
Graz
Rába
Villach
Tarvisio
Klagenfurt
Maribor
3342
Nagykanizsa
Varazdin
Kranj
Udine
Ljubljana
Sava
Zagreb
SLOVENIA
Monfalcone
Treviso
Trieste
Venezia
Karlovac
Sisak
Vrbovsko
G. di Venezia
Rijeka
CROATIA
Istra
Krk
Senj
Ferrara
Pula
Cres
Rab.
Banja Luka
BOSNIA - HERZEGOVINA
Reno
Lošinj
Karlobag
Gospić
Ravenna
ADRIATIC SEA
Pag
Jajce
Forli
Rimini
SAN MARINO
San Marino
Fano
Dugi
Zadar
DALMATIA
Kornat
Livno
Šibenik
Citta di Castello
Ancona
Split
Civitanova Marche
Brač
Makarska
Perugia
San Benedetto del Tronto
Vis
Hvar
Foligno
Korčula
Terni
Lastovo
Viterbo
2912
Pescara
L'Aquila
Vasto
Avezzano
Termoli
Roma (Rome)
Ostia
Frosinone
S. Severo
Manfredonia

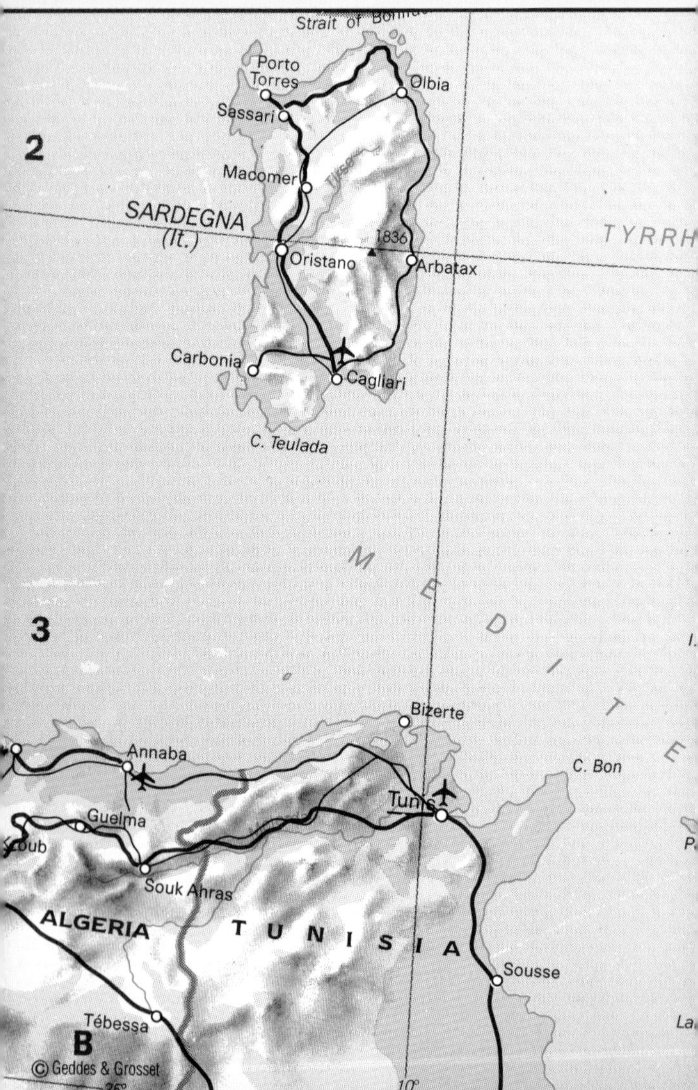
Strait of Bonifac
Porto Torres
Olbia
Sassari
2
Macomer
Tirso
SARDEGNA (It.)
1836
Oristano
Arbatax
TYRRH
Carbonia
Cagliari
C. Teulada
M E D I T E
3
Bizerte
Annaba
C. Bon
Tunis
Guelma
Souk Ahras
ALGERIA
T U N I S I A
Sousse
Tébessa
B
10°
35°

Foggia
Barletta
Formia
Caserta
Benevento
Cerignola
Bari
Monopoli
Napoli
Avellino
ITALY
Ischia
Vesuvio
1277
Salerno
Brindisi
Potenza
Capri
Sorrento
Eboli
Polla
Taranto
Agropoli
Sapri
Golfo
di
Taranto
Gallipoli
G. di Policastro
2248
Castrovillari
Corigliano
C. Sta Maria
di Leuca
Cosenza
1929
Crotone
C. Rizzuto
Vibo
Valentia
Catanzaro
1423
I. Lipari
(Eolie)
Palmi
Messina
Palermo
Locri
Cefalû
Reggio di
Calabria
C. Spartivento
Mti Nebrodi
Mt. Etna
3323
Str. di Messina
Enna
SICILIA
Catania
Gela
Siracusa
C. Passero
Malta Channel
Gozo
MALTA
Valletta
N
A
N
S
E
A
D
(It.)
15°

Tiranë
Durrës
Gevgelija
Ohrid
Bitola
Monopoli
Berat
2480
Brindisi
Kastoria
Vlorë
Korçë
Taranto
ALBANIA
2503
Kateríni
Olimbos
2917
Strait of Otranto
Gallipoli
Golfo di Taranto
Kalabáka
Ioannina
C. Sta Maria di Leuca
Kérkira
Kérkira (Corfu)
GREECE
Piniós
Igoumenítsa
IÓNIOI NÍSOI
Árta
Lamía
C. Rizzuto
Amfilokhía
Levkás
Mesolóngian
Pátrai
Kefallinía
IONIAN SEA
Pelopónnisos
Pírgos
Zákinthos
Tripolis
Kalámai
Pílos
Messiniakós Kólpos
20°

Kavála
Alexandroúpolis
Thásos
Samothráki
Strimonikós
Gökçeada
2033
Singitikós
Límnos
Sea of Marmara
Marmara
Bandirma
Bursa
2
40°
Gelibolu
Eceabat
Çanakkale
Balikesir
Edremit
Ayvalik
Áyios Evstrátios
Iliodhrómia
Lésvos
Akhisar
TURKEY
Manisa
Skiros
AEGEAN SEA
Izmir
Khalkis
Khíos
Selçuk
Athínai (Athens)
Ándros
Sámos
3
Kéa
Tinos
Ikaría
Mikonos
Muğla
Síros
Léros
Bodrum
Kíthnos
KIKLÁDHES
DHODHEKÁNISOS
Kálimnos
Marmaris
Sérifos
Páros
Náxos
Kós
Sífnos
Amorgós
Ródhos
Sea
Síkinos
Íos
Mílos
Astipálaia
Tílos
Ródhos (Rhodes)
Thíra
Anáfi
Kárpathos
Sea of Crete
Kásos
Akr. Sídheros
Khaniá
Kríti (Crete)
Iráklion
35°
2456
Timbákion
F
25°

D
E
20°
Győr
Budapest
Debrecen
Karcag
Tisza
Oradea
Szekesfehérvar
Szolnok
Kecskemet
HUNGARY
Salonta
1836
Turd
Balaton
Kiskunfelegyháza
Duna
1849
Szekszárd
Arad
Szeged
Makó
Pécs
Deva
Subotica
Timişoara
R O M
Caransebes
Osijek
CROATIA
Bosanski Brod
Dunav
Novi Sad
Vršac
Ruma
Dobreta-Turnu-Severin
Beograd (Belgrade)
Šabac
Sava
Tuzla
Bosna
Loznica
Morava
BOSNIA-HERZEGOVINA
YUGOSLAVIA
Drina
Svetozarevo
Zenica
Kragujevac
Vidin
Sarajevo
Paraćin
Čačak
SERBIA
Konjic
Kruščevac
2169
2032
Niš
Pirot
Mostar
Novi Pazar
Leskovac
2522
Kosovska-Mitrovica
Ivangrad
Priština
Mljet
Dubrovnik
MONTENEGRO
Peć
Vranje
Titograd
Uroševac
2692
Kotor
2252
Shkodër
2702
Kumanovo
ALBANIA
Skopje
Titov Veles
Drin

Iaşi
F
Kishinev
G
30°
Roman
MOLDAVIA
Odessa
Bacău
Mureş
Siret
Prut
RUSSIAN FED.
1
Bîrlad
Carpathian Mts.
Tecuci
Focşani
Braşov
Izmail
A
Galati
N
I
45°
2543
Meridionali
Brăila
Buzău
Cîmpina
Ploieşti
Urziceni
Hîrşova
Medgidia
Bucureşti
(Bucharest)
Constanţa
Dunărea
Videle
Mangalia
Giurgiu
Ruse
Ludogorie
Tolbukhin
Olt
Razgrad
Pleven
Byala
Šumen
Varna
2
BLACK
SEA
30°
Veliko Turnovo
Planina
Sliven
Kazanlŭk
Burgas
A
I
R
Michurin
Stara Zagora
L
G
A
Dimitrovgrad
Plovdiv
Edirne
Babaeski
TURKEY
Çorlu
Istanbul
Üsküdar
Planina
Néstos
Xanthi
Komotiní

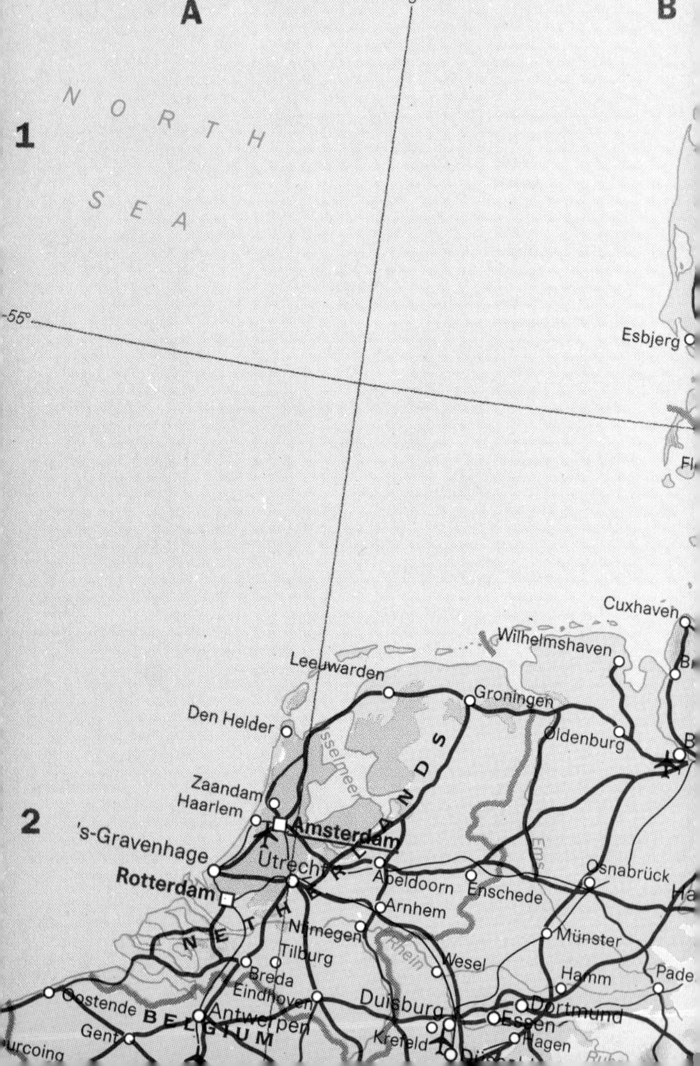
A
B
1
2
5°
55°
NORTH SEA
Esbjerg
Cuxhaven
Wilhelmshaven
Leeuwarden
Groningen
Den Helder
Oldenburg
IJsselmeer
Zaandam
Haarlem
Amsterdam
's-Gravenhage
Utrecht
Rotterdam
Apeldoorn
Enschede
Osnabrück
Arnhem
Nijmegen
Münster
Tilburg
Wesel
Breda
Hamm
Eindhoven
Duisburg
Dortmund
Oostende
Antwerpen
Essen
Gent
Krefeld
Hagen
NETHERLANDS
BELGIUM
Rhein
Ems

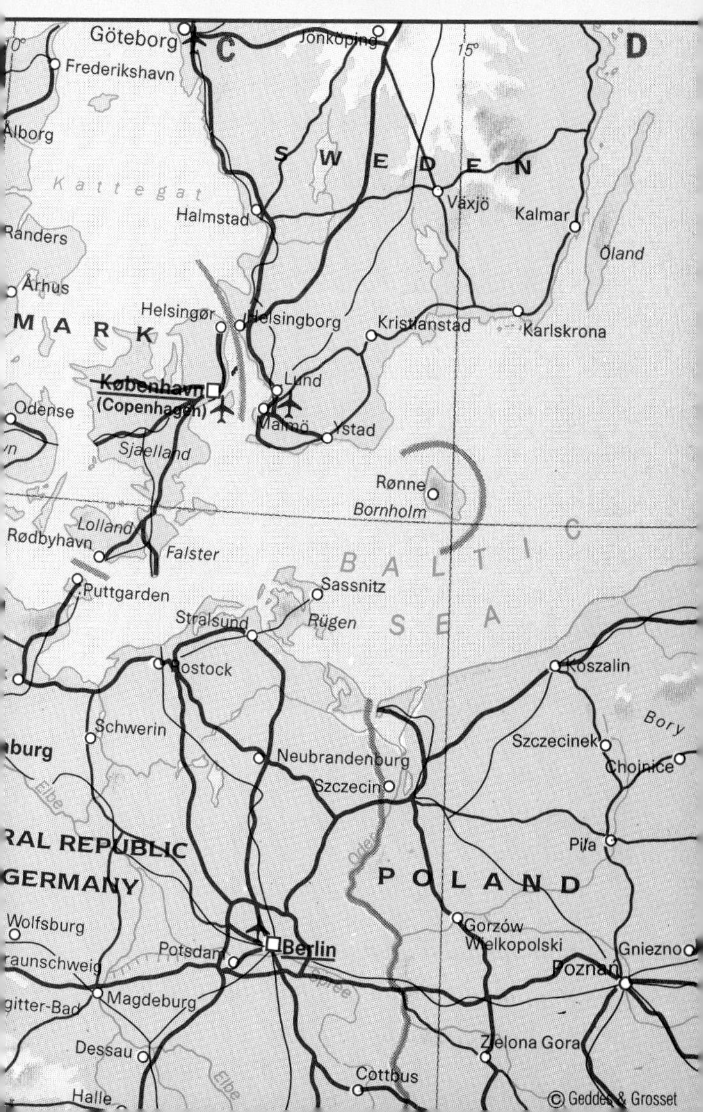
Göteborg
C
Jönköping
15°
D
Frederikshavn
Ålborg
S W E D E N
Kattegat
Växjö
Halmstad
Kalmar
Randers
Öland
Århus
Helsingør
Helsingborg
Kristianstad
Karlskrona
M A R K
København
(Copenhagen)
Lund
Odense
Malmö
Ystad
Sjælland
Rønne
Bornholm
Lolland
Rødbyhavn
Falster
B A L T I C
Puttgarden
Sassnitz
Stralsund
Rügen
S E A
Rostock
Koszalin
Schwerin
Bory
Szczecinek
Neubrandenburg
Chojnice
Szczecin
Elbe
RAL REPUBLIC
GERMANY
Piła
Oder
P O L A N D
Wolfsburg
Gorzów
Wielkopolski
Potsdam
Berlin
Gniezno
raunschweig
Poznań
Magdeburg
Spree
gitter-Bad
Dessau
Zielona Gora
Elbe
Cottbus
Halle

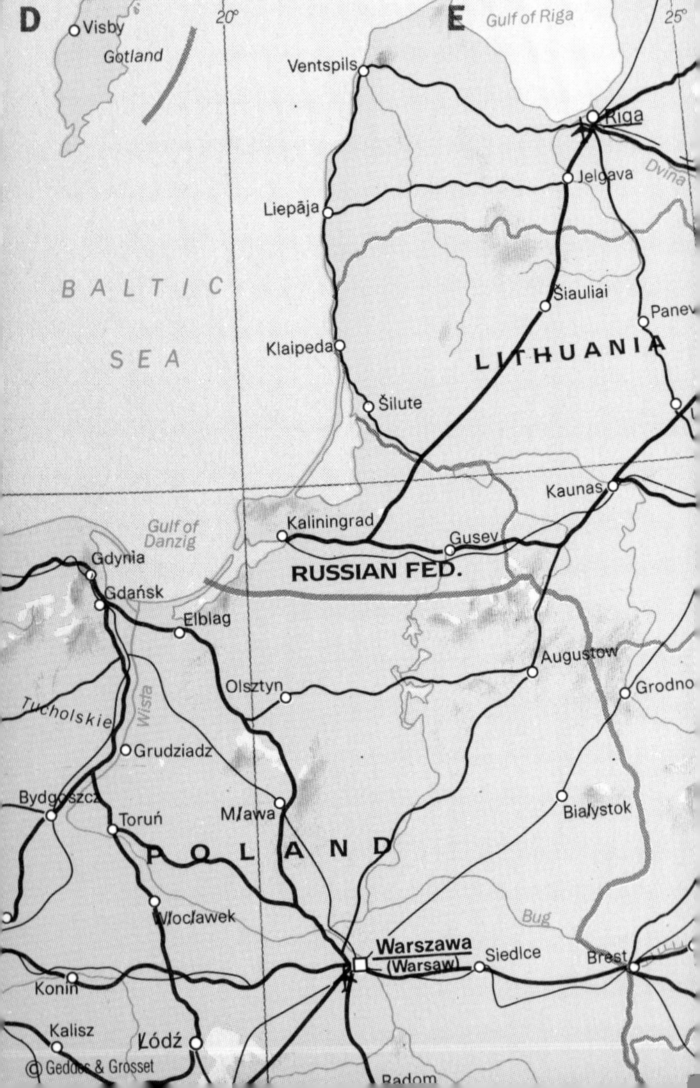
D
E
20°
25°
Visby
Gotland
Gulf of Riga
Ventspils
Riga
Jelgava
Dvina
Liepāja
BALTIC
SEA
Šiauliai
Panev
Klaipeda
LITHUANIA
Šilute
Kaunas
Kaliningrad
Gusev
Gulf of Danzig
Gdynia
RUSSIAN FED.
Gdańsk
Elblag
Augustow
Olsztyn
Grodno
Tucholskie
Wisła
Grudziadz
Bydgoszcz
Mława
Białystok
Toruń
POLAND
Włocławek
Bug
Warszawa
(Warsaw)
Siedlce
Brest
Konin
Kalisz
Łódź
Radom
© Geddes & Grosset

F
G
Ostrov
30°
RUSSIAN
FEDERATION
Rzhev
1
Velikiye-Luki
Rezekne
Polotsk
Novopolotsk
Dvina
Vitebsk
55°
Smolensk
Lepel'
Orsha
Borisov
Molodechno
Mogilev
Minsk
BELORUSSIA
Bobruysk
aranovichi
Dneprovskaya
2
Gomel
Soligorsk
Rechitsa
Dnepr
Mozyr
Pripyat
Nizmennost'
Chernigov
Sarny
UKRAINE
Nezhin

Lublin
Kepno
Kielce
Częstochowa
Opole
POLAND
Wisła
Bytom
Sosnowiec
Gliwice
Katowice
Rybnik
Kraków
Rzeszów
Tarnów
Przemys'l
Ostrava
THE CZECH LANDS
Beskidy Zachodnie
Žilina
2655
SLOVAKIA
Košice
Uzhgorod
Nitra
Miskolc
Nyíregyháza
Satu Mare
HUNGARY
Győr
Budapest
Tisza
Debrecen
Karcag
Székesfehérvár
Szolnok
Oradea
Balaton
Kecskemét
Salonta
1836
Duna
Kiskunfélegyháza
1849
Szekszárd
Szeged
Makó
Arad
Mureş
Pécs
Deva
Timisoara
YUGOSLAVIA
R
O
Caransebeş
Osijek
Novi Sad
20°
© Geddes & Grosset

Korosten
Kiyevskoye Vdkhr
Kiyev
Rovno
Zhitomir
Shepetovka
Belaya Tserkov
Berdichev
Cherkassy
Smela
UKRAINE
Khmel'nitskiy
Vinnitsa
Ternopol
Podol'skaya Vozv.
Pridneprovskaya Vozv.
Uman
Kamenets Podolskiy
Chernovtsy
MOLDAVIA
Prut
Dnestr
Bel'tsy
Suceava
Iaşi
Kishinev
Odessa
Roman
Bacău
Mureş
Siret
Bîrlad
Tecuci
Focşani
Braşov
Galati
Izmail
BLACK SEA
Brăila
Buzău
Cîmpina
A
F
G
2
3
50°
45°
25°
30°

Bruxelles
(Brussels)
Lille
Maastricht
Aachen
Köln
Siegen
Marbu
Kas
Bonn
Liège
Charleroi
Valenciennes
BELGIUM
Ardennes
St-Quentin
Koblenz
Frankfurt
Offenb
Mainz
Darmstad
LUXEMBOURG
Luxembourg
Mosel
Thionville
FEDERA
Reims
Marne
Meuse
Châlons-sur-Marne
Metz
Saarbrücken
Mannheim
Heidelberg
Vitry-le-François
Sézanne
CHAMPAGNE
Rhein
Karlsruhe
Stuttgar
Nancy
St. Dizier
Troyes
Sens
LORRAINE
FRANCE
Strasbourg
Seine
Chaumont
Vosges
Colmar
ALSACE
Schwarzwald
Langres
Freiburg
BOURGOGNE
Mulhouse
Belfort
Montbéliard
Dijon
Basel
Besançon
Zürich
Biel
LIECHTENSTEIN
FRANCHE-COMTE
Jura
Bern
Luzern
Mâcon
Lausanne
SWITZERLAND
Genève
Rhône
Lyon
SAVOIE
Domodossola
Matterhorn
4477
Aosta
Como
4807
Bergam
4061
Grenoble
Novara
Milano
Valence
Torino
Piacenza
A
B
2
3
50°
45°
5°

Leipzig
Jena
Gera
Dresden
Chemnitz
Zwickau
POLAND
Wrocław
Odra
Liberec
Jelenia
Góra
Erzgebirge
Ústí
Kladno
Praha
(Prague)
Hradec
Králové
1490
Jeseníky
Bayreuth
Plzeň
Erlangen
Nürnberg
Böhmer
wald
THE CZECH LANDS
Olomouc
Jihlava
Regensburg
1452
Danube
České
Budějovice
Brno
Znojmo
Donau
Linz
Wien
(Vienna)
München
Bratislava
Salzburg
Enns
Bruck an
der Mur
Rába
Brenner P.
A U S T R I A
3798
Grossglockner
Graz
Villach
Klagenfurt
Drava
Maribor
Tarvisio
Nagyka
Kranj
Varazdin
Udine
Ljubljana
Sava
Monfalcone
SLOVENIA
Zagreb
Treviso
Trieste
CROATIA
Venezia
Padova
C
Rijeka
15°
© Geddes & Grosset

SCANDINAVIA & THE BALTIC (N)

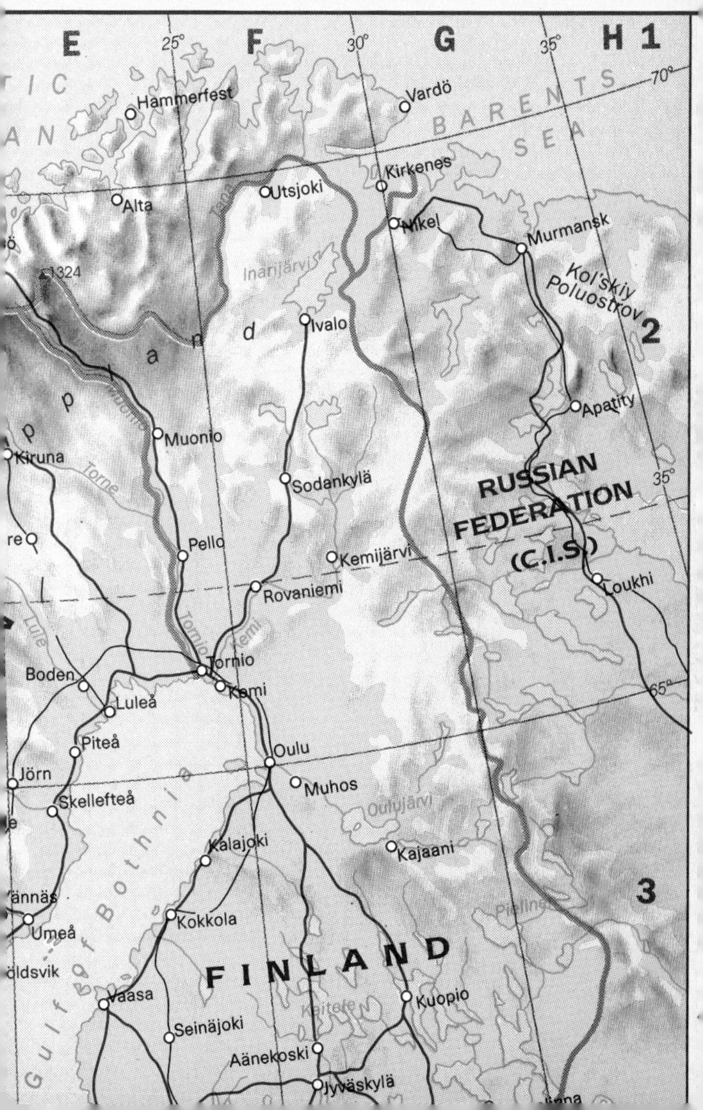
E
F
G
H
1
2
3
25°
30°
35°
70°
65°
BARENTS SEA
Hammerfest
Vardö
Kirkenes
Utsjoki
Alta
Nikel
Murmansk
Inarijärvi
Kol'skiy Poluostrov
Ivalo
Apatity
Muonio
Kiruna
Torne
Sodankylä
RUSSIAN FEDERATION (C.I.S.)
Pello
Kemijärvi
Loukhi
Rovaniemi
Tornio
Kemi
Lule
Boden
Luleå
Piteå
Oulu
Jörn
Muhos
Skellefteå
Oulujärvi
Kalajoki
Kajaani
Kokkola
Umeå
FINLAND
Vaasa
Kuopio
Seinäjoki
Äänekoski
Jyväskylä
Gulf of Bothnia
Lapland
1324

SCANDINAVIA & THE BALTIC (S)

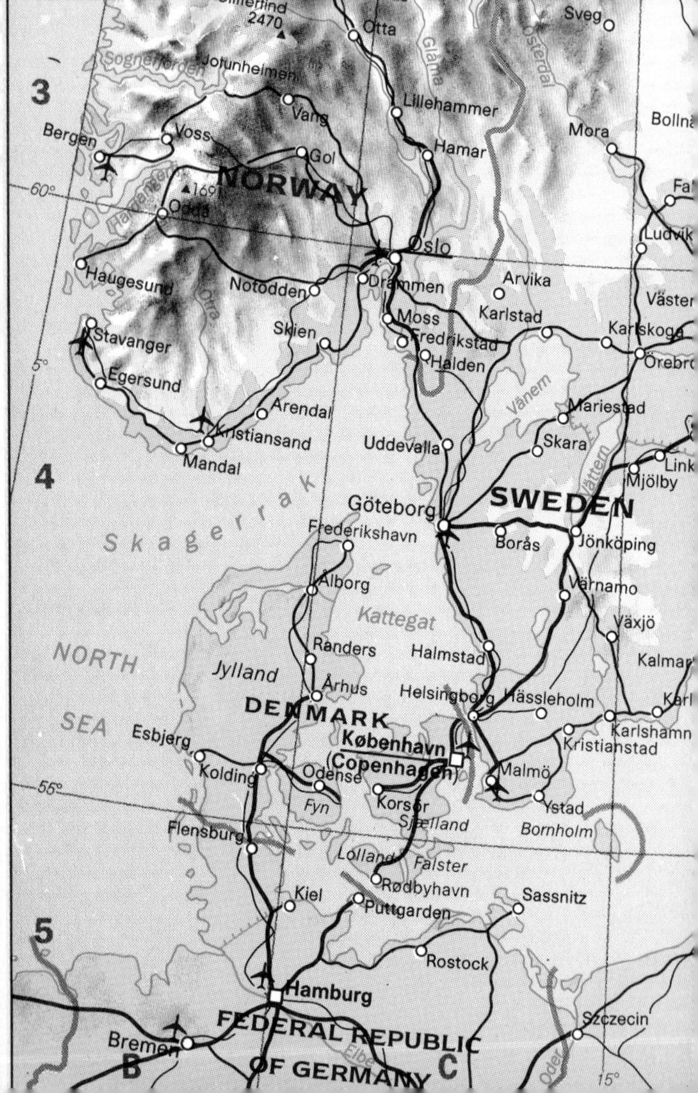

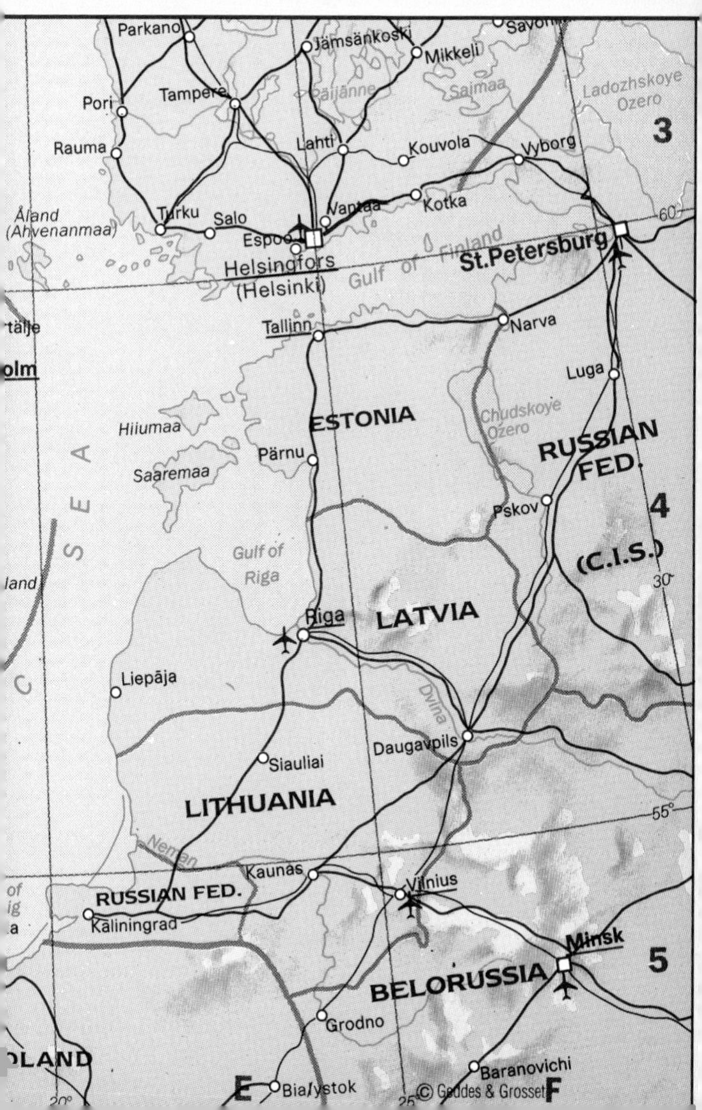
Parkano
Jämsänkoski
Mikkeli
Savonlinna
Pori
Tampere
Päijänne
Saimaa
Ladozhskoye Ozero
3
Rauma
Lahti
Kouvola
Vyborg
Kotka
Åland (Ahvenanmaa)
Turku
Salo
Vantaa
Espoo
Helsingfors (Helsinki)
Gulf of Finland
St.Petersburg
60°
Tallinn
Narva
Luga
ESTONIA
Chudskoye Ozero
RUSSIAN FED.
Hiiumaa
Pärnu
Saaremaa
Pskov
4
SEA
Gulf of Riga
(C.I.S.)
30°
Riga
LATVIA
Liepāja
Dvina
Daugavpils
Siauliai
LITHUANIA
55°
Neman
Kaunas
Vilnius
RUSSIAN FED.
Kaliningrad
Minsk
5
BELORUSSIA
Grodno
Baranovichi
E
Bialystok
F
20°
25°
© Geddes & Grosset

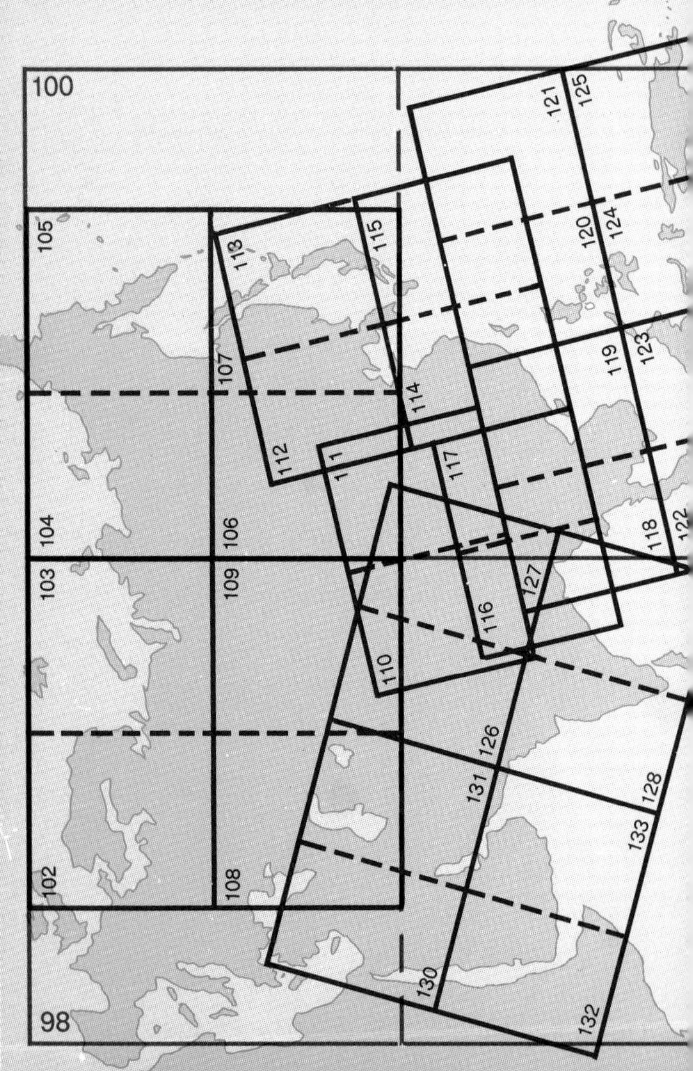
100
105
113
115
121
125
120
124
107
114
119
123
112
111
117
104
106
118
122
103
109
127
116
110
126
131
128
133
102
108
130
98
132

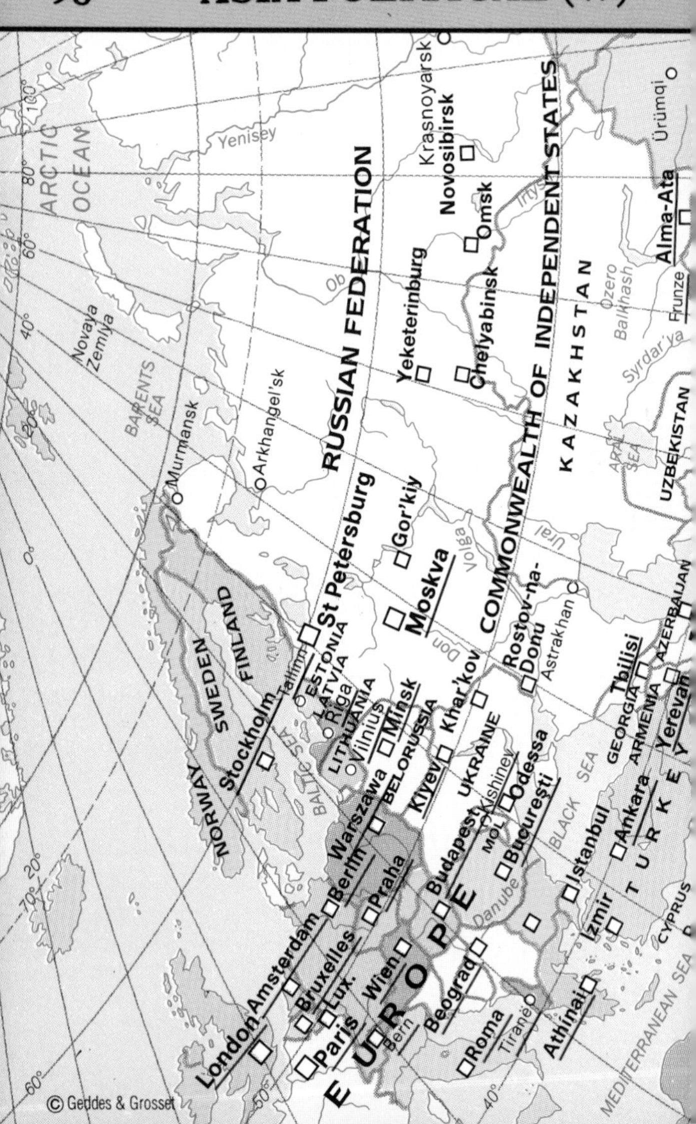

ARCTIC OCEAN
Yenisey
Krasnoyarsk
Novosibirsk
Ürümqi
RUSSIAN FEDERATION
COMMONWEALTH OF INDEPENDENT STATES
Omsk
Irtysh
Alma-Ata
Ob
Yeketerinburg
Chelyabinsk
KAZAKHSTAN
Ozero Balkhash
Frunze
Syrdar'ya
Novaya Zemlya
BARENTS SEA
Arkhangel'sk
Murmansk
ARAL SEA
UZBEKISTAN
St Petersburg
Gor'kiy
Moskva
Volga
Ural
Rostov-na-Donu
Astrakhan
AZERBAIJAN
Tbilisi
GEORGIA
ARMENIA
Yerevan
FINLAND
SWEDEN
NORWAY
Stockholm
Tallinn
ESTONIA
LATVIA
Riga
LITHUANIA
Vilnius
Minsk
BELORUSSIA
Khar'kov
Don
UKRAINE
Kiyev
Kishinev
Odessa
BALTIC SEA
BLACK SEA
Warszawa
Berlin
Praha
Budapest
București
Istanbul
Ankara
TURKEY
Izmir
CYPRUS
Danube
EUROPE
Amsterdam
London
Bruxelles
Lux.
Paris
Wien
Bern
Beograd
Roma
Tirane
Athínai
MEDITERRANEAN SEA

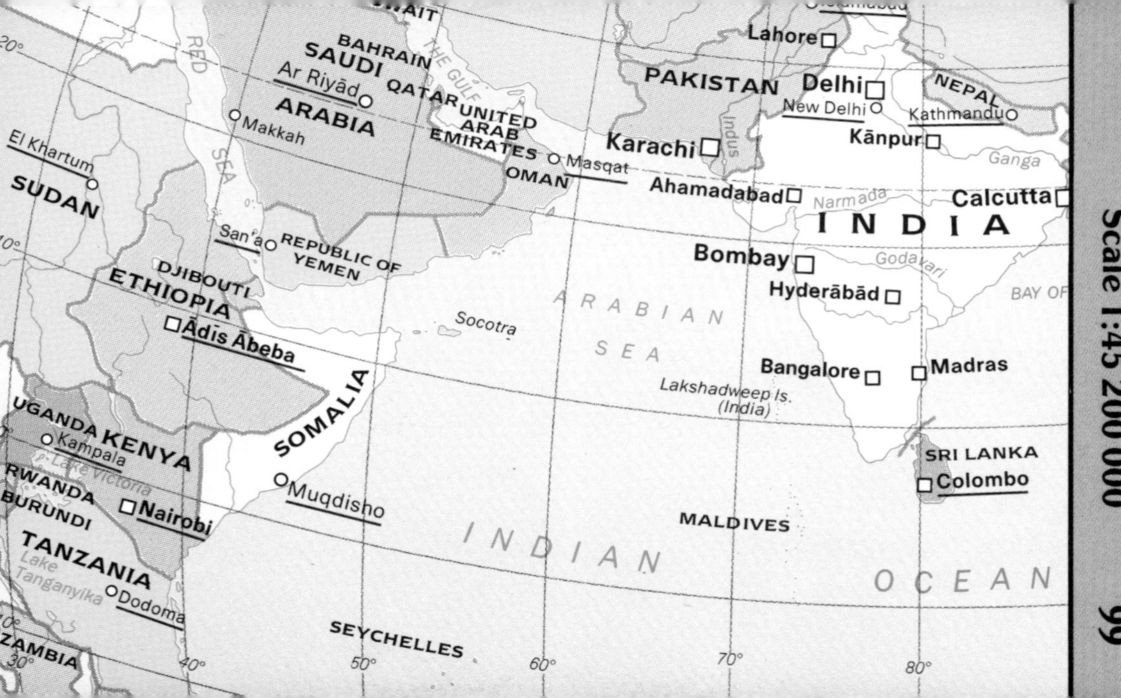
Lahore
PAKISTAN
Delhi
New Delhi
NEPAL
Kathmandu
Kānpur
Ganga
Karachi
Indus
Ahamadabad
Narmada
Calcutta
INDIA
Bombay
Godavari
Hyderābād
BAY OF
Bangalore
Madras
Lakshadweep Is.
(India)
SRI LANKA
Colombo
MALDIVES
ARABIAN
SEA
Socotra
INDIAN
OCEAN
BAHRAIN
SAUDI
Ar Riyād
QATAR
THE GULF
UNITED
ARAB
EMIRATES
ARABIA
Makkah
Masqat
OMAN
RED
SEA
El Khartum
SUDAN
San'a
REPUBLIC OF
YEMEN
DJIBOUTI
ETHIOPIA
Ādis Ābeba
SOMALIA
Muqdisho
UGANDA
Kampala
KENYA
Lake Victoria
RWANDA
BURUNDI
Nairobi
TANZANIA
Lake
Tanganyika
Dodoma
SEYCHELLES
ZAMBIA
20°
10°
0°
10°
30°
40°
50°
60°
70°
80°

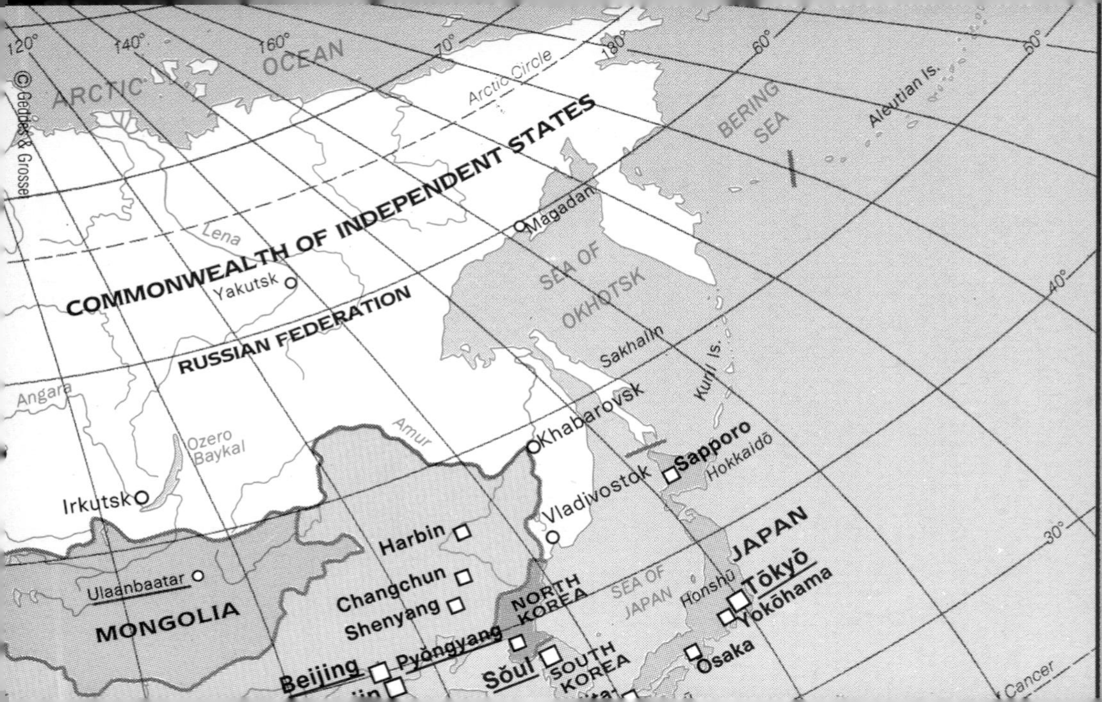
120°
140°
160°
70°
180°
60°
50°
40°
30°
Cancer
ARCTIC OCEAN
Arctic Circle
BERING SEA
Aleutian Is.
COMMONWEALTH OF INDEPENDENT STATES
RUSSIAN FEDERATION
Lena
Yakutsk
Magadan
SEA OF OKHOTSK
Sakhalin
Kuril Is.
Angara
Ozero Baykal
Irkutsk
Amur
Khabarovsk
Sapporo
Hokkaidō
Vladivostok
JAPAN
Tōkyō
Yokohama
Honshū
SEA OF JAPAN
Ōsaka
Harbin
Changchun
Shenyang
NORTH KOREA
Pyŏngyang
Sŏul
SOUTH KOREA
Beijing
Ulaanbaatar
MONGOLIA
© Geddes & Grosset

Lhasa
BHUTAN
Thimphu
Brahmaputra
BANGLADESH
Dhāka
MYANMAR (BURMA)
Chongqing
Kunming
Guangzhou
T'ai-pei
TAIWAN
HONG KONG (U.K.)
Macau (Port.)
PACIFIC
Hanoi
Hainan Dao
Luzon
SOUTH CHINA SEA
Manila
PHILIPPINES
Vientiane
LAOS
VIETNAM
BENGAL
Rangoon
THAILAND
Bangkok
CAMBODIA
Phnom Penh
Ho Chi Minh City
Gulf of Thailand
SULU SEA
Mindanao
Equator
0°
10°
Andaman Is. (India)
Nicobar Is. (India)
Halmahera
New Guinea
CELEBES SEA
BRUNEI
MALAYSIA
Kuala Lumpur
Irian Jaya
PAPUA NEW GUINEA
Medan
SINGAPORE
Borneo
Sulawesi
INDONESIA
Sumatera
Ujung Pandang
ARAFURA SEA
Palembang
JAVA SEA
Timor
AUSTRALIA
Jakarta
Jawa
Surabaya
90°
100°
110°
120°
130°
140°

4
3
60°
70°
10°
0°
Arctic Circle
West from Greenwich East from Greenwich
NORWEGIAN SEA
UNITED KINGDOM
Glasgow
Aberdeen
NORTH SEA
Bergen
Trondheim
NORWAY
Narvik
Oslo
Göteborg
SWEDEN
København (Copenhagen)
DENMARK
Malmö
Hamburg
FEDERAL REPUBLIC OF GERMANY
Berlin
Gulf of Bothnia
Stockholm
Oulu
Turku
FINLAND
Tampere
Helsingfors (Helsinki)
BALTIC SEA
Kaliningrad
Klaipeda
LATVIA
ESTONIA
Tallinn
Petrozavodsk
Ladozhskoye Ozero
LITHUANIA
Riga
St.Petersburg
POLAND
Poznan
Lodz
Wroclaw
Warszawa (Warsaw)
Kraków
Pskov
Vilnius
Daugavpils
Vitebsk
Minsk
BELARUS
Brest
Cherepovets
Vologda
Yaroslavl'
Andropov
Moskva (Moscow)
Kalinin
Ivanovo
Vladimir
Mogilev
Smolensk
Serpukhov
Tula
Gomel'
Chernigov
Kiyev
Zhitomir
Vinnitsa
UKRAINE
L'vov
Chernovtsy
Desna
Volga

A
B
C
D
E
F
G
H
J
K
1
80°
10°
20°
30°
40°
50°
60°
70°
80°
90°
Spitsbergen
Svalbard
(Norway)
Edgeøya
Nordaustlandet
ARCTIC
OCEAN
Zemlya Frantsa Iosifa
BARENTS
SEA
Novaya Zemlya
KARA
SEA
O. Kolguyev
O. Vaygach
Poluostrov
Yamal
Gydanskiy
Poluostrov
Nar'yan Mar
Pechora
Vorkuta
Labytnangi
Ob
Obskaya
Guba
Noril'sk
Yenisey
Igarka
Ukhta
Uralskiy
Khrebet
G. Narodnaya
1894
IAN FEDERATION
vkar
© Geddes & Grosset

1
U
T
S
R
Q
P
O
N
M
L
170°
160°
150°
140°
130°
120°
110°
100°
90°
80°
ARCTIC
OCEAN
O. Komsomolets
O. Oktyabr'skoy
Revolyutsii
Severnaya Zemlya
O. Bol'shevik
Novosibirskiye
Ostrova
O. Faddeyevskiy
O. Novaya Sibir
O. Bol'shoy
Lyakhovskiy
O. Kotel'nyy
LAPTEV
SEA
Gory Byrranga
Ozero
Taymyr
Poluostrov
Taymyr
Khrebet Orulgan
Lena
RUSSIAN FEDERAT
Verkhoya
Gory
Putorana
Sredne
Yaku

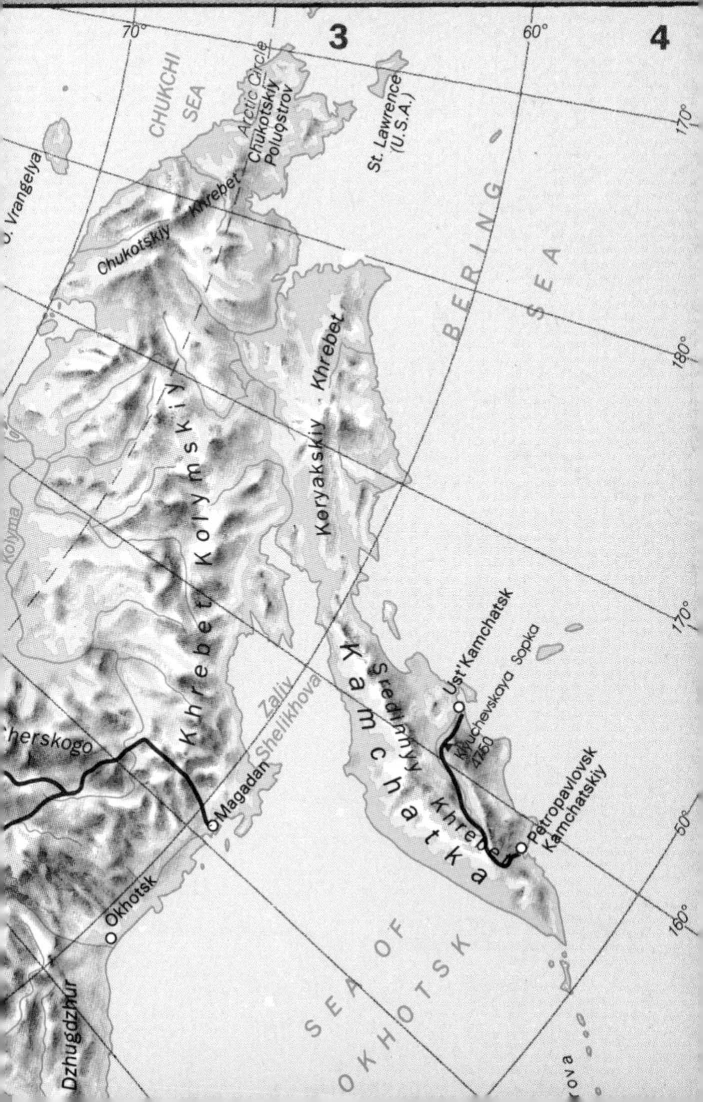
3
4
70°
60°
170°
180°
170°
50°
160°
CHUKCHI SEA
Arctic Circle
Chukotskiy Poluostrov
St. Lawrence (U.S.A.)
O. Vrangelya
Chukotskiy Khrebet
BERING SEA
Koryakskiy Khrebet
Khrebet Kolymskiy
Kolyma
Ust'Kamchatsk
Klyuchevskaya Sopka 4750
Sredinnyy Khrebet
Kamchatka
Petropavlovsk Kamchatskiy
Zaliv Shelikhova
Cherskogo
Magadan
Okhotsk
SEA OF OKHOTSK
Dzhugdzhur

3
Tunguska
Suntar
Sibirskoye
Ploskogorye
Yeniseysk
Angara
COMMONWEALTH OF INDEPENDENT S
RUSSIAN FEDERATION
Bratsk
Krasnoyarsk
Ozero Baykal
Shilka
Khrebet
Tulun
Cheremkhovo
Irkutsk
Angarsk
Ulan Ude
Chita
Yablonovyy
Borzya
Abakan
Zapadnyy Sayan
Vostochnyy Sayan
Kyzyl
Manzhouli
Choybalsan
Ulaanbaatar
(Ulan Bator)
Uvs Nuur
Hovd
Tsetserleg
MONGOLIA
GOBI
Altay
Saynshand
Hohhot
Baotou
Lop Nur
Yumen
CHINA
100°
110°

4
5
6
7
O
P
Khrebet
Sakhalin
Aleksandrovsk-Sakhalinskiy
Komsomol'sk na-Amure
Amur
Sovetskaya Gavan
Yuzhno-Sakhalinsk
Kuril'skiye Ostrova
(Kuril Is.)
Belogorsk
Blagoveshchensk
Birobidzhan
Khabarovsk
Sikhote-Alin
Hinggan Ling
Wakkanai
Hokkaido
Sapporo
Hakodate
Aomori
Qiqihar
Harbin
Ussuriysk
Nakhodka
Vladivostok
Jilin
Changchun
Ch'ŏngjin
SEA OF JAPAN
Sendai
Niigata
Tōkyō
Yokohama
JAPAN
Fushun
Shenyang
Anshan
Hamhŭng
NORTH KOREA
Honshū
Kyōto
Nagoya
Wŏnsan
SOUTH KOREA
Ōsaka
Kōbe
P'yŏngyang
Sŏul (Seoul)
Taegu
Pusan
Lüda
Taejŏn
Kwangju
Shikoku
Kita-Kyūshū
Kyūshū
Bo Hai
Qingdao
Mokp'o
YELLOW SEA
Fukuoka
Jinan
Kagoshima
150°
140°
40°
30°
120°
130°
© Geddes & Grosset

Kishinev
MOL.
UKRAINE
Odessa
Krivoy Rog
Nikolayev
Dnepropetrovsk
Sumy
Poltava
Kursk
Orel
Khar'kov
Donetsk
Zaporozh'ye
Melitopol'
Zhdanov
Sevastopol'
Kerch
Azovskoye More
Voroshilovgrad
Shakhty
Rostov-na-Donu
Voronezh
Tambov
Ryazan'
Gor'kiy
Ul'yanovsk
Penza
Syzran'
Saratov
Kuyb
Ural'sk
Oren
Volgograd
Don
Astrakhan'
Gur'yev
Ural
BLACK SEA
Novorossiysk
Krasnodar
Stavropol'
Samsun
Sukhumi
Batumi
Elbrus
GEORGIA
Caucasus
Groznyy
Makhachkala
TURKEY
Erzurum
Yerevan
Tbilisi
ARMENIA
Kirovabad
AZERBAIJAN
Baku
Diyarbakir
SYRIA
Araks
Tabriz
Al Mawşil
CASPIAN SEA
Plato Ustyurt
Krasnovodsk
Karakumy
TURKMENISTAN
IRAQ
Baghdād
Tehrān
Ashkhabad
Chardzh
Mashhad
Mary
Eşfahān
IRAN
Al Başra
KUWAIT
THE GULF
Herat
AFGH
30°
40°
50°
60°
5
6
7
F
G

Zapadno
Sibirskaya
Nizmennost
RUSSIAN FEDERATION
Sergino
Surgut
Serov
Nizhniy Tagil
Uralskiy Khrebet
Tyumen'
Tobol'sk
Yeketerinburg
Chelyabinsk
Petropavlovsk
Omsk
Novosibirsk
Tomsk
Kemerovo
Prokop'yevsk
Novokuznatsk
Barnaul
Pavlodar
Tselinograd
Semipalatinsk
Karaganda
AKHSTAN
Balkhash
Ozero Balkhash
Zaysan
Oz. Zaysan
Kzyl Orda
Dzhambul
Chimkent
Erunze
Alma-Ata
Ürümqi
shkent
KYRGYZSTAN
Namangan
Andizhan
Fergana
TAJIKISTAN
Pik Kommunizmo
7495
Pamir
Kashi
TIAN SHAN
Pik Pobedy
Turfan Depression
–154
Tarim
CHINA
Tarim Pendi
Ob
Irtysh
Ishim
Tobol
Syrdar'ya
70°
80°
90°
© Geddes & Grosset

A
B
1
2
3
70°
80
50°
40°
Semipalatinsk
Irtysh
Oz. Zaysan
Zaysan
KAZAKHSTAN (C.I.S.)
Balkhash
Ozero Balkhash
Dzhambul
Frunze
Alma-Ata
Namangan
Andizhan
Fergana
KYRGYZSTAN (C.I.S.)
Oz. Issyk-Kul
Pik Pobedy 7439
TIAN SHAN
Ürümqi
Turfan Depression
Kashi
Tarim
Yarkant
XINJIANG UYGUR ZIZHIQU
Bosten Hu
Tarim Pendi
Taklimakan Shamo
Hotan
Ruoqiang
Altun Shan
Karakoram
K2 8611
Kunlun
Xizang Gaoyuan
H
© Geddes & Grosset

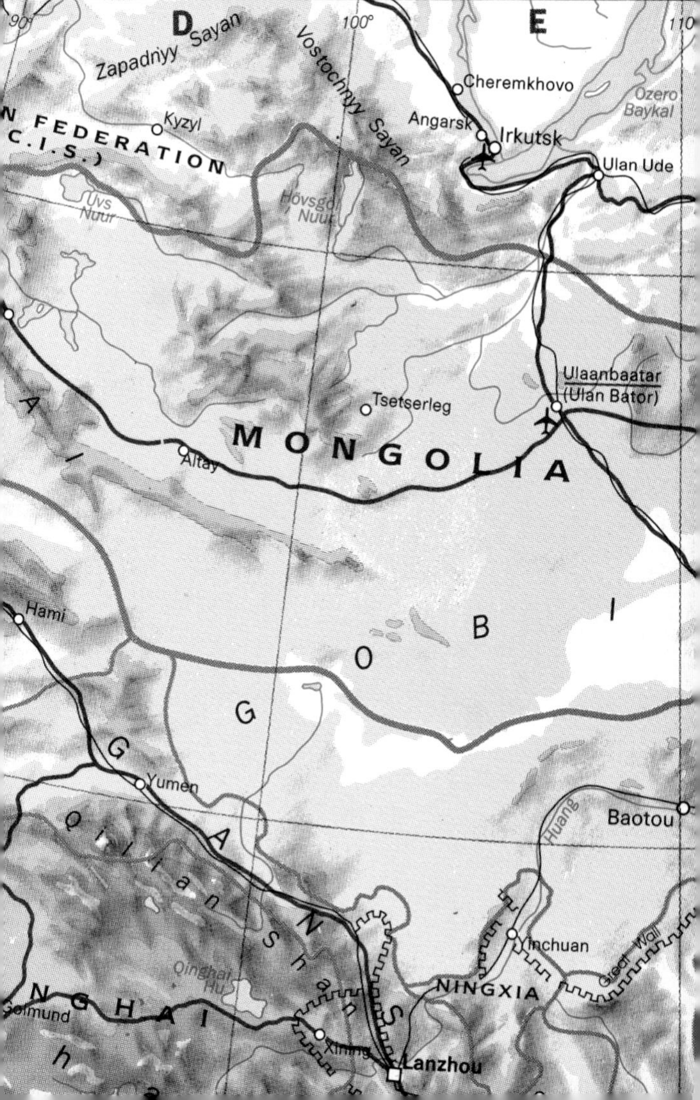
D
E
Zapadnyy Sayan
Vostochnyy Sayan
Cheremkhovo
Ozero Baykal
Angarsk
Irkutsk
Ulan Ude
Kyzyl
N FEDERATION
C.I.S.)
Uvs Nuur
Hövsgöl Nuur
Ulaanbaatar
(Ulan Bator)
Tsetserleg
MONGOLIA
Altay
Hami
G O B I
Yumen
Baotou
Huang
Qilian Shan
Yinchuan
Great Wall
Qinghai Hu
NINGXIA
Golmund
Xining
Lanzhou
100°
110

F
G
120°
130°
Skovorodino
Yablonovyy Khrebet
Shilka
Amur
Chita
Belogorsk
Blagoveshchensk
Ergun
Da Hinggan Ling
Borzya
Manzhouli
Hailar
Xiao Hinggan Ling
HEILONG
Nen
Qiqihar
Choybalsan
Songhua
Harbin
A
Baicheng
JILIN
Saynshand
NEI MONGOL ZIZHIQU
(INNER MONGOLIA)
Jilin
Changchun
Siping
Erenhot
Liaoyuan
Tonghua
Chifeng
Shenyang
Fushun
Fuxin
LIAONING
Benxi
Liaoyang
Jinzhou
Anshan
Zhangjiakou
Yingkou
Dandong
Liaodong
Hohhot
BEIJING
Qinhuangdao
Pyŏngyang
Datong
Tangshan
Beijing
(Peking)
Tianjin
Lüda
Bo Hai
Baoding
HEBEI
Cangzhou
Yantai
Shijiazhuang
Taiyuan
Yangquan
Xingtai
Dezhou
Huang He
Weifang
Handan
SHANXI
Jinan
Zibo
Qingdao
YELLOW
SEA
Changzhi
SHANDONG
Anyang

J
K
2
3
50°
140°
150°
40°
Aleksandrovsk-Sakhalinskiy
Sakhalin
Kuril Islands
Sovetskaya Gavan
Yuzhno-Sakhalinsk
Khabarovsk
Iturup
Kunashir
La Pérouse Strait
Wakkanai
Kushiro
Asahikawa
Sapporo
Hokkaidō
Otaru
Hakodate
Sikhote-Alin
Ussuriysk
Nakhodka
Hachinohe
Aomori
Morioka
Akita
Ishinomaki
Sendai
SEA OF JAPAN
Honshū
Yamagata
Niigata
Nagaoka
Utsunomiya
JAPAN
Tōkyō
Chiba
Nagano
Kanazawa
Kawasaki
Yokohama
Fukui
SOUTH KOREA
Nagoya
Shizuoka
Gifu
Tottori
Kyōto
Hamamatsu
Matsue
Ōsaka
Sakai
Okayama
Kōbe
Wakayama
Pusan
Tokushima
Hiroshima
Matsuyama
Kita-Kyūshū
Kōchi
© Geddes & Grosset

EASTERN ASIA (S.E.), CENTRAL JAPAN

Fukuoka
Sasebo
Kumamoto
Nagasaki
Kyūshū
Miyazaki
Kagoshima
Ōsumi-shotō
Shikoku
PACIFIC OCEAN
Amami Ō-shima
Okinawa
Hachinohe
Akita
Morioka
Miyako
Hanamaki
Mizusawa
Kamaishi
Sakata
Tsuruoka
Furukawa
Ishinomaki
Yamagata
Sendai
Sado shima
Niigata
Fukushima
Sanjō
Nagaoka
Aizu-Wakamatsu
Kōriyama
Mikuni-sammyaku
Noto-hantō
Takada
Iwaki
Takaoka
Nagano
Utsunomiya
Hitachi
Kanazawa
Toyama
Komatsu
Mito
Ashikaga
Matsumoto
Fukui
Takasaki
Tsuchiura
Wakasa wan
Okaya
Tsuruga
Kōfu
Tōkyō
Chiba
Kawasaki
Yokohama
Maizuru
Ogaki
Gifu
Fuji-san 3776
Kiso-sammyaku
Shimizu
Yokosuka
Kyōto
Nagoya
Okazaki
Odawara
Numazu
Toyohashi
Shizuoka
Bōsō-hantō
Kōbe
Ōsaka
Yokkaichu
Matsusaka
Hamamatsu
Sakai
Ise
Wakayama
Kii-sanchi
Kii-suidō
Shingū
CENTRAL JAPAN
1 : 10 000 000
0 100 200 km
0 50 100 150 miles

XIZANG ZIZHIQU
(TIBET)
Gangdise Shan
Tanggula
NEPAL
HIMALAYA
Annapurna
8078
Mt Everest
8848
Kangchenjunga
8598
Kathmandu
Thimphu
BHUTAN
Lhasa
Yarlung Zangbo
Dehra Dūn
Moradabad
Bareilly
Shahjahanpur
Lucknow
Kānpur
Allāhābād
Ghaghara
Ganga
Ganges
Gorakhpur
Vārānasi
Mirzapur
Patna
Son
INDIA
Tropic of Cancer
Bhagalpur
Rangpur
Shillong
Gauhati
Brahmaputra
Ranchi
Asansol
BANGLADESH
Mymensingh
Imphāl
Bilaspur
Jamshedpur
Hāora
Dhākā
(Dacca)
Raipur
Kharagpur
Calcutta
Khulna
Chittagong
Chin Hills
Cuttack
Sittwe
Arakan Yoma
Vishakhapatnam
BAY OF BENGAL
Henzada
3
4
5
C
D
30°
20°
90°

Pingliang
SHAANXI
Tianshui
Baoji
Xi'an
Wei
Qin Ling
Hanzhong
Bayan Har Shan
CHINA
Qamdo
Mianyang
Daba Shan
Nanchong
Wanxian
Chengdu
SICHUAN
Batang
Ya'an
Sichuan
Leshan Pendi
Chongqing
Yibin
Luzhou
Zunyi
Dalou Shan
Wu
Dukou
GUIZHOU
Guiyang
Duyun
Anshun
Dali
Kunming
YUNNAN
Nanpan
Lincang
Liuzhou
GUANGXI
Lashio
Gejiu
Lao Cai
Lai Chau
Nanning
Lang Son
Beihai
Kengtung
Hanoi
Haiphong
Nam Dinh
Gulf of Tongkin
Mekong
Luang Prabang
Chiang Mai
M. Lampang
LAOS
VIETNAM
AILAND
Vientiane
Vinh
Nong Khai
100°
110°

NEPAL
Thimphu
BHUTAN
A
B
90°
100°
Sadiya
Bhāgalpur
Rangpur
Brahmaputra
Dibrugarh
Gauhati
Shillong
Naga Hills
BANGLADESH
INDIA
Ganga
Myitkyina
Dali
Mymensingh
Imphāl
Dhākā
(Dacca)
Hāora
Khulna
Calcutta
Bhamo
Chin Hills
Chittagong
Lincang
MYANMAR
(BURMA)
Lashio
Myingyan
Mandalay
20°
Kengtung
Sittwe
Arakan
Yoma
Meiktila
Pegu
Yoma
Irrawaddy
BAY
OF
BENGAL
Prome
Chiang Mai
Henzada
Lampang
Dawna Ra.
Pegu
Ping
Nan
Bassein
Yangon
(Rangoon)
Phitsanulok
2
C. Negrais
Moulmein
THAIL
Ye
Nakhon Sawan
Nakhon Ratchasima
North Andaman
Thon Buri
Tavoy
Middle Andaman
ANDAMAN
SEA
Bangkok
(Krung Thep)
Andaman Islands
(India)
South Andaman
Mergui Archipelago
10°
Little Andaman
Gulf
of
Thailand
Ten Degree Channel
Isthmus of Kra
Chumphon
3
Nicobar Islands
(India)
Phuket
Nakhon Si Thammarat

C
D
Chongqing
Luzhou
110°
Dongting Hu
Poyang Hu
Nanchang
Jingdezhen
Changsha
Guiyang
Hengyang
C H I N A
Fuzhou
Guilin
Quanzhou
Liuzhou
Shaoguan
Wuzhou
Xiamen
Nanning
Shantou
Foshan
Guangzhou
Kowloon
Macau (Macao) (Port)
Victoria
HONG KONG (U.K.)
Lang Son
Haiphong
Zhanjiang
Gulf of Tongkin
Haikou
Vinh
Hainan Dao
V I E T N A M
Hue
Da Nang
Paracel Is.
Pakse
Qui Nhon
S O U T H
C H I N A
S E A
Da Lat
Nha Trang
Calamian Group
Ho Chi Minh City (Saigon)
My Tho
Spratly Islands
Palawan

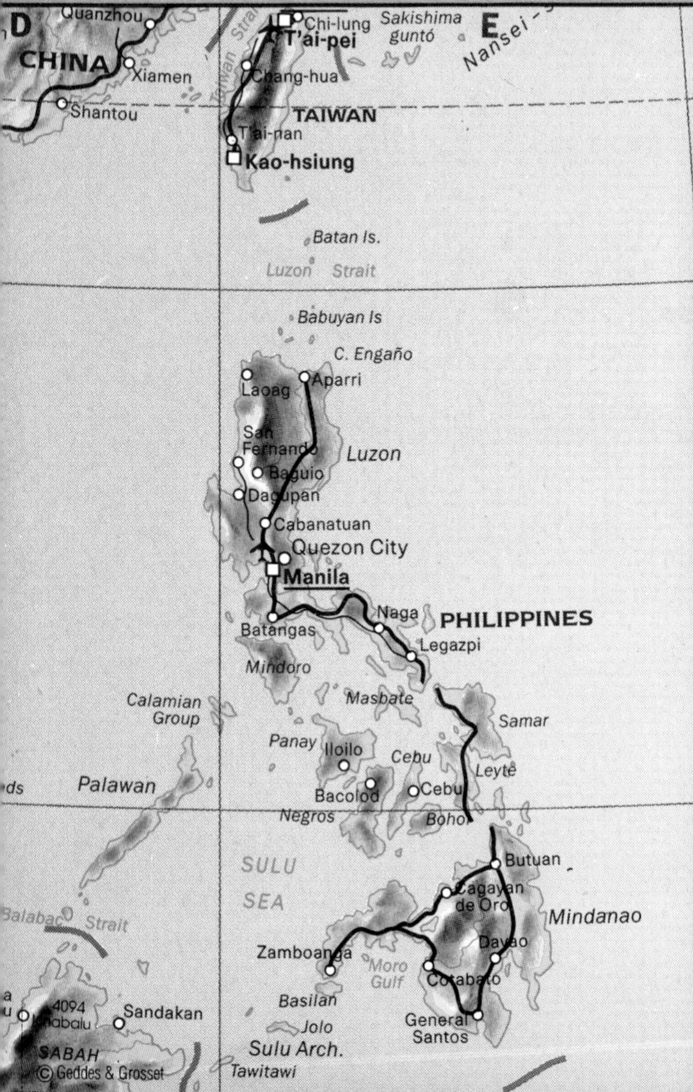
D
E
Quanzhou
CHINA
Xiamen
Shantou
Chi-lung
T'ai-pei
Chang-hua
TAIWAN
T'ai-nan
Kao-hsiung
Sakishima guntó
Nansei
Batan Is.
Luzon Strait
Babuyan Is
C. Engaño
Laoag
Aparri
San Fernando
Luzon
Baguio
Dagupan
Cabanatuan
Quezon City
Manila
Naga
PHILIPPINES
Batangas
Legazpi
Mindoro
Masbate
Calamian Group
Samar
Panay
Iloilo
Cebu
Leyte
Palawan
Bacolod
Cebu
Negros
Bohol
SULU SEA
Butuan
Cagayan de Oro
Mindanao
Balabac Strait
Davao
Zamboanga
Moro Gulf
Cotabato
Basilan
4094
Sandakan
General Santos
Jolo
SABAH
Sulu Arch.
© Geddes & Grosset
Tawitawi

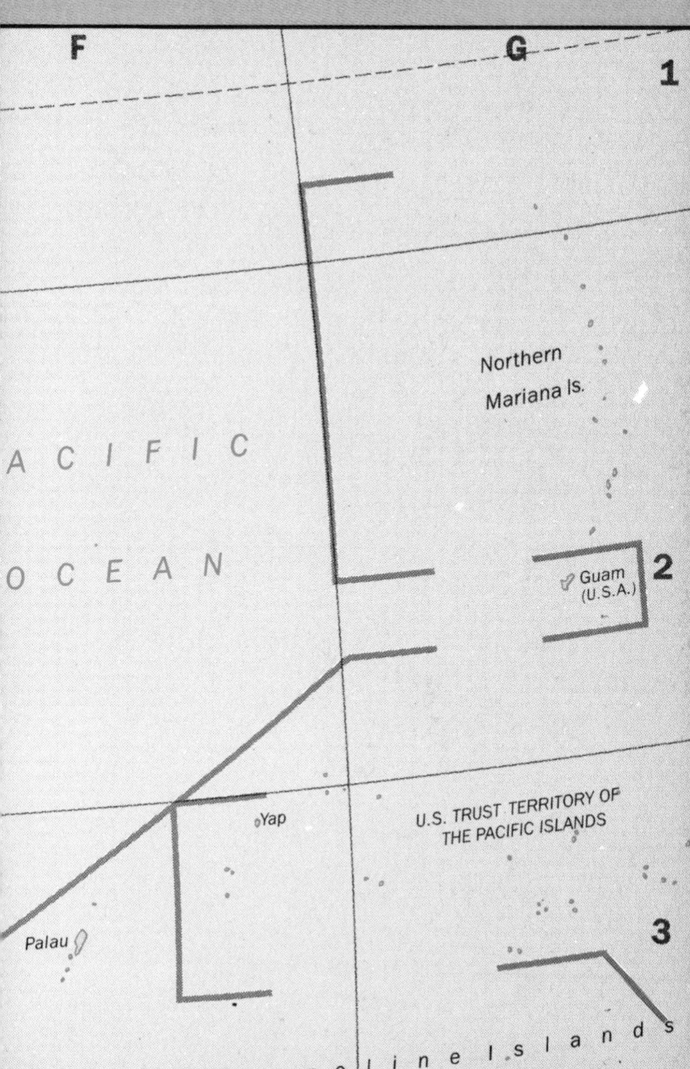
F
G
1
Northern
Mariana Is.
A C I F I C
O C E A N
Guam
(U.S.A.)
2
Yap
U.S. TRUST TERRITORY OF
THE PACIFIC ISLANDS
Palau
3
C a r o l i n e I s l a n d s

MALAYSIA & INDONESIA (W)

Con Son
Balabac Strait
Kota Kinabalu
4094 Kinabalu
Sandakan
Bandar Seri Begawan
BRUNEI
SABAH
A Y S I A
Miri
Natuna Besar
Tawau
Anambas
Kep. Natuna
Tarakan
Sibu
SARAWAK
Rajang
Peg. Iran
Singkawang
Kuching
G. Menyapa 2000
KALIMANTAN
Borneo
Pontianak
Samarinda
Balikpapan
Peg. Schwaner
Palu
Palangkaraya
Kandangan
Makassar Strait
Belitung
Majene
Banjarmasin
Tg. Puting
Laut
Parepare
INDONESIA
JAVA SEA
Ujung Pandang
Jakarta
Cirebon
Semarang
Madura
3428
Surakarta
FLORES
Surabaya
Lesser Sunda
Yogyakarta
Kediri
Bali
Lombok
Raba
Malang
Banyuwangi
Jawa (Java)
Mataram
Sumbawa
Sumba
D
110°
120

SULU
SEA
Butuan
Cagayan de Oro
Mindanao
Davao
PHILIPPINES
Zamboanga
Moro Gulf
Cotabato
Basilan
General Santos
Jolo
Sulu Arch.
Tawitawi
Kep. Talaud
CELEBES
SEA
Kep. Sangihe
Morotai
Manado
Halmahera
Gorontalo
MOLUCCA
SEA
Waigeo
Teluk
Kep. Togian
Tomini
MALUKU (MOLUCCAS)
Sorong
Obi
Poso
Misoöl
Kep. Banggai
Kep. Sula
SERAM SEA
Sulawesi (Celebes)
Fakfak
Seram
Buru
Ambon
Kendari
Muna
Butung
INDONESIA
Kep. Kai
BANDA
SEA
Salayar
SEA
Yamdena
Islands
Wetar
Babar
Kepulauan Tanimbar
Alor
Flores
Ruteng
Ende
Dili
Kep. Leti
SAWU SEA
Timor
Kupang
Roti
120°
130°
© Geddes & Grosset

3
Caroline Islands
Equator
0°
Admiralty Is.
Bismarck Archipelago
BISMARCK SEA
4
Jayapura
Wewak
IRIAN
JAYA
Maoke
Sepik
Central Range
PAPUA
Madang
Mt. Hagen
4508
Mt. Wilhelm
Lae
New Guinea
NEW GUINEA
New Britain
Wau
Fly
D'Entrecasteaux Is.
Owen Stanley Range
Dolak
Merauke
Daru
Port Moresby
10°
Alotau
Torres Strait
C. York
5
AUSTRALIA
CORAL SEA
G
H
140°
150°

NORTHERN INDIA & THE HIMALAYAS

MONGOLIA
Hami
Turfan Depression
Lop Nur
Yumen
Altun Shan
Qilian Shan
Qinghai Hu
Golmud
Kunlun Shan
Bayan Har Shan
Jinsha
Gaoyuan
CHINA
Tanggula Shan
Nu
Nam Co
Lhasa
Shan
HIMALAYA
Yarlung Zangbo
Kangchenjunga 8598
NEPAL
Kathmandu
Mt Everest 8848
Thimphu
BHUTAN
Sadiya
Dibrugarh
Brahmaputra
Naga Hills
Gauhati
Shillong
Myitkyina
Gorakhpur
Patna
Rangpur
Mymensingh
Imphāl
MYANMAR (BURMA)
Bhagalpur
Vārānasi
BANGLADESH
Dhāka (Dacca)
Tropic of Cancer

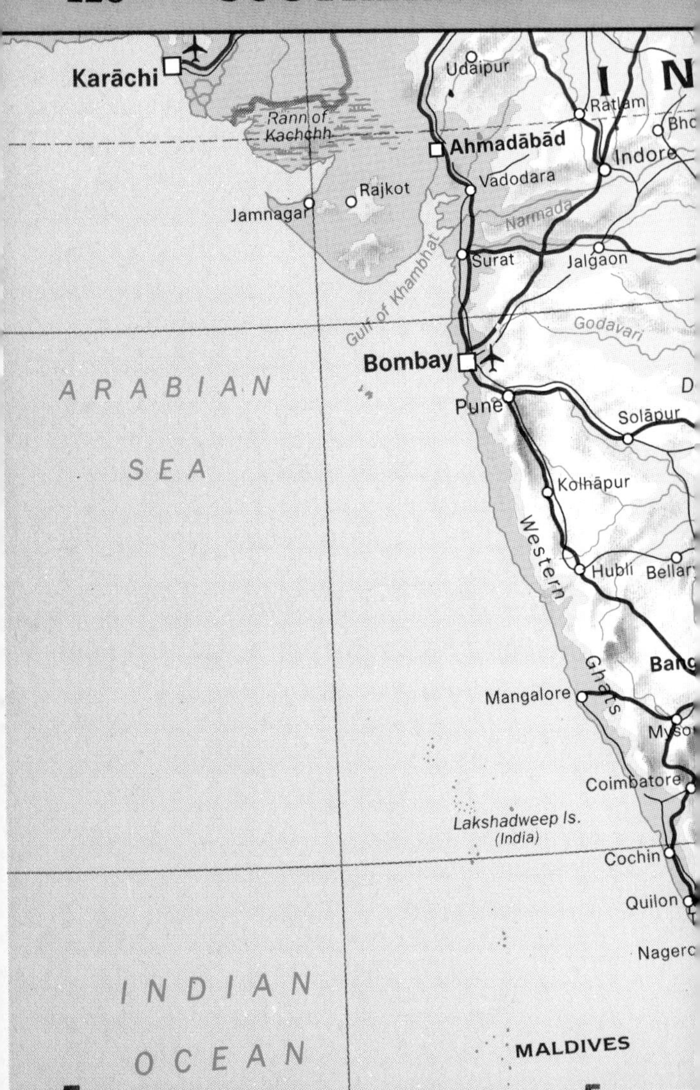
Karāchi
Udaipur
Rann of Kachchh
Ratlam
Bho
Ahmadābād
Indore
Vadodara
Rajkot
Jamnagar
Narmada
Surat
Jalgaon
Gulf of Khambhat
Godavari
Bombay
A R A B I A N
S E A
Pune
D
Solāpur
Kolhāpur
Western Ghats
Hubli
Bellar
Bang
Mangalore
Myso
Coimbatore
Lakshadweep Is. (India)
Cochin
Quilon
Nagerc
I N D I A N
O C E A N
MALDIVES
E
F
70°

A
Asansol
Calcutta
Khulna
Ranchi
Jamshedpur
Hāora
Kharagpur
Chittagong
Mandalay
MYANMAR (BURMA)
Arakan Yoma
Sittwe
20°
Cuttack
Prome
Bassein
BAY OF BENGAL
Vishakhapatnam
Kākināda
jayawada
C. Negrais
4
North Andaman
Middle Andaman
South Andaman
Andaman Islands (India)
dras
Little Andaman
10°
Ten Degree Channel
Nicobar Islands (India)
Trincomalee
SRI LANKA
Great Nicobar
5
Kandy
Galle
G
90°
H

BULGARIA
GREECE
BLACK SEA
Istanbul
Üsküdar
Bursa
Samsun
Sukhumi
Batumi
Trabzon
Eskişehir
Ankara
TURKEY
Izmir
Sivas
Erzurum
Denizli
Konya
Kayseri
Malatya
Antalya
Toros Dağlari
Adana
Diyarbakir
Gaziantep
Ródhos
Halab
CYPRUS
Nicosia
Al Lādhiqīyah
SYRIA
MEDITERRANEAN SEA
LEBANON
Beyrouth
(Beirut)
Hims
Dimashq
(Damascus)
Haifa
Dar'ā
Bādiyat ash Shām
IRAQ
El Iskandarîya
Port Said
Tel Aviv Yafo
Jerusalem
ISRAEL
Ammān
Karbalā
Tanta
El Gîza
Dead Sea
An Najaf
El Qâhira
(Cairo)
Suez
JORDAN
Ma'ān
Sinai
Aqaba
Al Jawf
G. Katherina 2637
El Minya
Tabūk
An Nafūd
Asyût
Nile
Qena
Hā'il
SAUDI ARABIA
EGYPT
Hijāz
Buraydah
Aswân
Tropic of Cancer
Al Madīnah
Ar Ri
(Riya
Gulf of Suez
Al Furāt (Euphrates)
A
B
1
2
3
30°
40°

D
50°
60°
ARAL SEA
Groznyy
Makhachkala
Plato
Ustyurt
UZBEKISTAN
(C.I.S.)
Amurdar'ya
CASPIAN
SEA
Kirovabad
Baku
ZERBAIJAN
(C.I.S.)
Krasnovodsk
Karakumy
TURKMENISTAN
(C.I.S.)
Chardzhou
Ardabīl
Ashkhabad
Rasht
Mary
Reshteh-ye Kūhhā ye Alborz
Qazvīn
Damavand
5671
Mashhad
Tehrān
Qom
Dasht-e-Kavir
Herāt
AFGHANISTAN
IRAN
Eşfahān
Yazd
Dasht-e-Lūt
Farāh
Ahvāz
Kūhhā-ye Zagros
Kermān
Helmand
Shīrāz
Zāhedān
THE GULF
Bandar 'Abbās
Al Manāmah
QATAR
Ad Dawhah
(Doha)
Str. of Hormuz
OMAN

Lake Nasser
Nubian Desert
20°
Nile
SUDAN
Atbara
Atbara
El Khartum
(Khartoum)
Kassala
Wad Medani
Gedaref
Port Sudan
Jiddah
Makkah
At Ta'if
RED SEA
Mits'iwa
Asmera
Danakil
-116
Ras Dashen
4620
Gonder
L. Tana
Ethiopian
Debre Mark'os
Desē
Āseb
San'ā
Al Hudaydah
Ta'izz
Adan
DJIBOUTI
Djibouti
Dirē Dawa
Berbera
Hargeysa
Hārer
10°
Ādīs Ābeba
(Addis Ababa)
Highlands
Jima
ETHIOPIA
Shebele
KENYA
L. Turkana
40°
A
B
C
5

Dubayy
Abū Zabi
(Abu Dhabi)
Gulf of Oman
Al Khābūrah
UNITED
ARAB
EMIRATES
Masqat
(Muscat)
Ra's al Ḥadd
OMAN
Maşīrah
al Knālī
ARABIAN
SEA
Şalālah
YEMEN
ukallā
Socotra
(Suqutra)
(Rep. of Yemen)
INDIAN OCEAN
D
60°

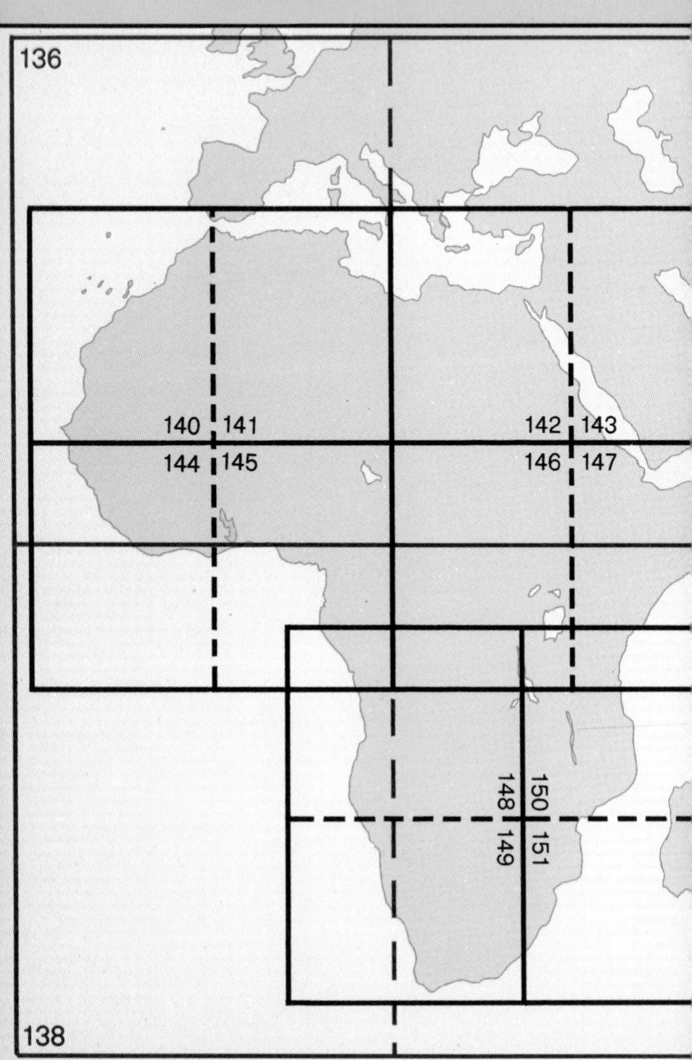
136
140
141
142
143
144
145
146
147
148
149
150
151
138

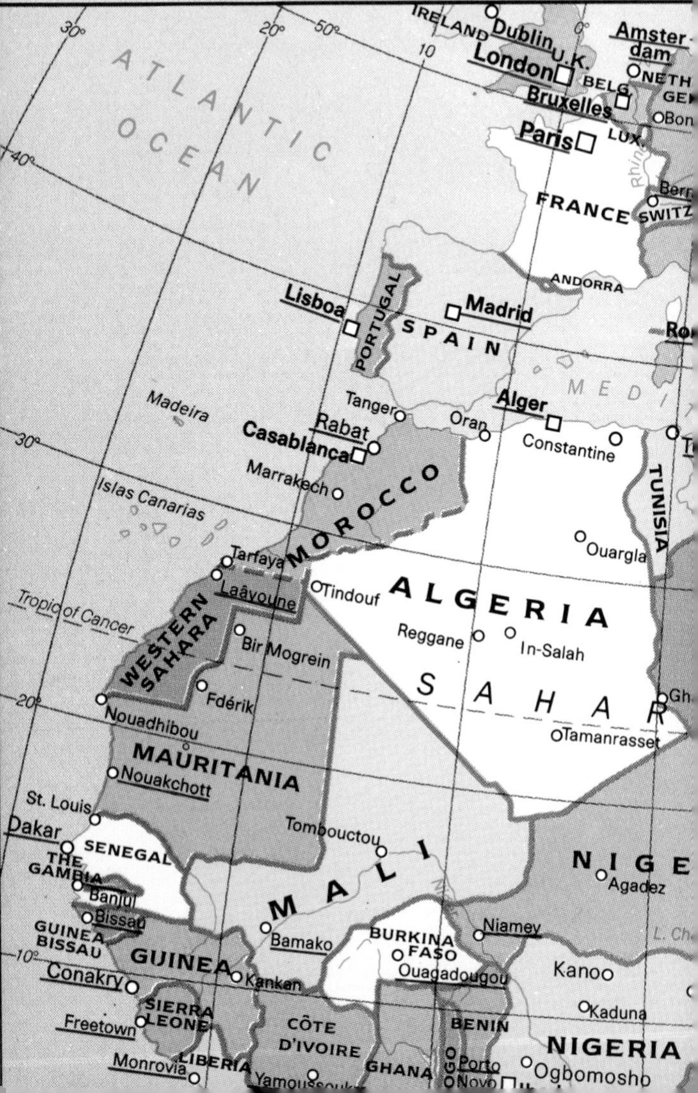

ATLANTIC OCEAN
IRELAND
Dublin
U.K.
London
Amster-dam
NETH
BELG.
Bruxelles
Bon
LUX.
Paris
FRANCE
Rhine
Bern
SWITZ
ANDORRA
Lisboa
PORTUGAL
Madrid
SPAIN
MEDI
Madeira
Tangier
Rabat
Casablanca
Oran
Alger
Constantine
Marrakech
MOROCCO
TUNISIA
Islas Canarias
Ouargla
Tarfaya
Laâyoune
Tindouf
ALGERIA
Tropic of Cancer
WESTERN SAHARA
Bir Mogrein
Reggane
In-Salah
SAHAR
Fdérik
Nouadhibou
Tamanrasset
MAURITANIA
Nouakchott
St. Louis
Dakar
SENEGAL
Tombouctou
THE GAMBIA
Banjul
MALI
NIGE
Agadez
Bissau
GUINEA BISSAU
Bamako
BURKINA FASO
Ouagadougou
Niamey
GUINEA
Kankan
Conakry
Kano
Kaduna
SIERRA LEONE
Freetown
CÔTE D'IVOIRE
BENIN
NIGERIA
Monrovia
LIBERIA
GHANA
Porto Novo
Ogbomosho
30°
20°
50°
10
0°
40°
30°
20°
10°

LITH.
Minsk
BELORUSSIA
RUSSIAN FED.
Warszawa
Kiyev
COMMONWEALTH OF INDEPENDENT STATES
KAZAKHSTAN
ARAL SEA
UKRAINE
Kishinev
MOLDAVIA
ROMANIA
UZBEK.
CASPIAN SEA
Bucureşti
BLACK SEA
GEOR.
Tbilisi
Baku
TURKMENISTAN
Sofiya
BULGARIA
ARM.
AZER.
Ashkabad
Ankara
Yerevan
Tehrān
TURKEY
Athínai
GREECE
SYRIA
Baghdád
IRAN
CYPRUS
LEB.
Dimashq
Euphrates
IRAQ
Beyrouth
Jerusalem
Ammān
KUWAIT
Al Kuwayt
The Gulf
El Iskandarîya
ISR.
JORDAN
El Qâhira
As Suez
BAHRAIN
Ad Dawḥah
SAUDI ARABIA
QATAR
Abū Zabī
U.A.E.
Ar Riyad
Nile
EGYPT
Aswân
RED SEA
Wadī Ḥalfa
Port Sudan
'Atbara
San'ā
REP. OF YEMEN
El Khartum
Asmera
Wad Medanī
Gulf of Aden
El Obeid
DJIBOUTI
Djibouti
SUDAN
SOMALIA
Ādis Ābeba
ETHIOPIA
© Geddes & Grosset

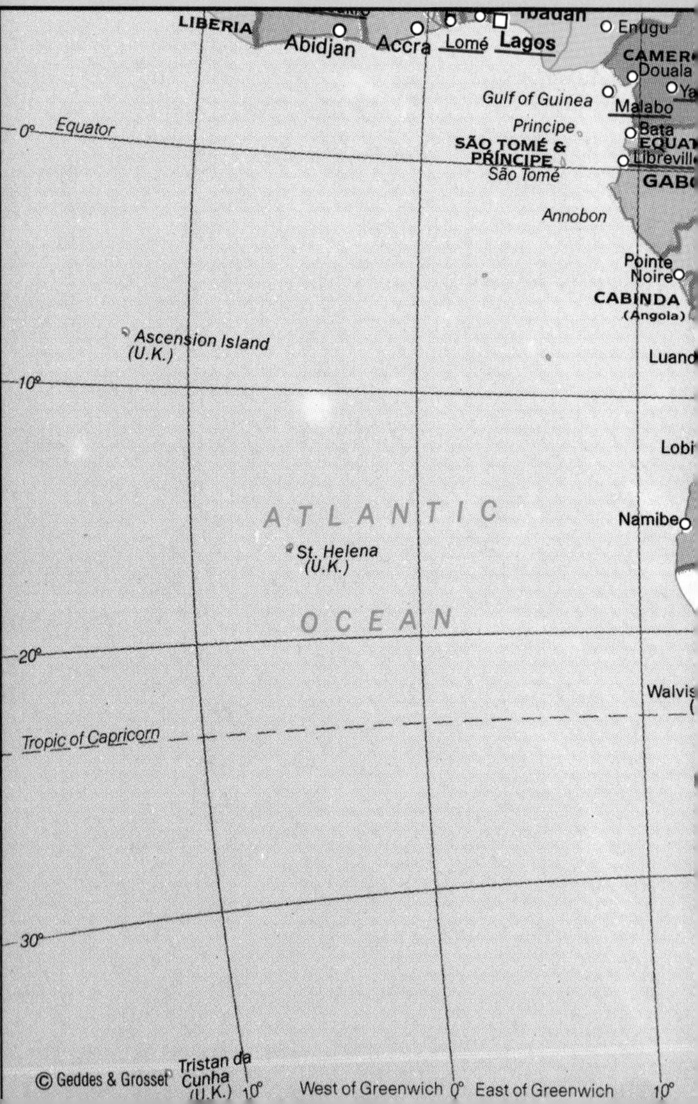
LIBERIA
Abidjan
Accra
Lomé
Lagos
Ibadan
Enugu
CAMER
Douala
Ya
Gulf of Guinea
Malabo
0° Equator
Principe
Bata
SÃO TOMÉ & PRÍNCIPE
EQUAT
São Tomé
Libreville
GAB
Annobon
Pointe Noire
CABINDA (Angola)
Ascension Island (U.K.)
Luand
10°
Lobi
ATLANTIC
Namibe
St. Helena (U.K.)
OCEAN
20°
Walvis
Tropic of Capricorn
30°
Tristan da Cunha (U.K.)
10°
West of Greenwich 0° East of Greenwich
10°

ETHIOPIA
SOMALIA
Wau
Jūbā
Bangassou
Turkana
Mugdisho
UGANDA
Kisangani
Kampala
KENYA
0°
Kismaayo
L. Victoria
Nairobi
RWANDA
Kigali
Mwanza
Kindu
BURUNDI
Arusha
Bujumbura
Mombasa
Kigoma
Kananga
Dodoma
Zanzibar
L. Tanganyika
Kalemie
TANZANIA
Dar es Salaam
Lualaba
Kamina
Mbeya
10°
Likasi
COMOROS
Lubumbashi
MALAWI
L. Malawi
Antsiranana
Ndola
Pemba
Lichinga
ZAMBIA
Lilongwe
Moçambique
Lusaka
Blantyre
Mozambique Channel
Zambezi
Nampula
MOZAMBIQUE
MADAGASCAR
Harare
Livingstone
ZIMBABWE
Beira
Antananarivo
Bulawayo
20°
Limpopo
BOTSWANA
Toliara
Gaborone
Inhambane
Pretoria
Maputo
Johannesburg
Mbabane
SWAZILAND
Bloemfontein
Maseru
Durban
LESOTHO
INDIAN
OCEAN
SOUTH AFRICA
30°
East London
Port Elizabeth
30°
40°
50°

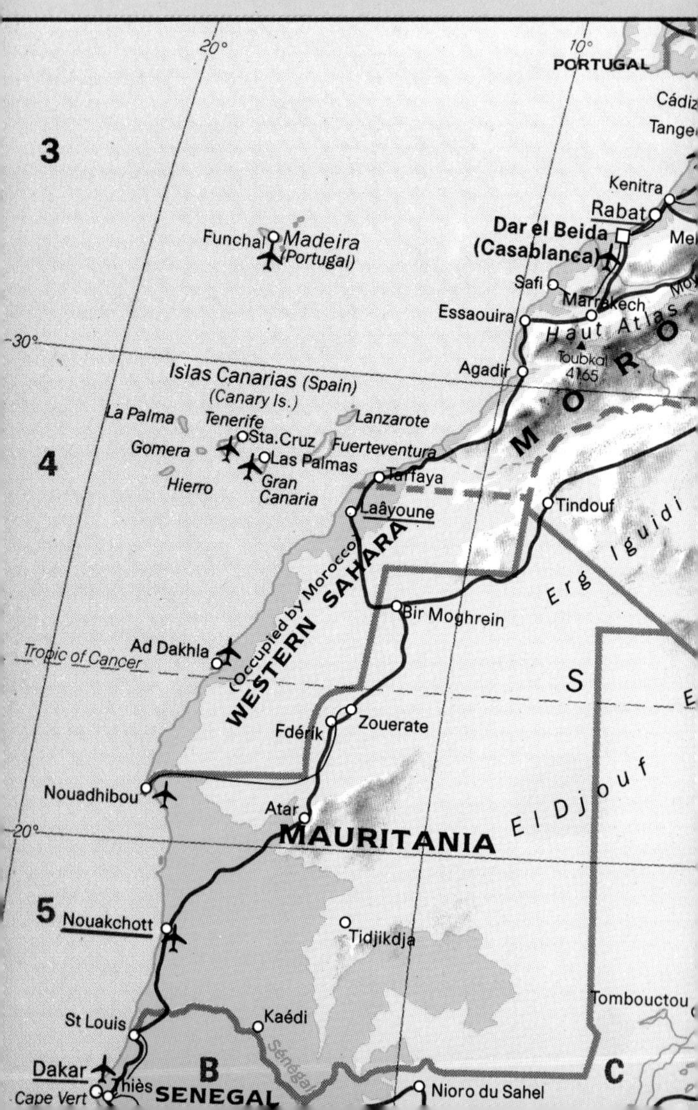
20°
10°
PORTUGAL
Cádiz
Tange
3
Kenitra
Rabat
Dar el Beida
(Casablanca)
Funchal
Madeira
(Portugal)
Safi
Marrakech
Essaouira
Haut Atlas
Toubkal
4165
-30°
Agadir
Islas Canarias (Spain)
(Canary Is.)
La Palma
Tenerife
Lanzarote
Sta.Cruz
Gomera
Fuerteventura
4
Las Palmas
Hierro
Gran
Canaria
Tarfaya
Laâyoune
Tindouf
MORO
WESTERN SAHARA
(Occupied by Morocco)
Erg Iguidi
Bir Moghrein
Ad Dakhla
Tropic of Cancer
S
Zouerate
Fdérik
Nouadhibou
Atar
-20°
MAURITANIA
El Djouf
5
Nouakchott
Tidjikdja
Tombouctou
St Louis
Kaédi
Sénégal
Dakar
Thiès
B
SENEGAL
C
Cape Vert
Nioro du Sahel

MEDITERRANEAN SEA
Cartagena
Alger
(Algiers)
Oran
Blida
Sétif
Skikda
Annaba
Bizerte
Tunis
Sicilia
Constantine
Sousse
Valleta
MALTA
Sidi Bel Abbès
Tlemcen
Djelfa
Biskra
Kairouan
Sfax
Tozeur
Gabès
Tarābulus
(Tripoli)
Atlas Saharien
TUNISIA
Touggourt
Az Zawiyah
Misrātah
Ouargla
Grand Erg Occidental
El Golea
Grand Erg Oriental
Ghadāmis
Timimoun
Plateau du Tademaït
GERIA
In Salah
Sabhā
LIBYA
Ghāt
Hoggar
H
A
R
A
Tamanrasset
Plateau du Djado
Aïr
T
Agadez
NIGER
D
E
© Geddes & Grosset

ITALY
E
20°
Athinai
GREECE
F
Izmir
30°
TURKEY
Kriti
Nicos
CYPRUS
LEBA
Beyr
(Bei
MEDITERRANEAN SEA
ISRA
Al Baydā'
Banghāzī
Gulf of Sirte
Tubruq
El Iskandarîya
(Alexandria)
Port
Said
Tanta
Suez
El Gîza
Qattara
Depression
– 133
El Qâhira
(Cairo)
El Faiyûm
El Minya
Asyût
Nile
LIBYA
Libyan Desert
EGYPT
Lu
Wadi Halfa
3415
Emi Koussi
Faya-
Largeau
Nile
SUDAN
Bodélé
Omdurman
CHAD

H
J
Al Mawşil
Tehrān
Dijlah
Al Furāt
Baghdād
IRAQ
Eşfahān
(Euphrates)
Al Başrah
Abādān
KUWAIT
An Nufūd
BAHRAIN
Ad Dammām
SAUDI
QATAR
Ar Riyāḍ
(Riyadh)
Al Madīnah
Tropic of Cancer
U.A.E.
ARABIA
Makkah
Jiddah
Rub al Khālī
Port Sudan
REPUBLIC OF YEMEN
Mits'iwa
Kassala
Asmera
© Geddes & Grosset
1
2
3

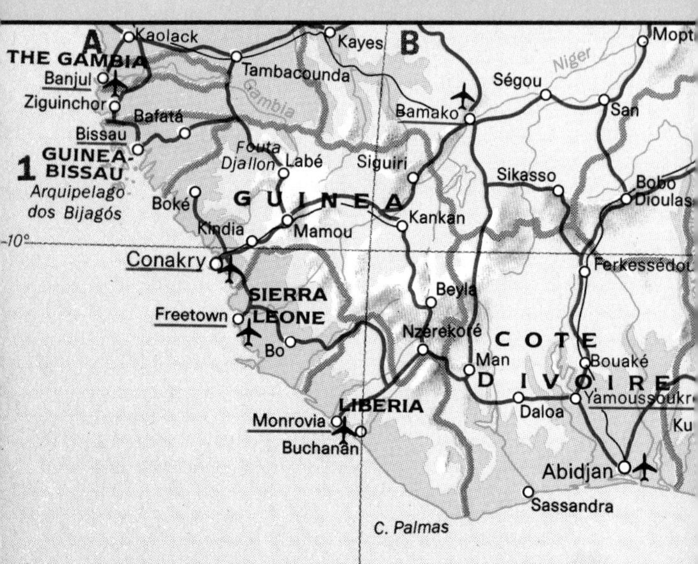
A
B
Kaolack
Kayes
THE GAMBIA
Banjul
Tambacounda
Ségou
Niger
Gambia
Ziguinchor
Bamako
San
Bafatá
Bissau
GUINEA-BISSAU
Fouta Djallon
Labé
Siguiri
Sikasso
Bobo
Arquipelago dos Bijagós
Boké
GUINEA
Kankan
Kindia
Mamou
10°
Conakry
SIERRA LEONE
Freetown
Beyla
Nzerekoré
COTE D'IVOIRE
Bo
Man
Bouaké
LIBERIA
Daloa
Monrovia
Buchanan
Abidjan
Sassandra
C. Palmas
2
0° Equator
ATLANTIC
3
10° West from Greenwich

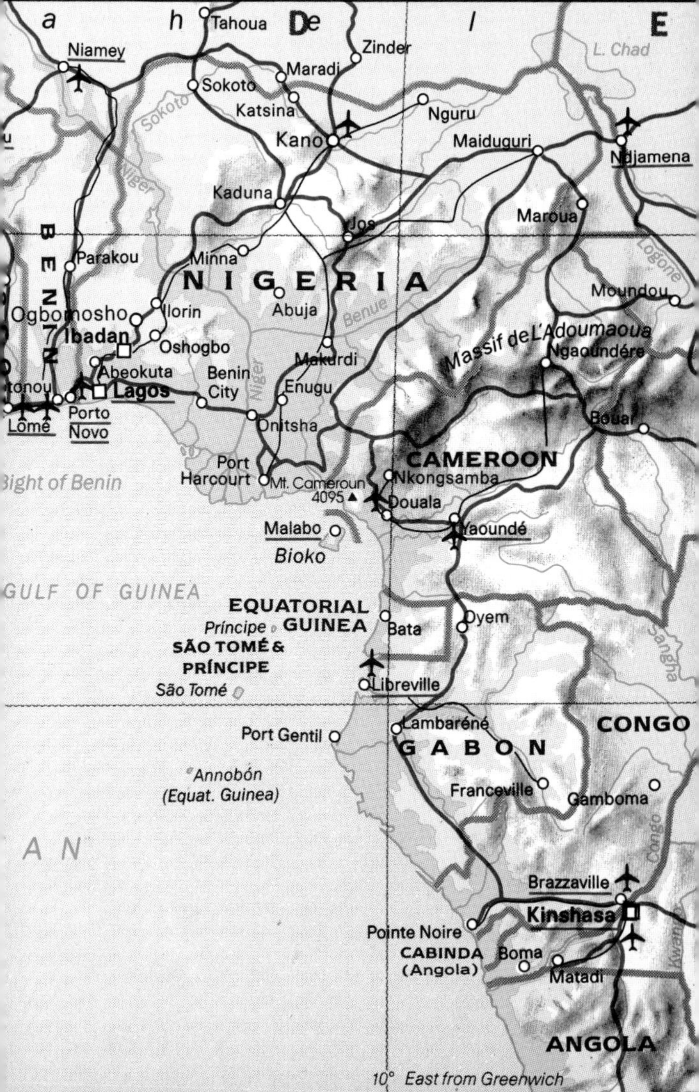
Tahoua
Zinder
L. Chad
Niamey
Maradi
Sokoto
Katsina
Nguru
Kano
Maiduguri
Ndjamena
Kaduna
Maroua
Jos
Parakou
Minna
NIGERIA
Moundou
Ogbomosho
Ilorin
Abuja
Benue
Ibadan
Oshogbo
Massif de L'Adoumaoua
Ngaoundére
Abeokuta
Makurdi
Benin City
Lagos
Enugu
Lomé
Porto Novo
Onitsha
Bouar
Port Harcourt
CAMEROON
Bight of Benin
Mt. Cameroun 4095
Nkongsamba
Douala
Yaoundé
Malabo
Bioko
GULF OF GUINEA
EQUATORIAL GUINEA
Príncipe
Bata
Oyem
SÃO TOMÉ & PRÍNCIPE
São Tomé
Libreville
Port Gentil
Lambaréné
GABON
CONGO
Annobón (Equat. Guinea)
Franceville
Gamboma
Brazzaville
Kinshasa
Pointe Noire
CABINDA (Angola)
Boma
Matadi
ANGOLA
10° East from Greenwich

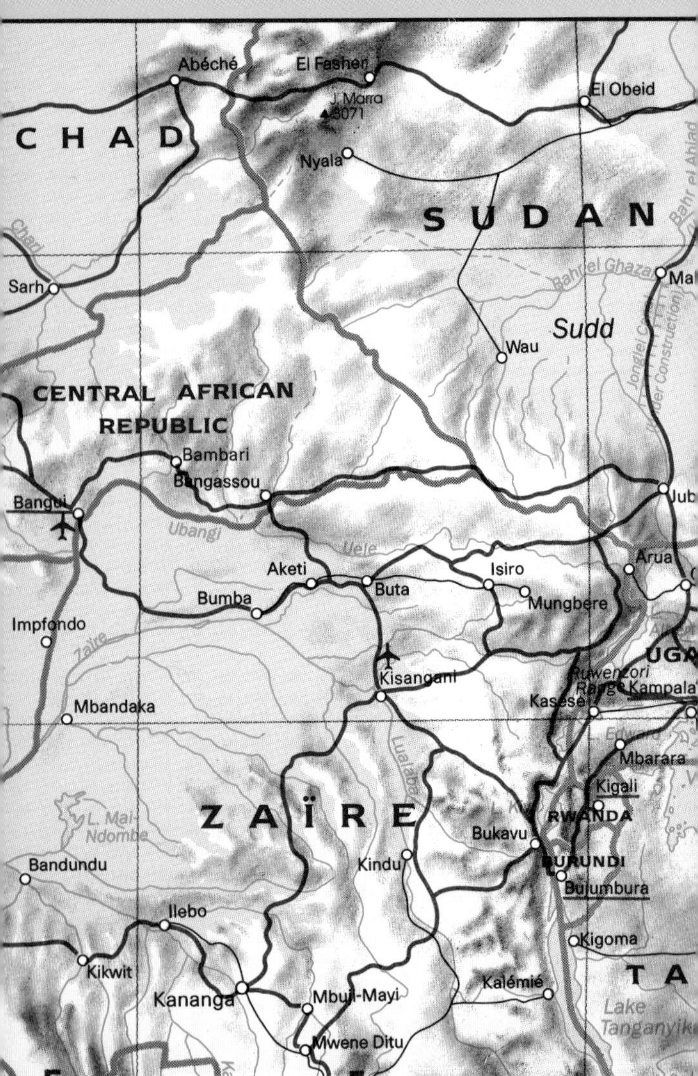

Abéché
El Fasher
J. Marra
3071
El Obeid
C H A D
Nyala
S U D A N
Bahr el Ahiad
Chari
Sarh
Bahr el Ghazal
Mal
Sudd
Wau
Jonglei Canal (under Construction)
CENTRAL AFRICAN
REPUBLIC
Bambari
Bangassou
Bangui
Jub
Ubangi
Uele
Arua
Aketi
Isiro
Buta
Mungbere
Bumba
Impfondo
Zaire
UGA
Kisangani
Ruwenzori
Range
Kampala
Kasese
Mbandaka
Mbarara
Lualaba
Kigali
L. Mai-
Ndombe
Z A Ï R E
RWANDA
Bukavu
BURUNDI
Bandundu
Kindu
Bujumbura
Ilebo
Kigoma
Kikwit
T A
Kalémié
Kananga
Mbuji-Mayi
Lake
Mwene Ditu
Kasai
E
F
20°
30°

Danakil
▼–116
Ta'izz
Ras
Dashen
4620
Āseb
'Adan
Gulf of Aden
Gonder
DJIBOUTI
Djibouti
Desē
Debre
Berbera
Ethiopian
Dirē Dawa
Burco
THIOPIA
Hārer
Hargeysa
Ādīs Ābeba
(Addis Ababa)
Highlands
Shebele
SOMALIA
Lake
Jubbe
Muqdisho
(Mogadishu)
KENYA
Equator
Mt. Kenya
5200
Kismaayo
INDIAN
OCEAN
Mombasa
Masai
Steppe
Tanga
Pemba
Zanzibar
Dodoma
Dar es Salaam
H
J
40°
50°
10°
0°
3
4
5

A
B
C
1
2
10°
20°
GABON
Port Gentil
Franceville
Gamboma
L. Mai-Ndombe
ZAÏRE
RWANDA
Bukavu
BURUNDI
Kindu
CONGO
Congo
Bandundu
Kasai
Lualaba
Brazzaville
Ilebo
Kinshasa
Pointe Noire
CABINDA (Angola)
Boma
Matadi
Kikwit
Kananga
Kalémié
Mbuji-Mayi
Kwango
Mwene Ditu
Kasai
Kamina
L. Mweru
Luanda
Cuanza
Malanje
Kolwezi
Likasi
L. Bangweulu
Lubumbashi
ANGOLA
Chingola
Mufulira
Lobito
Huambo
Kitwe
Ndola
Benguela
Bié Plateau
ZAMBIA
Menongue
Guando
Lusaka
Namibe
Lubango
Mongu

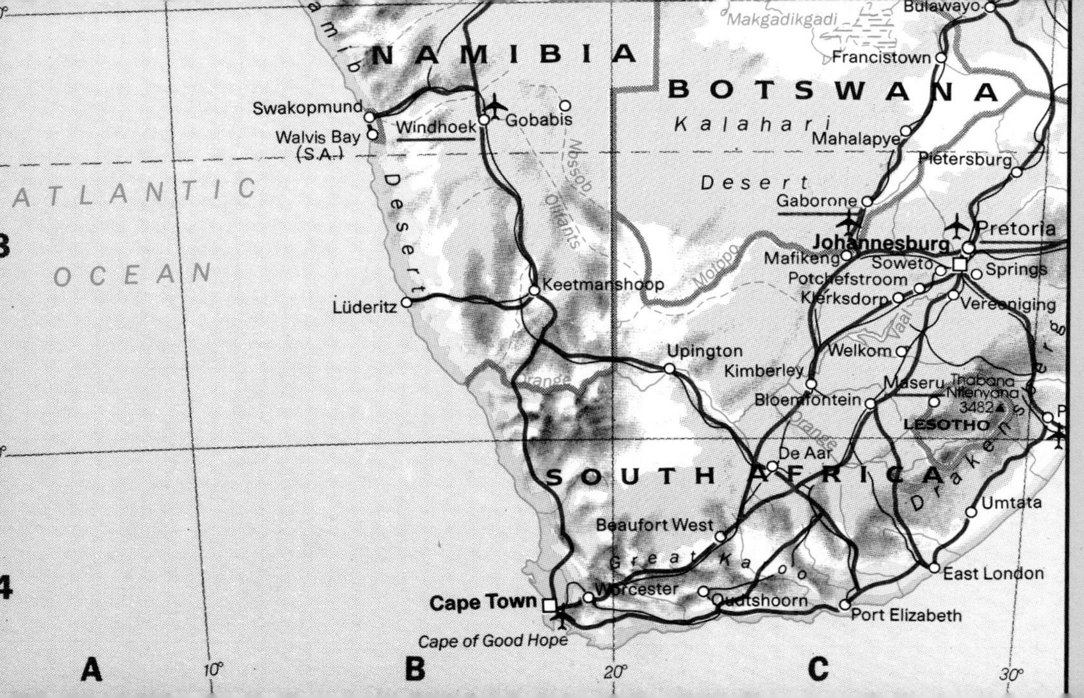

NAMIBIA
Namib Desert
BOTSWANA
Kalahari
Desert
SOUTH AFRICA
LESOTHO
ATLANTIC
OCEAN
Great Karoo
Drakensberg
Makgadikgadi
Bulawayo
Francistown
Mahalapye
Pietersburg
Gaborone
Pretoria
Johannesburg
Mafikeng
Soweto
Springs
Potchefstroom
Klerksdorp
Vereeniging
Vaal
Welkom
Kimberley
Maseru
Thabana Ntlenyana
3482
Bloemfontein
Orange
De Aar
Umtata
East London
Port Elizabeth
Oudtshoorn
Beaufort West
Worcester
Cape Town
Cape of Good Hope
Upington
Molopo
Keetmanshoop
Nossob
Olifants
Lüderitz
Swakopmund
Walvis Bay (S.A.)
Windhoek
Gobabis
20°
30°
10°
3
4
A
B
C

D
E
F
1
2
40°
50°
10°
Kigali
RWANDA
Lake Victoria
Mwanza
BURUNDI
Nairobi
KENYA
Mosi
Mombasa
Tabora
Masai Steppe
Pemba
Zanzibar
TANZANIA
Dodoma
Lake Tanganyika
Dar es Salaam
Mafia I.
L. Rukwa
Iringa
Mbeya
INDIAN OCEAN
SEYCHELLES
Amirante Is.
Farquhar Is.
Kasama
Muchinga Mts.
ZAMBIA
Luangwa
MALAWI
Mtwara
Cape Delgado
Moroni
COMOROS
Mayotte (France)
Antsirañana
Massif du Tsaratanana
Pemba
Lichinga
Lilongwe
Cabora Bassa Dam
Zomba
Blantyre
Tete
Nampula
Moçambique
Mahajanga

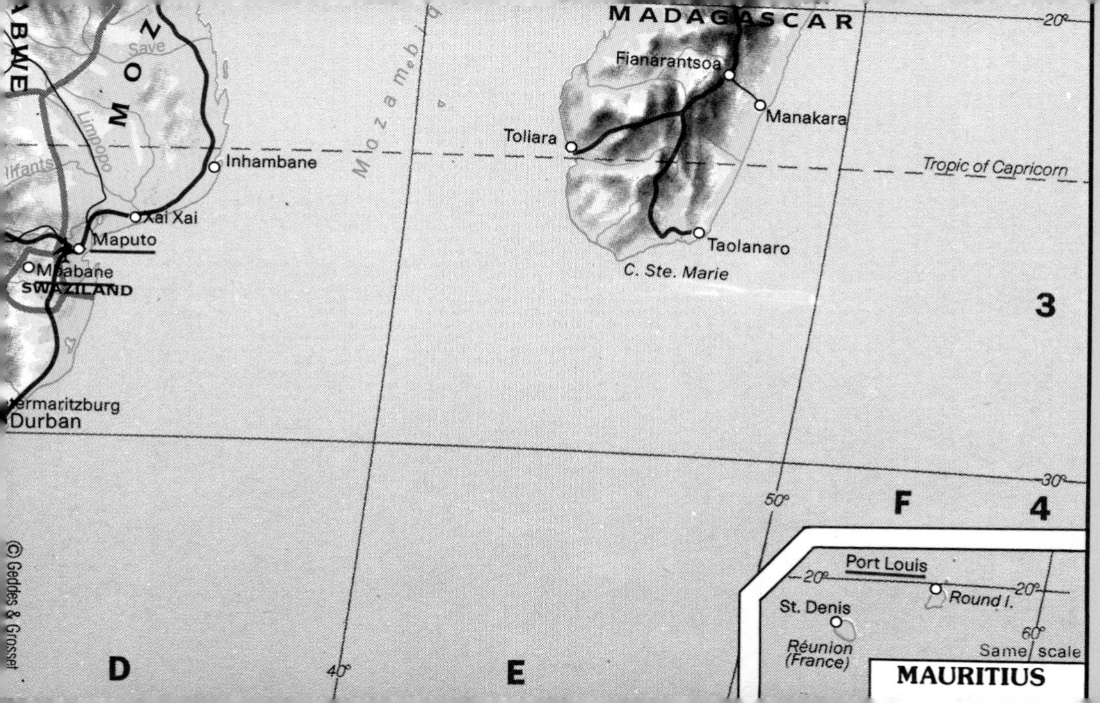
MADAGASCAR
Fianarantsoa
Manakara
Toliara
Taolanaro
C. Ste. Marie
Tropic of Capricorn
Inhambane
Xai Xai
Maputo
SWAZILAND
Save
Limpopo
Durban
MAURITIUS
Port Louis
Round I.
St. Denis
Réunion (France)
Same scale
3
4
D
E
F
20°
30°
40°
50°
60°
© Geddes & Grosset

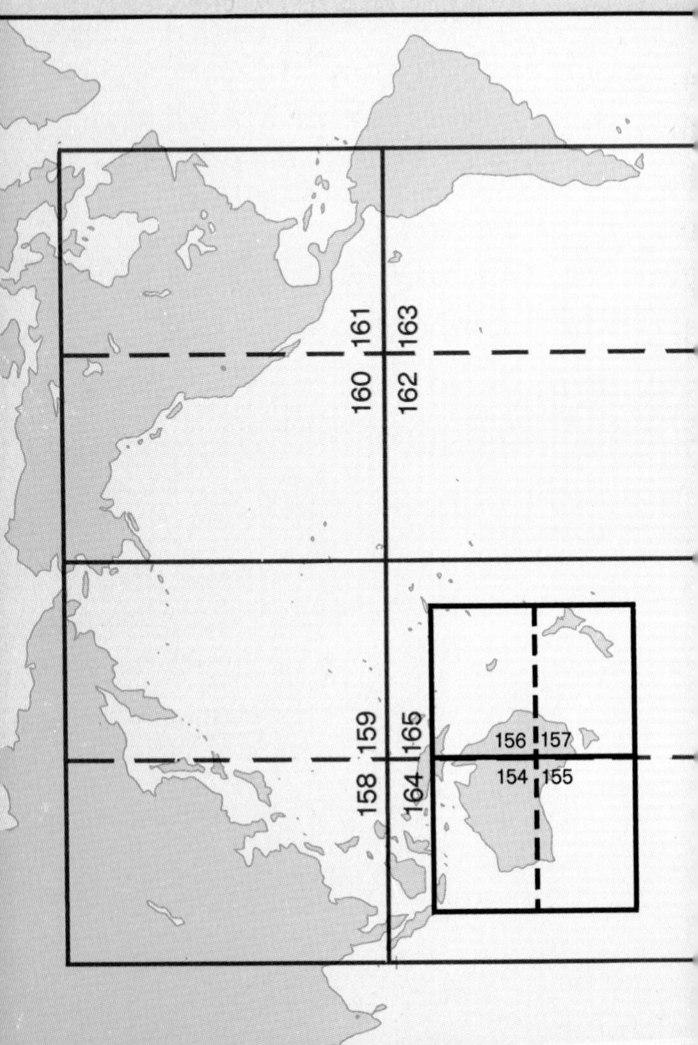
161
163
160
162
159
165
158
164
156
157
154
155

A
B
C
1
2
INDONESIA
FLORES SEA
Lombok
Bali
Sumbawa
Sumba
Flores
Wetar
Timor
TIMOR SEA
Roti
ARAFURA SEA
New Guinea
Torres Strait
C.York
Cape York Penins
Mitch
Melville I.
Bathurst I.
Wessel Is.
Darwin
Arnhem Land
Katherine
Gulf of Carpentaria
Groote Eylandt
Wellesley Is.
Joseph Bonaparte Gulf
Wyndham
Kimberley Plateau
King Leopold Ra.
INDIAN OCEAN
Broome
Fitzroy Crossing
NORTHERN TERRITORY
Barkly Tableland
Flinders
Tennant Creek
Mount Isa
Cloncurry
Hughen
Great Sandy Desert
Port Headland
L. Mackay
Macdonnell Ranges
Mt. Ziel 1510
Alice Springs
WESTERN
AUSTRALIA
Fortescue
Hamersley Ra.
Ashburton
L. Disappointment
Gibson Desert
Ayers Rock 867
Simpson Desert
Finke
Diamantina
Tropic of Capricorn
10°
20°
120°
130°
140°

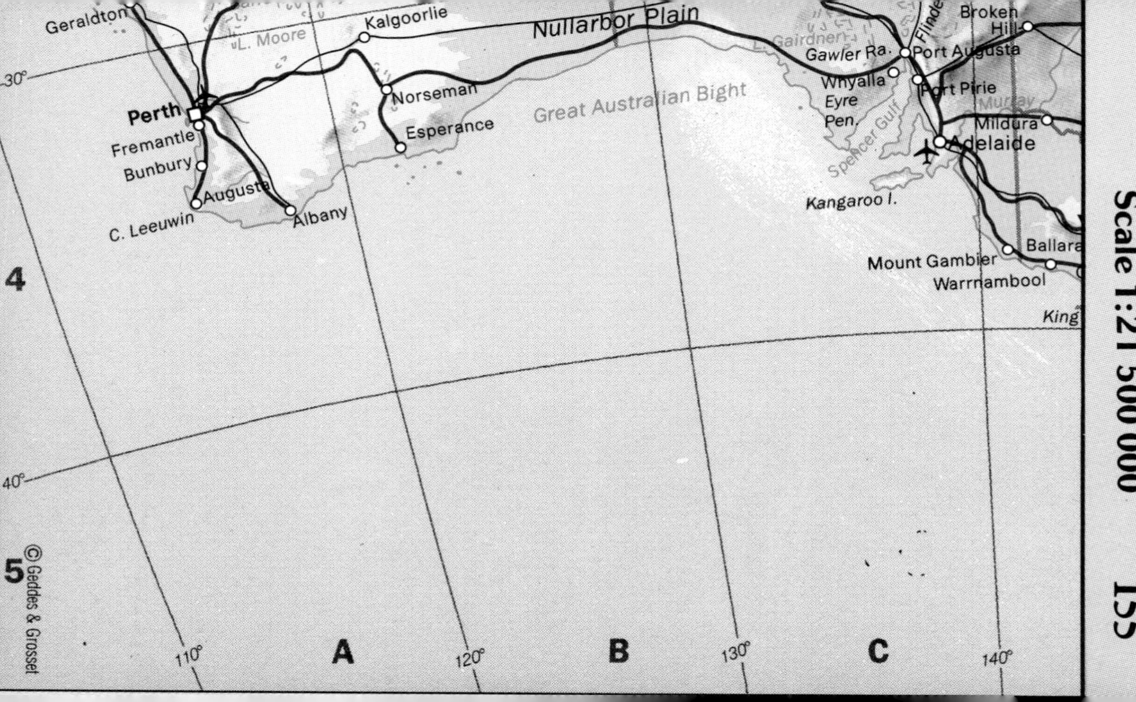
Geraldton
L. Moore
Kalgoorlie
Nullarbor Plain
Gairdner
Gawler Ra.
Port Augusta
Broken Hill
Perth
Fremantle
Bunbury
Augusta
C. Leeuwin
Albany
Norseman
Esperance
Great Australian Bight
Whyalla
Eyre Pen.
Spencer Gulf
Port Pirie
Murray
Mildura
Adelaide
Kangaroo I.
Mount Gambier
Ballara
Warrnambool
King
30°
40°
4
5
110°
A
120°
B
130°
C
140°
© Geddes & Grosset

D
E
F
1
2
150°
160°
170°
10°
20°
PAPUA NEW GUINEA
Port Moresby
Owen Stanley Ra.
D'Entrecasteaux Islands
Louisiade Arch.
New Georgia
Santa Isabel
Honiara
Guadalcanal
SOLOMON ISLANDS
Malaita
San Cristobal
Santa Cruz Is.
Rennell
CORAL SEA
CORAL SEA ISLANDS TERRITORY
Great Barrier Reef
Cooktown
Cairns
Townsville
Mackay
QUEENSLAND
GREAT DIVIDING
Rockhampton
Bundaberg
Fraser I.
Charleville
Banks Is.
Espiritu Santo
VANUATU
Malekula
Epi
Vila
Efate
Erromanga
Tanna
Îs. Chesterfield
Nouvelle Calédonie (Fr.)
Nouméa
Îs. Loyauté
Tropic of Capricorn

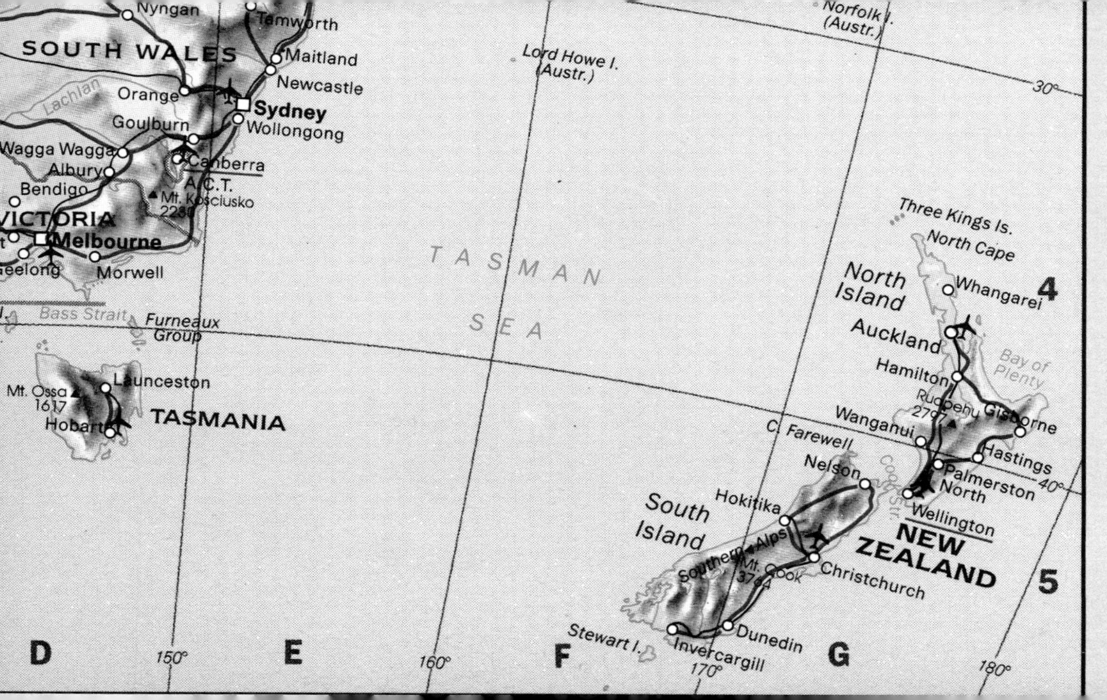
SOUTH WALES
Nyngan
Tamworth
Maitland
Newcastle
Orange
Sydney
Wollongong
Lachlan
Goulburn
Wagga Wagga
Canberra
Albury
A.C.T.
Bendigo
Mt. Kosciusko
2230
VICTORIA
Melbourne
Geelong
Morwell
Bass Strait
Furneaux Group
Mt. Ossa
1617
Launceston
Hobart
TASMANIA
Lord Howe I.
(Austr.)
Norfolk I.
(Austr.)
TASMAN
SEA
Three Kings Is.
North Cape
North Island
Whangarei
Auckland
Hamilton
Bay of Plenty
Ruapehu
2797
Gisborne
Wanganui
C. Farewell
Hastings
Nelson
Palmerston North
Wellington
Cook Str.
Hokitika
South Island
NEW ZEALAND
Southern Alps
Mt. Cook
3764
Christchurch
Stewart I.
Dunedin
Invercargill
30°
40°
150°
160°
170°
180°
4
5
D
E
F
G

30°
40°
50°
60°
70°
80°
90°
East of Greenwich
Ob
Yenisey
RUSSIAN FEDERATION
60°
COMMONWEALTH OF INDEPEN
Yeketerinburg
Krasnoyarsk
Omsk
Novosibirsk
Oz. Baykal
Irkutsk
Chita
50°
KAZAKHSTAN
Karaganda
Oz. Balkhash
Ulaanbaatar
MONGOLIA
Harbi
Ürümqi
Changchun
Alma-Ata
Shenyang
Beijing
40°
Huang
Tianjin
Lüda
Jinan
Qingdao
Lanzhou
SOUTH KOREA
YELLOW SEA
Xi'an
C H I N A
Nanjing
Kita-
Kyūsh
Chengdu
Wuhan
Shanghai
Chang
30°
Chongqing
EAST CHINA SEA
NEPAL
BHUTAN
Ryūkyū Is.
INDIA
Brahmaputra
Irrawaddy
Fuzhou
Salween
Mekong
BANG.
Kunming
T'ai-pei
Dhākā
Guangzhou
Calcutta
TAIWAN
MYANMAR (BURMA)
Hanoi
MACAU (Port.)
HONG KONG (U.K.)
20°
Vientiane
Hainan Dao
LAOS
Rangoon
Luzon
VIETNAM
THAILAND
Manila
Andaman Is. (India)
Bangkok
CAMB.
SOUTH CHINA SEA
Mindoro
PHILIPPINES
Samar
Phnom Penh
Ho Chi Minh City
Palawan
10°
Gulf of Thailand
Nicobar Is. (India)
SULU SEA
Mindanao
Pal
BRUNEI

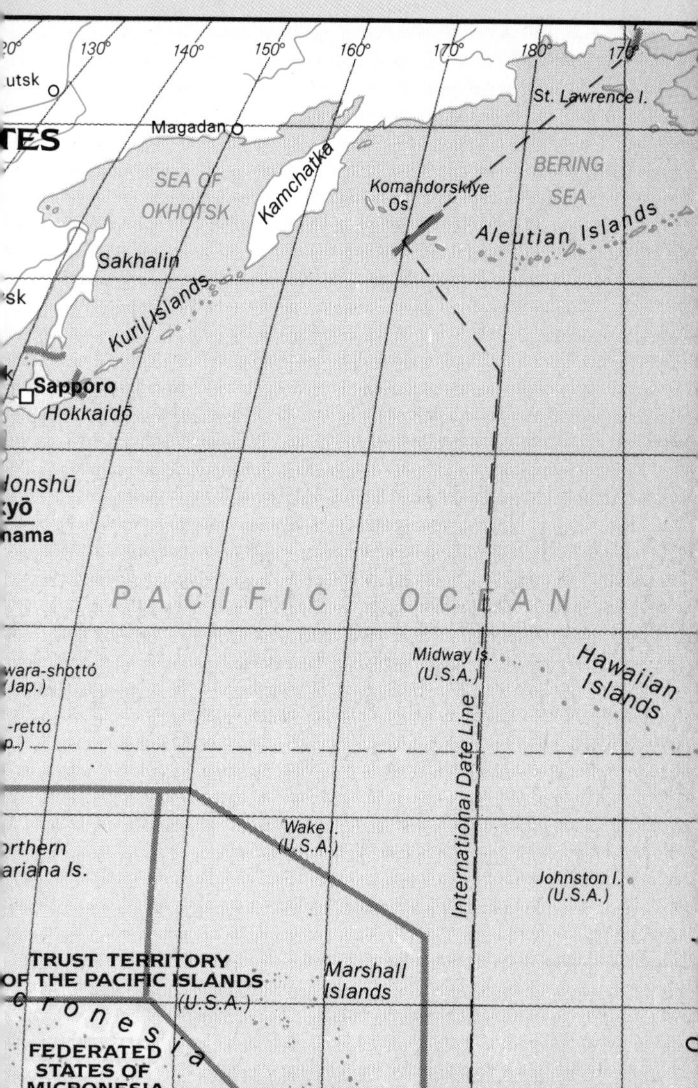
130°
140°
150°
160°
170°
180°
170°
utsk
Magadan
TES
St. Lawrence I.
SEA OF
OKHOTSK
Kamchatka
Komandorskiye
Os.
BERING
SEA
Aleutian Islands
Sakhalin
sk
Kuril Islands
Sapporo
Hokkaidō
Honshū
kyō
nama
PACIFIC OCEAN
Midway Is.
(U.S.A.)
Hawaiian
Islands
wara-shottó
(Jap.)
-rettó
p.)
International Date Line
Wake I.
(U.S.A.)
orthern
ariana Is.
Johnston I.
(U.S.A.)
TRUST TERRITORY
OF THE PACIFIC ISLANDS
(U.S.A.)
Marshall
Islands
cronesia
FEDERATED
STATES OF
MICRONESIA

160°
150°
140°
130°
120°
110°
100°
90°
Yukon
Great Bear Lake
Mackenzie
Great Slave Lake
L. Athabasca
Anchorage
Gulf of Alaska
Kodiak I.
Alexander Arch.
Queen Charlotte Is.
CANA
Edmonton
Calgary
Vancouver
Vancouver I.
Seattle
Portland
Snake
UNIT
San Francisco
Los Angeles
San Diego
Guadalupe (Mex.)
PACIFIC
OCEAN
Hawaiian Islands
Honolulu
Hawaii
P
O
Palmyra (U.S.A.)

60° 50° 40° 30° 20° 10° 0° 10°
West of Greenwich
GREENLAND
(Den.)
Davis Str.
ICELAND
Reykjavik
60°
LABRADOR
SEA
50°
St. Lawrence
Newfoundland
L. Superior
L. Huron
L. Michigan
Montréal
Ottowa
olis
L. Ontario
Detroit
Toronto
Boston
Chicago
L. Erie
New York
A T E S
Pittsburgh
Philadelphia
Cincinnati
40°
Baltimore
St. Louis
Washington
Ohio
ATLANTIC
M E R I C A
Atlanta
Dallas
Mississippi
New
Orleans
Bermuda
(U.K.)
30°
Houston
OCEAN
GULF OF
Miami
terrey
THE
BAHAMAS
MEXICO
MEXICO
Tropic of Cancer
La Habana
CUBA
Guadalajara
Greater
DOMINICAN
REPUBLIC
México
HAITI
20°
Antilles
BELIZE
JAMAICA
Puerto
Rico
(U.S.A.)
Lesser Antilles
GUATEMALA
Guatemala
HONDURAS
CARIBBEAN SEA
Tegucigalpa
San Salvador
EL SALVADOR
NICARAGUA
Managua
lipperton I.
(Fr.)
COSTA RICA
San José
Panamá
Caracas
10°
PANAMA
VENEZUELA
Medellín
de Coco
(C.R.)
Bogotá

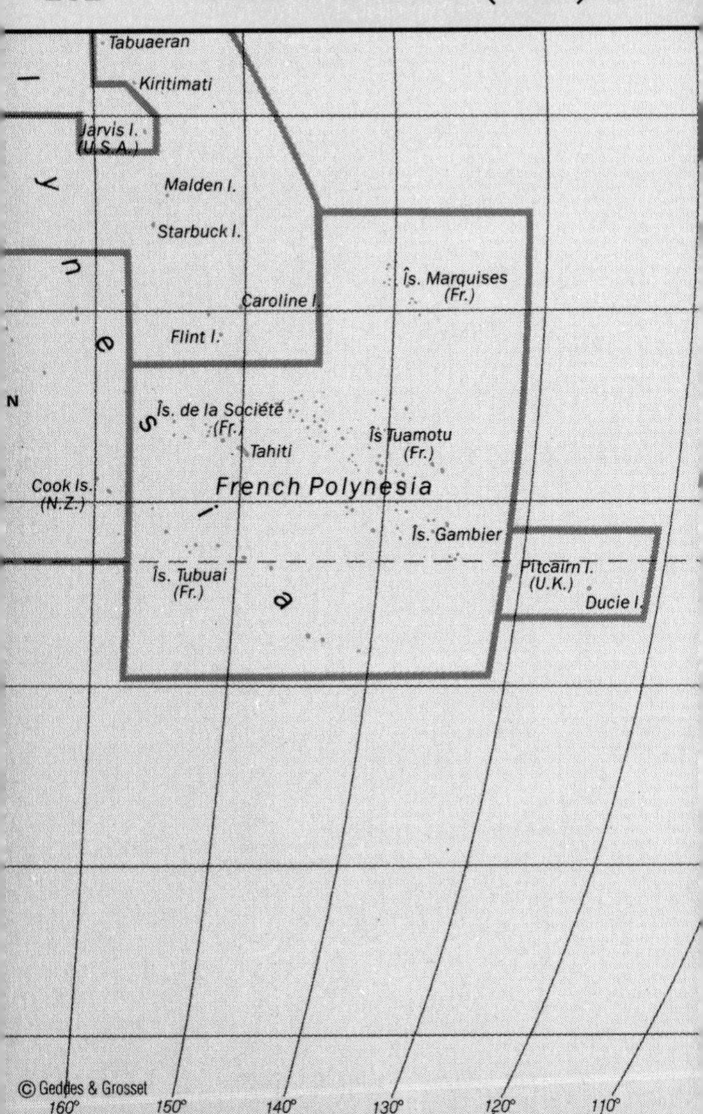
Tabuaeran
Kiritimati
Jarvis I.
(U.S.A.)
Malden I.
Starbuck I.
Caroline I.
Flint I.
Îs. Marquises
(Fr.)
Îs. de la Société
(Fr.)
Tahiti
Îs Tuamotu
(Fr.)
French Polynesia
Cook Is.
(N.Z.)
Îs. Gambier
Îs. Tubuai
(Fr.)
Pitcairn I.
(U.K.)
Ducie I.
N
160°
150°
140°
130°
120°
110°

COLOMBIA
Equator
0°
Quito
Islas Galápagos
(Ecuador)
Guayaquil
ECUADOR
Amazonas
BRAZIL
Trujillo
PERU
10°
Callao
Lima
Titicaca
Arequipa
La Paz
BOLIVIA
IC OCEAN
Sucre
20°
PAR.
Tropic of Capricorn
Antofagasta
Asunción
Sala-y-Gomez (Ch.)
scua
CHILE
30°
Córdoba
URUGUAY
Rosario
Montevideo
Is. Juan Fernández
(Ch.)
Santiago
Buenos
Aires
Concepción
ARGENTINA
Bahía Blanca
40°
Puerto Montt
Patagonia
50°
Falkland Is.
(Islas Malvinas)
(U.K.)
Punta Arenas
Tierra del
Fuego
South Georgia
(U.K.)
80°
70°
60°
50°
40°
30°

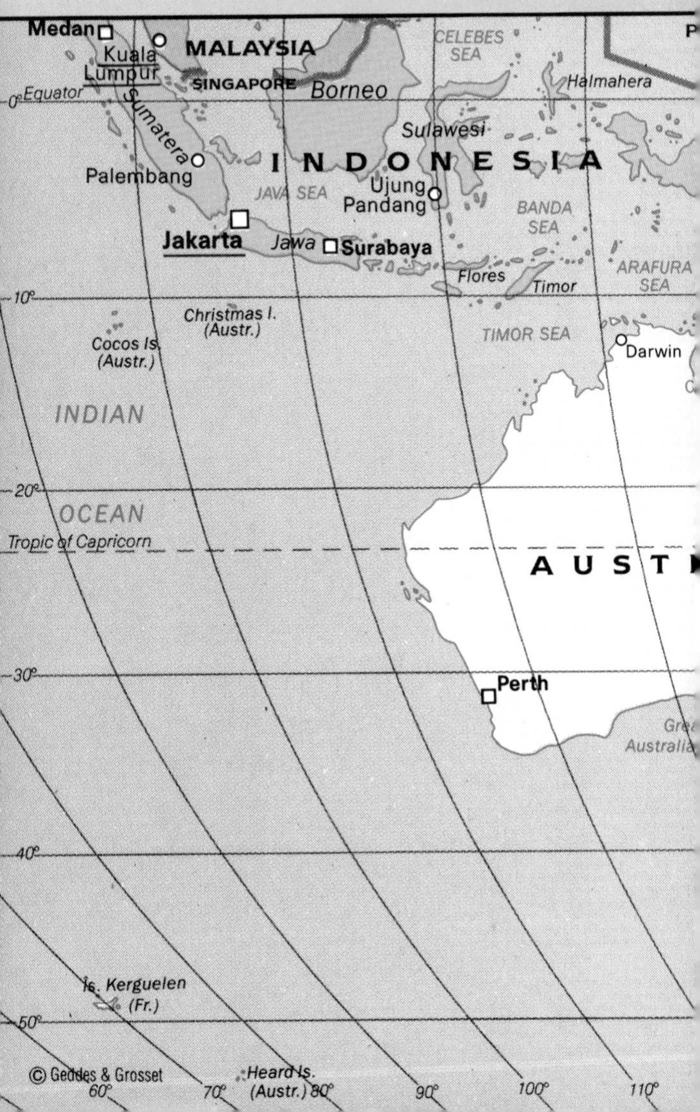
Medan
Kuala Lumpur
MALAYSIA
SINGAPORE
Borneo
CELEBES SEA
Halmahera
Equator
Sumatera
Sulawesi
Palembang
INDONESIA
JAVA SEA
Ujung Pandang
BANDA SEA
Jakarta
Jawa
Surabaya
ARAFURA SEA
Flores
Timor
Christmas I. (Austr.)
TIMOR SEA
Darwin
Cocos Is. (Austr.)
INDIAN
OCEAN
Tropic of Capricorn
AUST
Perth
Australia
Is. Kerguelen (Fr.)
Heard Is. (Austr.)
0°
10°
20°
30°
40°
50°
60°
70°
80°
90°
100°
110°

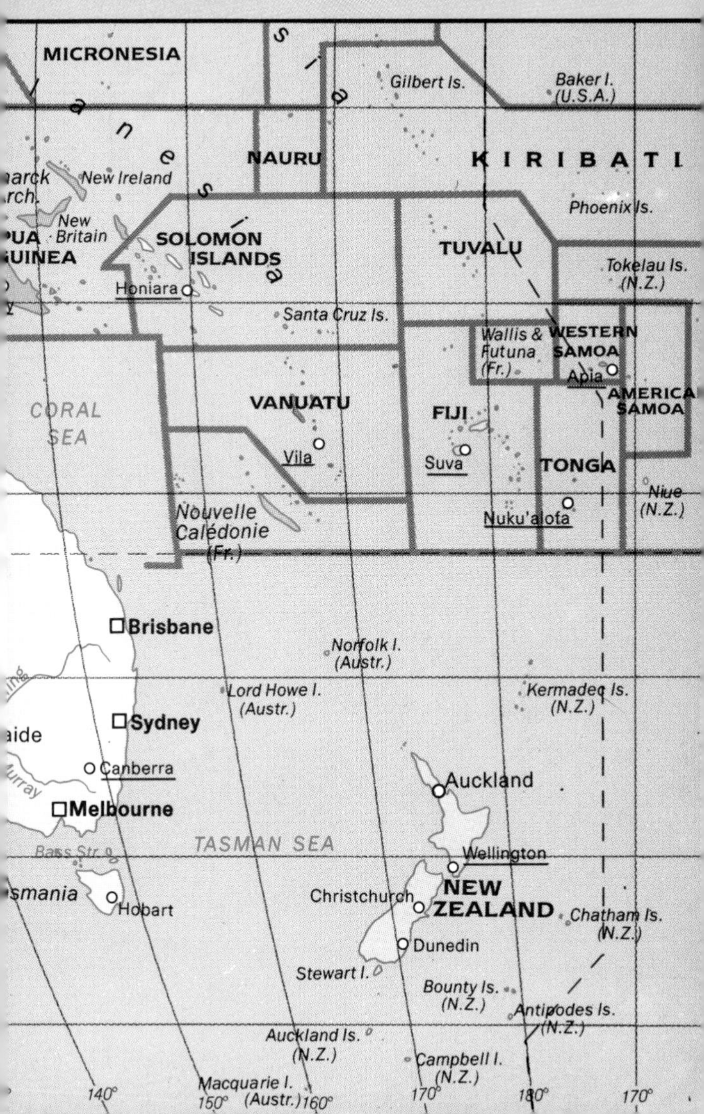

MICRONESIA
Gilbert Is.
Baker I. (U.S.A.)
NAURU
KIRIBATI
New Ireland
New Britain
SOLOMON ISLANDS
Honiara
Phoenix Is.
TUVALU
Tokelau Is. (N.Z.)
Santa Cruz Is.
Wallis & Futuna (Fr.)
WESTERN SAMOA
Apia
AMERICAN SAMOA
CORAL SEA
VANUATU
Vila
FIJI
Suva
TONGA
Nuku'alofa
Niue (N.Z.)
Nouvelle Calédonie (Fr.)
Brisbane
Norfolk I. (Austr.)
Lord Howe I. (Austr.)
Kermadec Is. (N.Z.)
Sydney
Canberra
Murray
Auckland
Melbourne
TASMAN SEA
Bass Str.
Wellington
NEW ZEALAND
Christchurch
Hobart
Chatham Is. (N.Z.)
Dunedin
Stewart I.
Bounty Is. (N.Z.)
Antipodes Is. (N.Z.)
Auckland Is. (N.Z.)
Campbell I. (N.Z.)
Macquarie I. (Austr.)
140°
150°
160°
170°
180°
170°

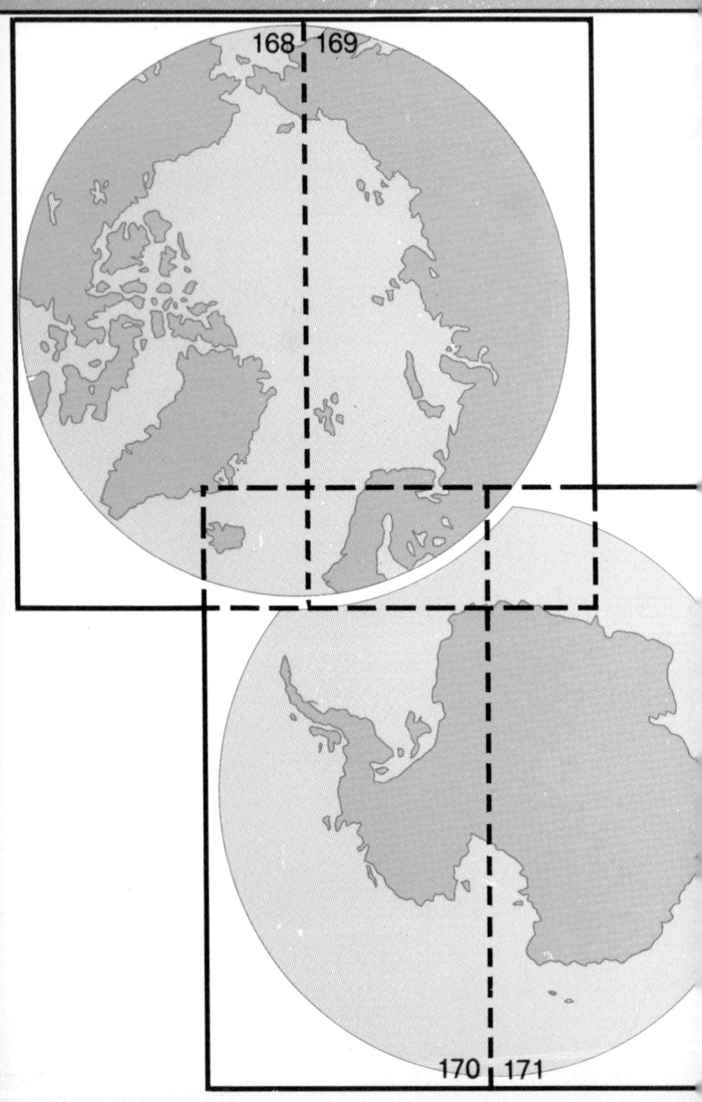
168
169
170
171

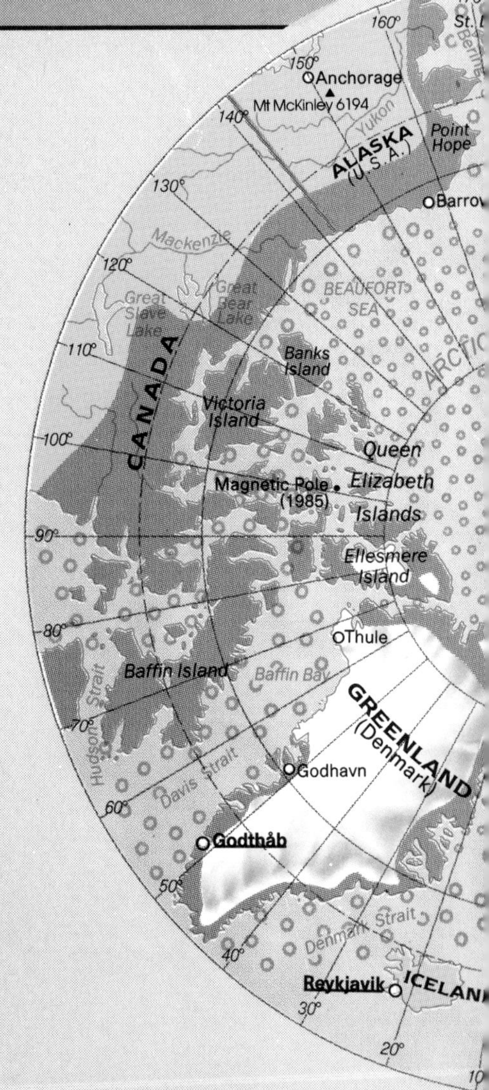
Anchorage
Mt McKinley 6194
Yukon
ALASKA
(U.S.A.)
Point Hope
Barrow
Mackenzie
Great Bear Lake
Great Slave Lake
BEAUFORT SEA
CANADA
Banks Island
Victoria Island
Queen Elizabeth Islands
Magnetic Pole (1985)
Ellesmere Island
Thule
Baffin Island
Baffin Bay
Hudson Strait
Davis Strait
GREENLAND
(Denmark)
Godhavn
Godthåb
Denmark Strait
Reykjavik
160°
150°
140°
130°
120°
110°
100°
90°
80°
70°
60°
50°
40°
30°
20°

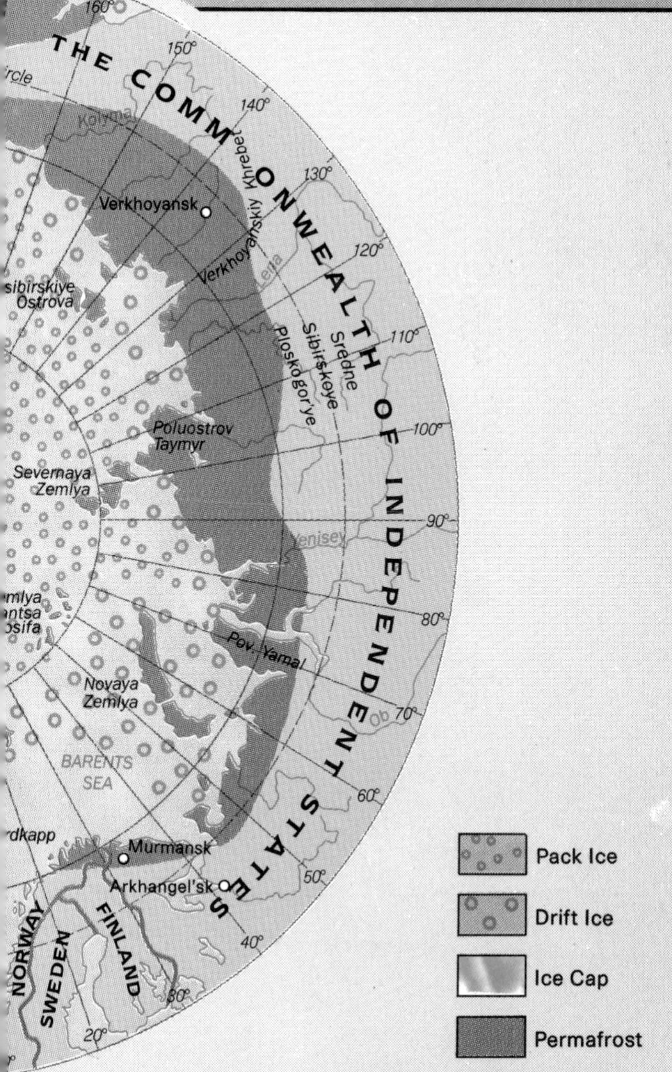

THE COMMONWEALTH OF INDEPENDENT STATES
Verkhoyansk
Verkhoyanskiy Khrebet
Kolyma
Lena
Sredne Sibirskoye Ploskogor'ye
sibirskiye Ostrova
Poluostrov Taymyr
Severnaya Zemlya
Yenisey
Pov. Yamal
Ob
Novaya Zemlya
BARENTS SEA
rdkapp
Murmansk
Arkhangel'sk
NORWAY
SWEDEN
FINLAND
Pack Ice
Drift Ice
Ice Cap
Permafrost

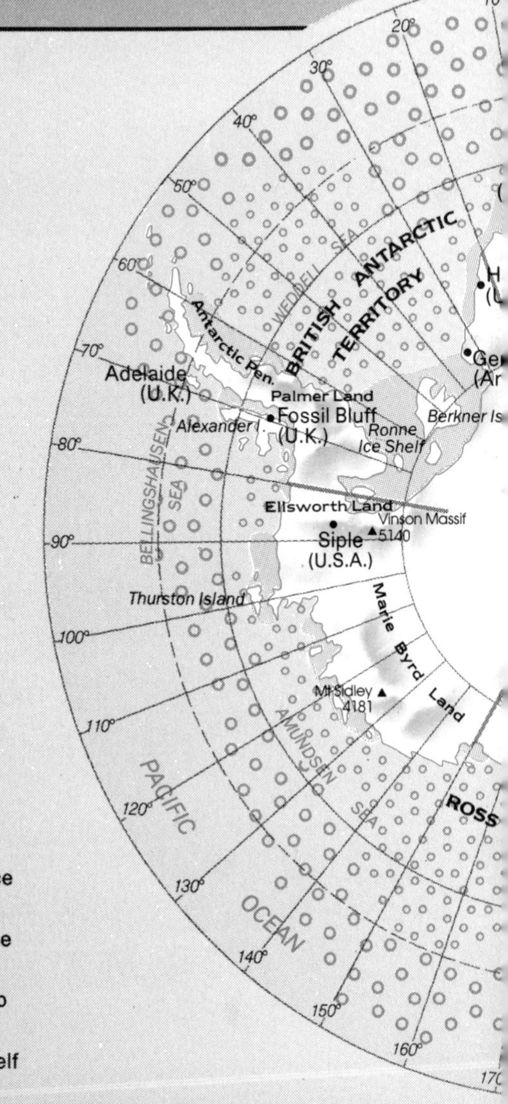

Pack Ice

Drift Ice

Ice Cap

Ice Shelf

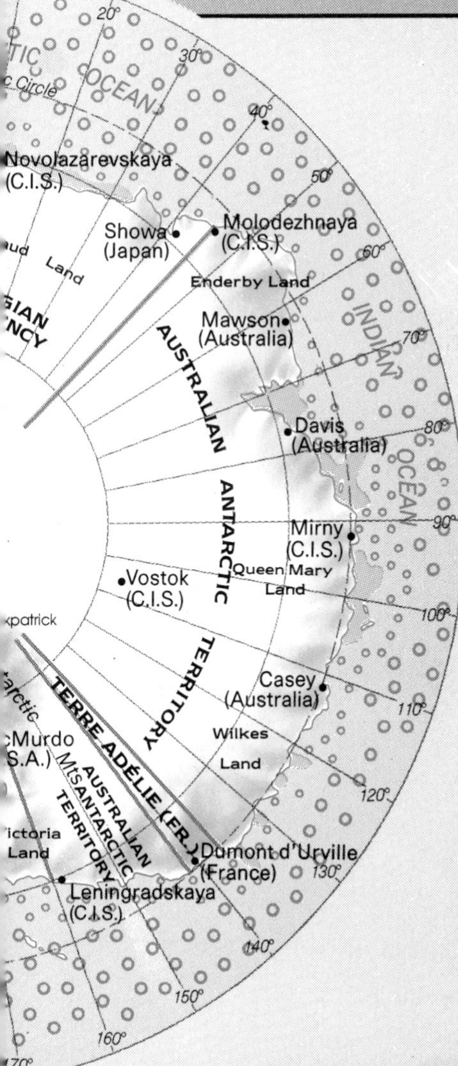
10°
20°
30°
40°
50°
60°
70°
80°
90°
100°
110°
120°
130°
140°
150°
160°
170°
OCEAN
c Circle
Novolazarevskaya
(C.I.S.)
Showa
(Japan)
Molodezhnaya
(C.I.S.)
Land
Enderby Land
Mawson
(Australia)
INDIAN
OCEAN
AUSTRALIAN
ANTARCTIC
TERRITORY
Davis
(Australia)
Mirny
(C.I.S.)
Queen Mary
Land
Vostok
(C.I.S.)
Casey
(Australia)
Wilkes
Land
TERRE ADÉLIE (FR.)
cMurdo
S.A.)
AUSTRALIAN
ANTARCTIC
TERRITORY
ictoria
Land
Dumont d'Urville
(France)
Leningradskaya
(C.I.S.)

Index

In the index, the first number refers to the page, and the following letter and number to the section of the map in which the index entry can be found. For example, London 56G6 means that London can be found on page 56 where column G and row 6 meet.

Abbreviations used in the index

Afghan	Afghanistan
Alb	Albania
Alg	Algeria
Arg	Argentina
Aust	Australia
Bang	Bangladesh
Belg	Belgium
Bol	Bolivia
Bos. Herz.	Bosnia Herzegovina
Bulg	Bulgaria
CAR	Central African Republic
Camb	Cambodia
Can	Canada
CIS	Commonwealth of Independent States
Cro	Croatia
Czech L.	Czech Lands
Den	Denmark
Dom Rep	Dominican Republic
El Sal	El Salvador
Eng	England
Eq Guinea	Equatorial Guinea
Est	Estonia
Eth	Ethiopia
FRG	Federal Republic of Germany
Fin	Finland
Hung	Hungary
Indon	Indonesia
Lat	Latvia
Leb	Lebanon
Lib	Liberia
Liech	Liechtenstein
Lith	Lithuania
Lux	Luxembourg
Madag	Madagascar
Malay	Malaysia
Maur	Mauritania
Mor	Morocco
Mozam	Mozambique
N Ire	Northern Ireland
N Korea	North Korea
NZ	New Zealand
Neth	Netherlands
Nic	Nicaragaua
Nig	Nigeria
Nor	Norway
PNG	Papua New Guinea
Pak	Pakistan
Par	Paraguay
Phil	Phillipines
Pol	Poland
Port	Portugal
Rep.Yem.	Republic of Yemen
Rom	Romania
S Africa	South Africa
S Arabia	Saudi Arabia
S Korea	South Korea
Scot	Scotland
Sen	Senegal
Slo	Slovenia
Slov.	Slovakia
Switz	Switzerland
Tanz	Tanzania
Thai	Thailand
Turk	Turkey
UAE	United Arab Emirates
UK	United Kingdom
USA	United States of America
Urug	Uruguay
Ven	Venezuela
Viet	Vietnam
Yugos	Yugoslavia
Zim	Zimbabwe

A

B

C

D

E

F

G

H

L

M

N

O

P

Q

R

S

T

U

V

Gazetteer

hanistan

652,090 sq km (251,772 sq miles); *population* 15,810,000; *capital* Kabul; *other r cities* Herat, Kandahar, Mazar-i-Sharif; *form of government* People's Republic; *ons* Sunni Islam, Shia Islam; *currency* Afghani

ıanistan is a landlocked country in southern Asia. The greater part of country is mountainous with several peaks over 6000 m (19,686 ft) in central region. The climate is generally arid with great extremes of perature. There is considerable snowfall in winter. The main economic vity is agriculture, and although predominantly pastoral, successful vation takes place in the fertile plains and valleys. Natural gas is luced in northern Afghanistan, and over 90% of this is piped across the ler to the former USSR.

ania

28,748 sq km (11,100 sq miles); *population* 3,200,000; *capital* Tirana (Tiranë); *major cities* Durrës, Shkodër, Elbasan; *form of government* Socialist Republic; *on* Constitutionally atheist but mainly Sunni Islam ; *currency* Lek

nia is a small mountainous country in the eastern Mediterranean. Its ediate neighbours are Greece and the former Yugoslavian republics rbia and Macedonia, and it is bounded to the west by the Adriatic Sea. climate is typically Mediterranean, although winters are severe in the and areas. All land is state-owned, with the main agricultural areas along the Adriatic coast and in the Korce Basin. Industry is also nalized and output is small. The principal industries are agricultural uct processing, textiles, oil products and cement.

eria

2,381,741 sq km (919,590 sq miles); *population* 25,360,000; *capital* Algiers r); *other major cities* Oran, Constantine, Annaba; *form of government* Republic; *n* Sunni Islam; *currency* Algerian dinar

ia is a huge country in northern Africa, which fringes the Mediterra- Sea. Over four-fifths of Algeria is covered by the Sahara Desert. Near orth coastal area the Atlas Mountains run east-west in parallel ranges. limate in the coastal areas is warm and temperate with most of the alling in winter. Inland conditions become more arid, and tempera- range from 49°C during the day to 10°C at night. Most of Algeria is oductive agriculturally, but it does possess one of the largest reserves tural gas and oil in the world.

Andorra

Area 453 sq km (175 sq miles); *population* 51,400; *capital* Andorra-la-Vella; *for* *government* Co-principality; *religion* RC; *currency* Franc, Peseta

Andorra is a tiny state, situated high in the eastern Pyrénées, betv France and Spain. The state consists of deep valleys and high mou peaks which reach heights of 3000 m (9843 ft). Although only 20 kn miles) wide and 30 km (19 miles) long, the spectacular scenery and cli attract many tourists. About 6 million visitors arrive each winter whe cold weather with heavy snowfalls makes for ideal skiing. Tourism an duty-free trade are now Andorra's chief sources of income.

Angola

Area: 1,246,700 sq km (481,351 sq miles); *population* 10,020,000; *capital* Luar *other major cities* Huambo, Lobito, Benguela; *form of government* People's Republic; *religions* RC, Animism; *currency* Kwanza

Angola is situated on the Atlantic coast of west-central Africa and lies a 10° south of the Equator. Its climate is tropical with temperatures stantly between 20°C and 25°C. The rainfall is heaviest in inland a where there are vast equatorial forests. The country is also rich in mine Oil production is the most important aspect of the economy.

Antigua and Barbuda

Area 440 sq km (170 sq miles); *population* 85,000; *capital* St. John's; *form of government* Constitutional Monarchy; *religion* Christianity (mainly Anglicanism) *currency* East Caribbean dollar

Antigua and Barbuda, located on the eastern side of the Leeward Isla is a tiny state comprising three islands—Antigua, Barbuda, an uninhabited Redonda. The climate is tropical although its average ra of 100 mm (4 inches) makes it drier than most of the other islands West Indies. On Antigua, many palm-fringed sandy beaches make ideal tourist destination. Barbuda is surrounded by coral reefs, and is to a wide range of wildlife.

Argentina

Area 2,766,889 sq km (1,068,296 sq miles); *population* 32,690,000; *capital* Bu Aires; *other major cities* Cordoba, Rosaria, Mendoza, La Plata; *form of govern* Federal Republic; *religion* RC; *currency* Austral

Argentina, the world's eighth largest country, stretches from the Tro Capricorn to Cape Horn on the southern tip of the South Ame continent. To the west a massive mountain chain, the Andes, form border with Chile. The climate ranges from warm temperate ove pas in the central region, to a more arid climate in the north and west, in the extreme south conditions although also dry are much cooler. ries of military regimes has resulted in an unstable economy.

ienia

29,800 sq km (11,500 sq miles); *population* 3,267,000; *capital* Yerevan; *other city* Kumayri (Leninakan); *form of government* Republic; *religion* Armenian dox; *currency* Rouble

enia is the smallest republic of the former USSR and part of the former dom of Armenia which was divided between Turkey, Iran and the er USSR. It declared independence from the USSR in 1991. It is a ocked Transcaucasian republic, and its neighbours are Turkey, Iran, gia and Azerbaijan. The country is very mountainous with many s over 3000 m (13,418 ft). Agriculture is mixed in the lowland areas. g of copper, zinc and lead is important, and industrial development reasing.

tralia

,686,848 sq km (2,967,892 sq miles); *population* 17,100,000; *capital* rra; *other major cities* Adelaide, Brisbane, Melbourne, Perth, Sydney; *form of nment* Federal Parliamentary State; *religion* Christianity; *currency* Australian

alia, the world's smallest continental landmass, is a vast and sparsely lated island state in the southern hemisphere. The most mountainous n is the Great Dividing Range which runs down the entire east coast. use of its great size, Australia's climates range from tropical monsoon ol temperate, and there are also large areas of desert. Much of alia's wealth comes from agriculture, with huge sheep and cattle ns extending over large parts of the interior. Mineral extraction is also mportant.

ria

3,853 sq km (32,376 sq miles); *population* 7,600,000; *capital* Vienna (Wien); *najor cities* Graz, Linz, Salzburg; *form of government* Federal Republic; RC; *currency* Schilling

a is a landlocked country in central Europe and is surrounded by nations. The wall of mountains that runs across the centre of the y dominates the scenery. In the warm summers tourists come to the forests and mountains, and in the cold winters skiers come to ountains, which now boast over 50 ski resorts. Agriculture in Austria ed on small farms, many of which are run by a single family. Dairy products, and beef and lamb from the hill farms, contribute to exp More than 37% of Austria is covered in forest.

Azerbaijan

Area 87,000 sq km (33,600 sq miles); *population* 6,506,000; *capital* Baku; *othe major cities* Kirovabad, Sumgait; *form of government* Republic; *religions* Shia I Russian Orthodox; *currency* Rouble

Azerbaijan, a republic of the former USSR, declared itself independe 1991. It is situated on the southwest coast of the Caspian Sea and sh borders with Iran, Armenia, Georgia and the Russian Federation. country is semi-arid, and 70% of the land is irrigated for the producti cotton, wheat, maize, potatoes, tobacco, tea and citrus fruits. It has mineral deposits, the most important being oil, which is found in the area.

Bahamas

Area 13,878 sq km (5358 sq miles); *population* 256,000; *capital* Nassau; *other important city* Freeport; *form of government* Constitutional Monarchy; *religion* Christianity; *currency* Bahamian dollar

The Bahamas consist of an archipelago of 700 islands located i Atlantic Ocean off the southeast coast of Florida. The largest isla Andros, and the two most populated are Grand Bahama and Providence. Winters in the Bahamas are mild and summers warm islands have few natural resources. Tourism, which employs ove thirds of the work force, is the most important industry. About three n tourists, the great majority from North America, visit the Bahamas year.

Bahrain

Area 678 sq km (262 sq miles); *population* 486,000; *capital* Manama; *form of government* Monarchy (Emirate); *religions* Shia Islam, Sunni Islam; *currency* Bahraini dollar

Bahrain is a Gulf State comprising 33 low-lying islands situated bet the Qatar peninsula and the mainland of Saudi Arabia. Bahrain Isla the largest, and a causeway linking it to Saudi Arabia was opened in The climate is pleasantly warm between December and March, bu hot from June to November. Most of Bahrain is sandy and fertile imported from other islands. Oil was discovered in 1931, and reve from oil now account for about 75% of the country's total rev Traditional industries include pearl fishing, boat building, weavin pottery.

ngladesh

ı 143,998 sq km (55,598 sq miles); *population* 113,340,000; *capital* Dacca
ıka); *other major cities* Chittagong, Khulna; *form of government* Republic;
ion Sunni Islam; *currency* Taka

ıgladesh is bounded almost entirely by India and to the south by the Bay engal. The country is extremely flat and is virtually a huge delta formed ne Ganges, Brahmaputra and Meghna rivers. The country is subject levastating floods and cyclones. Most villages are built on mud forms to keep them above water. The climate is tropical monsoon with t, extreme humidity and heavy rainfall. The combination of rainfall, sun silt from the rivers makes the land productive, and it is often possible row three crops a year.

·bados

430 sq km (166 sq miles); *population* 260,000; *capital* Bridgetown; *form of*
·rnment Constitutional Monarchy; *religions* Anglicanism, Methodism; *currency*
ados dollar

›ados is the most easterly island of the West Indies. Most of the island w-lying. The climate is tropical, but the cooling effect of the northeast e winds prevents the temperatures rising above 30°C (86°F). There only two seasons, the dry and the wet, when rainfall is very heavy. ough the industry is now declining, sugar is still the principal export. rism has now taken over as the main industry, and it employs 40% of sland's labour force.

orussia (Byelorussia)

207,600 sq km (80,150 sq miles); *population* 9,878,000; *capital* Minsk; *other*
r cities Gomel, Vitebsk, Mogilev; *form of government* Republic; *religions*
ian Orthodox, RC; *currency* Rouble

›russia, a republic of the former USSR, declared itself independent in 1. It borders Poland to the west, Ukraine to the south, Latvia and ıania to the north, and the Russian Federation to the east. The country ısists mainly of a low-lying plain, and forests cover approximately one of it. The climate is continental with long severe winters and short n summers. The main economic activity is agriculture. The production ›at is the main industry.

gium

30,519 sq km (11,783 sq miles); *population* 9,930,000; *capital* Brussels
sel, Bruxelles); *other major cities* Antwerp, Ghent, Charleroi, Liege; *form of*
rnment Constitutional Monarchy; *religion* RC; *currency* Belgian franc

Belgium is a relatively small country in northwest Europe with a s coastline on the North Sea. The Meuse River divides Belgium intc distinct geographical regions. To the north, the land slopes until it rea the flat and grassy coastlands. To the south of the river is the fore plateau area of the Ardennes. Belgium is a densely populated indu country with few natural resources. Agriculture is based on lives production but employs only 3% of the work force. Nearly all raw mat are now imported through the main port of Antwerp.

Belize

Area 22,965 sq km (8867 sq miles); *population* 193,000; *capital* Belmopan; *oth major city* Belize City; *form of government* Constitutional Monarchy; *religion* RC *currency* Belize dollar

Belize is a small Central American country located on the southeast c Yucatan Peninsula. Its coastline on the Gulf of Honduras is approa through some 550 km (342 miles) of coral reefs and keys (cayo). coastal area and north of the country are low-lying and swampy with d forests inland. The subtropical climate is warm and humid, and the winds bring cooling sea breezes. Rainfall is heavy, and hurricanes occur in summer. The dense forests that cover most of the country pr valuable hardwoods such as mahogany. Most of the population ma living from forestry, fishing or agriculture.

Benin

Area 112,622 sq km (43,483 sq miles); *population* 4,760,000; *capital* Porto-No *other major city* Contonou; *form of government* Republic; *religions* Animism, RC Sunni Islam; *currency* Franc CFA

Benin is an ice cream cone-shaped country in West Africa with a very coastline on the Bight of Benin. The coastal area has white sandy bea backed by lagoons and low-lying fertile lands. In the northwest are g plateaux. The climate is tropical, and there are nine rainy months year so crops rarely fail. Farming is predominantly subsistence, with y cassava, maize, rice, groundnuts and vegetables forming most c produce. The country is very poor, and lack of foreign investment pre diversification of the economy.

Bermuda

Area 53 sq km (21 sq miles); *population* 59,066; *capital* Hamilton; *form of gove ment* Colony under British administration; *religion* Protestantism; *currency* Berr dollar

Bermuda consists of a group of 150 small islands in the western At ɪan. The hilly limestone islands are the caps of ancient volcanoes rising ı the sea bed. The climate is pleasantly warm and humid, with rain ead evenly throughout the year. Many foreign banks and financial tutions operate from the island to take advantage of the lenient tax ;. Its proximity to the US and the pleasant climate have led to a rishing tourist industry.

ɹtan

47,000 sq km (18,147 sq miles); *population* 1,400,000; *capital* Thimphu; *form* ·*vernment* Constitutional Monarchy; *religion* Buddhism; *currency* Ngultrum

tan is surrounded by India to the south and China to the north. It rises ı foothills overlooking the Brahmaputra River to the southern slopes of Himalayas, which rise to over 7500 m (24,608 ft) and make up most of country. The climate is hot and wet on the plains, but temperatures drop ressively with altitude, resulting in glaciers and permanent snow cover e north. The valleys in the centre of the country are wide and fertile, about 95% of the work force are farmers. Bhutan has little contact with rest of the world.

ivia

1,098,581 sq km (424,162 sq miles); *population* 6,410,000; *capital* La Paz inistrative capital), Sucre (legal capital); *other major city* Cochabamba; *form of rnment* Republic; *religion* RC; *currency* Boliviano

via is a landlocked republic of central South America through which the t mountain range of the Andes runs. On the undulating Altiplano ression is the highest capital city in the world, La Paz. To the east and neast of the mountains is a huge area of lowland containing tropical orests and wooded savanna. The northeast has a heavy rainfall while e southwest it is negligible. Temperatures vary with altitude from emely cold on the summits to cool on the Altiplano, where at least half population lives. Although rich in natural resources, eg oil, tin, Bolivia ot rich because of lack of funds for their extraction.

;nia-Herzegovina

51,129 sq km (19,736 sq miles); *population* 4,124,000; *capital* Sarajevo; *other r cities* Banja Luka, Tuzla; *form of government* Republic; *religions* Eastern odox, Sunni Islam, RC; *currency* Dinar

nia-Herzegovina, a republic of former Yugoslavia, was formally recog-d as an independent state in 1992. It is very mountainous, and half the ıtry is forested. One quarter of the land is cultivated, and corn, wheat flax are the principal products of the north. In the south, tobacco, cotton, fruits and grapes are the main products. It has large deposit lignite, iron ore and bauxite, but little industrialization.

Botswana

Area 581,730 sq km (224,606 sq miles); *population* 1,260,000; *capital* Gaborone *other major cities* Mahalapye, Serowe, Francistown; *form of government* Republ *religions* Animism, Anglicanism; *currency* Pula

Botswana is a landlocked republic in southern Africa, which straddles Tropic of Capricorn. Much of the west and southwest of the country fo part of the Kalahari Desert. In the north the land is marshy around the b of the Okavango river. With the exception of the desert area, most of country has a subtropical climate. The people are mainly farmers, cattle rearing is the main activity. Diamonds are an important reve earner. About 17% of the land is set aside for wildlife preservatio national parks, game reserves, game sanctuaries and controlled hur areas.

Brazil

Area 8,511,965 sq km (3,285,470 sq miles); *population* 115,600,000; *capital* Brasília; *other major cities* Belo Horizonte, Porto Alegre, Recife, Rio de Janeiro, Salvador, São Paulo; *form of government* Federal Republic; *religion* RC; *curren* Cruzeiro

Brazil is the fifth largest country in the world and covers nearly half of S America. The climate is mainly tropical, but droughts may occur in northeast, where it is hot and arid. About 14% of the populatio employed in agriculture and the main products exported are coffee, s beans and cocoa. Brazil is rich in minerals and is the only source of grade quartz crystal in commercial quantities. It is also a major prod of chrome ore.

Brunei

Area 5,765 sq km (2,226 sq miles); *population* 267,000; *capital* Bandar Seri Begawan; *other major cities* Kuala Belait, Seria; *form of government* Monarchy (Sultanate); *religion* Sunni Islam; *currency* Brunei dollar

Brunei is a sultanate located on the northwest coast of Borneo, bour on all sides by the Sarawak territory of Malaysia, which splits it intc separate parts. Broad tidal swamplands cover the coastal plains, inland Brunei is hilly and covered with tropical forest. The climate is tro with rainfall heaviest (5000 mm/197 inches) inland. The main crops g are rice, vegetables and fruit, but economically the country depends c oil industry, which accounts for almost all exports.

lgaria

a 110,912 sq km (42,823 sq miles); *population* 8,970,000; *capital* Sofia (Sofiya); *r major cities* Burgas, Plovdiv, Ruse, Varna; *form of government* Republic; *ion* Eastern Orthodox; *currency* Lev

garia is located on the east Balkan peninsula and has a coast on the ck Sea. It is bounded to the north by Romania, west by Serbia and cedonia of the former Yugoslavia, and south by Greece and Turkey. centre of Bulgaria is crossed from west to east by the Balkan untains. The south of the country has a Mediterranean climate with hot summers and mild winters. Further north the temperatures become e extreme, and rainfall is higher in summer. Traditionally Bulgaria is an cultural country, and a revolution in farming during the 1950s has led reat increases in output. This was due to the collectivization of farms the use of more machinery, fertilizers and irrigation.

rkina (Burkina Faso)

274,200 sq km (105,869 sq miles); *population* 8,760,000; *capital* gadougou; *form of government* Republic; *religions* Animist, Sunni Islam; *ency* Franc CFA

kina, a landlocked state in West Africa, on the southern fringe of the ara Desert, is made up of vast monotonous plains and low hills. cipitation is generally low, the heaviest rain falling in the southwest, e the rest of the country is semi-desert. About 90% of the people live arming, and food crops include sorghum, beans and maize. There is eat shortage of work, and many of the younger population go to Ghana Côte d'Ivoire for employment.

ma (Myanmar)

676,578 sq km (261,227 sq miles); *population* 39,300,000; *capital* Yangon erly Rangoon); *other major cities* Mandalay, Moulmein, Pegu; *form of rnment* Republic; *religion* Buddhism; *currency* Kyat

Union of Myanmar (formerly Burma) is the second largest country in th-East Asia. Its heartland is the valley and delta of the Irrawaddy. The h and west of the country are mountainous, and in the east the Shan eau runs along the border with Thailand. The climate is mainly tropical soon. Rice is the staple food and accounts for half the export earnings. na is rich in timber and minerals although not yet fully exploited.

undi

27,834 sq km (10,747 sq miles); *population* 5,540,000; *capital* Bujumbura; *form vernment* Republic; *religion* RC; *currency* Burundi franc

Burundi is a small densely populated country in central east Afr bounded by Rwanda to the north, Tanzania to the east and south, Zaïre to the west. It has a mountainous terrain, with much of the cou above 1500 m (4921 ft). The climate is equatorial but modified by altitu The soils are not rich, but there is enough rain to grow crops in most are The main food crops are bananas, sweet potatoes, peas, lentils beans. The main cash crop is coffee, accounting for 90% of Burur export earnings.

Cambodia

Area 181,035 sq km (69,898 sq miles); *population* 8,300,000; *capital* Phnom Pe *other major cities* Kampong Cham, Battambang; *form of government* People's Republic; *religion* Buddhism; *currency* Riel

Cambodia is a southeast Asian state on the Gulf of Thailand. The hea the country is saucer-shaped, and gently rolling alluvial plains are drai by the Mekong river. The Dangrek Mountains form the frontier Thailand in the northwest. It has a tropical monsoon climate, and abou the land is tropical forest. Crop production depends entirely on the rai and floods, but production was badly disrupted during the civil war, yields still remain low.

Cameroon

Area 475,442 sq km (183,568 sq miles); *population* 11,540,000;*capital* Yaoundé *other major city* Douala; *form of government* Republic; *religions* Animism, RC, S Islam; *currency* Franc CFA

Cameroon is a triangular-shaped country of diverse landscapes in w central Africa. It stretches from Lake Chad at its apex to the nort borders of Equatorial Guinea, Gabon and the Congo in the south. climate is equatorial with high temperatures and plentiful rain. The ma of the population lives in the south where they grow maize and vegetal In the drier north, where drought and hunger are well known, life is ha Bananas, coffee and cocoa are the major exports.

Canada

Area 9 ,976,139 sq km (3,851,787 sq miles); *population* 26,600,000; *capital* Ott *other major cities* Toronto, Montreal, Vancouver, Quebec; *form of government* Federal Parliamentary State; *religions* RC, United Church of Canada, Anglicani *currency* Canadian dollar

Canada, the second largest country in the world, is a land of great clin and geographical extremes. It lies to the north of the United States anc both Pacific and Atlantic coasts. Climates range from polar conditio north, to cool temperate in the south with considerable differences from st to east. More than 80% of its rich cultivated farmland is in the prairies t stretch from Alberta to Manitoba. Forest reserves cover more than half total land area. The most valuable mineral deposits (oil, gas, coal and ı ore) are found in Alberta. Most industry in Canada is associated with cessing its natural resources.

pe Verde

a 4033 sq km (240,534 sq miles); *population* 369,000; *capital* Praia; *form of* *ernment* Republic; *religion* RC; *currency* Cape Verde escudo

pe Verde, one of the world's smallest nations, is situated in the Atlantic ean, about 640 km (400 miles) northwest of Senegal. It consists of 10 nds and five islets. Over 50% of the population live on the island of São go on which is situated Praia, the capital. Rainfall is sparse, and the nds suffer from periods of severe drought. Agriculture is mostly fined to irrigated inland valleys. Fishing for tuna and lobsters is an ortant industry, but in general the economy is shaky, and Cape Verde es heavily on foreign aid.

ntral African Republic

a 622,984 sq km (240,534 sq miles); *population* 2,900,000; *capital* Bangui; *form* *overnment* Republic; *religions* Animism, RC; *currency* Franc CFA

e Central African Republic is a landlocked country in central Africa. The ain consists of an undulating plateau with dense tropical forest in the th and a semi-desert area in the east. The climate is tropical with little iation in temperature throughout the year. Most of the population live in west and in the hot, humid south and southwest. Over 86% of the king population are subsistence farmers, and the main crops grown cassava, groundnuts, bananas, plantains, millet and maize. Gems and ustrial diamonds are mined and vast deposits of uranium have been covered.

ad

a 1,284,000 sq km (495,752 sq miles); *population* 5,540,000; *capital* Ndjamena jamena); *other major cities* Sarh, Moundou; *form of government* Republic; *ions* Sunni Islam, Animism; *currency* Franc CFA

ad, a landlocked country in the centre of northern Africa, extends from edge of the equatorial forests in the south to the middle of the Sahara sert in the north. It lies more than 1600 km (944 miles) from the nearest st. In the far north of the country, the Tibesti Mountains rise from the ert sand to heights of more than 3000 m (9843 ft). The southern part of Chad is the most densely populated and its relatively well-wat savanna has always been the country's most arable region. Rece however, even here the rains have failed. Cotton ginning is the prin industry.

Chile

Area 756,945 sq km (292,256 sq miles); *population* 12,960,000; *capital* Santiag *other major cities* Arica, Talcahuano, Viña del Mar; *form of government* Republi *religion* RC; *currency* Chilean peso

Chile lies like a backbone of the South American continent. Its Pa coastline is 4200 km (2610 miles) long. Because of its enormous ran latitude, it has almost every kind of climate from desert conditions t wastes. Some 60% of the population live in the central valley where climate is similar to southern California. The land here is fertile, and principal crops grown are wheat, sugar beet, maize and potatoes. Al the central valley is one of the largest copper mines in the world, w accounts for Chile's most important source of foreign exchange.

China

Area 9,596,961 sq km (3,705,387 sq miles); *population* 1,114,000,000; *capital* Beijing (Peking); *other major cities* Chengdu, Guangzhou, Shanghai, Tianjin, Wuhan; *form of government* People's Republic; *religions* Buddhism, Confuciani Taoism; *currency* Yuan

China, the third largest country in the world, covers a large area of Asia. In western China most of the terrain is very inhospitable—ir northwest there are deserts which extend into Mongolia and the Rus Federation, and much of the southwest consists of the ice-capped p of Tibet. The southeast has a green and well-watered landscape com ing terraced hillsides and paddy fields. Most of China has a tempe climate, but in such a large country wide ranges of latitude and alti produce local variations. China is an agricultural country, and inte cultivation and horticulture are necessary to feed its population of 1,000,000,000.

Colombia

Area 1,138,914 sq km (439,735 sq miles); *population* 33,000,000; *capital* Bogo *other major cities* Barranquilla, Cali, Cartagena, Medellin; *form of government* Republic; *religion* RC; *currency* Peso

Colombia is situated in the northwest of South America. The Ande north along its western, Pacific coast and gradually disappear toward Caribbean Sea. Half of Colombia lies east of the Andes, and much c on is covered in tropical grassland. Towards the Amazon Basin the etation changes to tropical forest. Very little of the country is under vation although much of the soil is fertile. The range of climates results n extraordinary variety of crops, of which coffee is the most important. ombia is rich in minerals and produces about half of the world's eralds.

moros

2235 sq km (863 sq miles); *population* 503,000; *capital* Moroni; *form of rnment* Federal Islamic Republic; *religion* Sunni Islam; *currency* Comorian franc

Comoros consist of three volcanic islands in the Indian Ocean situated veen mainland Africa and Madagascar. The islands are mostly forested, the tropical climate is affected by Indian monsoon winds from the h. Only small areas of the islands are cultivated, and most of this land ngs to foreign plantation owners. The chief product was formerly ar cane, but now vanilla, copra, maize, cloves and essential oils are the t important products.

ngo

342,000 sq km (132,046 sq miles) 2,260,000; *capital* Brazzaville; *other major* Pointe-Noire; *form of government* Republic; *religion* RC; *currency* Franc CFA

go is situated in west-central Africa, where it straddles the Equator. Bateke Plateau has a long dry season, but the Congo Basin is more id and rainfall approaches 2500 mm (98 inches) each year. About 62% e total land area is covered with equatorial forest from which valuable lwoods such as mahogany are exported. Cash crops such as coffee cocoa are mainly grown on large plantations. Oil discovered offshore ounts for most of the Congo's revenues.

sta Rica

51,100 sq km (19,730 sq miles); *population* 2,910,000; *capital* San José; *other r city* Límon; *form of government* Republic; *religion* RC; *currency* Costa Rican n

the Pacific Ocean to the south and west and the Caribbean Sea to the , Costa Rica is sandwiched between the Central American countries icaragua and Panama. Much of the country consists of volcanic ntain chains that run northwest to southeast. The climate is tropical a small temperature range and abundant rain. The most populated is the Valle Central, which was first settled by the Spanish in the 16th ury. Coffee and bananas are grown commercially and are the major cultural exports.

Côte d'Ivoire

Area 322,463 sq km (124,503 sq miles); *population* 12,100,000; *capital* Yamoussoukro; *other major cities* Abidjan, Bouaké, Daloa; *form of government* Republic; *religions* Animism, Sunni Islam, RC; *currency* Franc CFA

A former French colony in west Africa, Côte d'Ivoire is located on the of Guinea with Ghana to the east and Liberia to the west. In the east t are coastal plains which are the country's most prosperous region. climate is tropical and affected by distance from the sea. Côte d'Ivoi basically an agricultural country. It is the world's largest producer of c and the fourth largest producer of coffee. These two crops bring in ha country's export revenue.

Croatia (Hrvatska)

Area 56,538 sq km (21,824 sq miles); *population* 4,601,500; *capital* Zagreb; *oth major cities* Rijeka, Split; *form of government* Republic; *religions* RC, Eastern Orthodox; *currency* Dinar

Croatia, a republic of former Yugoslavia, declared itself independe 1991 and was formally recognized in 1992. Western Croatia lies ir Dinaric Alps. The eastern region is low-lying and agricultural. Over third of the country is forested and timber is a major export. Deposi coal, bauxite, copper, oil and iron ore are substantial, and most o republic's industry is based on the processing of these. In Istria ir northwest and on the Dalmatian coast tourism is a major industry.

Cuba

Area 110,861 sq km (42,803 sq miles); *population* 10,580,000; *capital* Havana (Habana); *other major cities* Camaguey, Holguin, Santiago de Cuba; *form of government* Socialist Republic; *religion* RC; *currency* Cuban peso

Cuba is the most westerly of the Greater Antilles and lies about 140 kr miles) south of the tip of Florida. Cuba is as big as all other Caribl islands put together and is home to a third of the whole West Ir population. The climate is warm and generally rainy, and hurricane liable to occur between June and November. The island consists m of extensive plains, and the soil is fertile. The most important agricu product is sugar, and the processing of it is the most important indu

Cyprus

Area 9251 sq km (3572 sq miles); *population* 698,800; *capital* Nicosia; *other m cities* Limassol, Larnaca; *form of government* Republic; *religions* Greek Orthod Sunni Islam; *currency* Cyprus pound

Cyprus is an island which lies in the eastern Mediterranean. It has a panhandle and is divided from west to east by two parallel ranges of ıntains, which are separated by a wide central plain open to the sea at er end. It has very hot dry summers and warm damp winters. This tributes towards the great variety of crops grown on the island. Fishing significant industry, but above all the island depends on visitors, and the tourist industry which has led to a recovery in the economy since 4.

ech Republic

78,864 sq km (30,449 sq miles); *population* 10,291,900; *capital* Prague ha); *other major cities* Brno, Ostrava, Plzen; *form of government* Republic; *ons* RC, Protestantism; *currency* Koruna

Czech Republic was newly constituted on January 1,1993, with the olution of the 74-year-old federal republic of Czechoslovakia that it had iously formed with Slovakia. It is a landlocked country at the heart of ral Europe. Natural boundaries are the Sudeten Mountains in the h, the Ore Mountains to the northwest, and the Bohemian Forest in the hwest. The climate is humid continental with warm summers and cold ers. Agriculture is highly developed and efficient. Major crops are ar beet, wheat and potatoes. Over a third of the labour force is loyed in industry, the most important being iron and steel, coal, hinery, cement and paper.

ımark

43,077 sq km (16,632 sq miles); *population* 5,140,000; *capital* Copenhagen enhavn); *other major cities* Ålborg, Århus, Odense; *form of government* titutional Monarchy; *religion* Lutheranism; *currency* Danish krone

mark is a small European state lying between the North Sea and the ance to the Baltic. It consists of a western peninsula and an eastern ipelago of 406 islands, only 89 of which are populated. It has warm ıy summers and cold cloudy winters. The scenery is very flat, low-lying monotonous, but the soils are good and a wide variety of crops can be vn. Animal husbandry is, however, the most important activity, its uce including the famous Danish bacon and butter. It produces a wide e of manufactured goods and is famous for its imaginative design of ture, silverware and porcelain.

outi

23,200 sq km (8958 sq miles); *population* 484,000; *capital* Djibouti; *form of rnment* Republic; *religion* Sunni Islam; *currency* Djibouti franc

outi is situated in northeast Africa and is bounded almost entirely by

Ethiopia, except in the southeast where it shares a border with Som[illegible] Its coastline is on the Gulf of Aden. The climate is hot, among the wo[illegible] hottest, and extremely dry. Only a tenth of the land can be farmed eve[illegible] grazing, so it has great difficulty supporting its modest, mostly nom[illegible] population.

Dominica

Area 751 sq km (290 sq miles); *population* 81,200; *capital* Roseau; *form of government* Republic; *religion* RC; *currency* Franc

Dominica is the most northerly of the Windward Islands in the West Inc[illegible] The island is very rugged and consists of inactive volcanoes. The clin[illegible] is tropical, and the wettest season is from June to October when h[illegible] canes often occur. The steep slopes are difficult to farm, but agricu[illegible] provides almost all Dominica's exports, eg bananas, copra, citrus fr[illegible] cocoa, bay leaves and vanilla. Industry is mostly based on the proces[illegible] of the agricultural products.

Dominican Republic

Area 48,734 sq km (18,816 sq miles); *population* 7,200,000; *capital* Santo Domi[illegible] *other major city* Santiago de los Caballeros; *form of government* Republic; *curre*[illegible] Dominican peso

The Dominican Republic forms the eastern two-thirds of the islan[illegible] Hispaniola in the West Indies. Although well endowed with fertile land, [illegible] about 30% is cultivated. Sugar is the main crop and mainstay of [illegible] country's economy. It is grown mainly on plantations in the south[illegible] plains. Other crops grown are coffee, cocoa and tobacco. The [illegible] industries are food processing and the manufacture of consumer go[illegible]

Ecuador

Area 283,561 sq km (109,483 sq miles); *population* 10,490,000; *capital* Quito; *o*[illegible] *major cities* Guayaquil, Cuenca; *form of government* Republic; *religion* RC; *curr*[illegible] Sucre

Ecuador is an Andean country situated in the northwest of South Ame[illegible] It is bounded to the north by Colombia and to the east and south by P[illegible] The country contains over thirty active volcanos. The climate varies [illegible] equatorial through warm temperate to mountain conditions, accordir[illegible] altitude. In the coastal plains plantations of bananas, cocoa, coffee [illegible] sugar cane are found. In contrast to this, the highland areas are ada[illegible] to grazing, dairying and cereal growing. The fishing industry is impo[illegible] on the Pacific Coast. Oil produced in the tropical eastern regio[illegible] Ecuador's most important export.

ypt

a 1,001,449 sq km (386,659 sq miles); *population* 50,740,000; *capital* Cairo (El ıira); *other major cities* Alexandria, El Gîza; *form of government* Republic; ɡions Sunni Islam, Christianity; *currency* Egyptian pound

ypt is situated in northeast Africa, straddling the River Nile and with vast serts either side. The climate is mainly dry, but there are winter rains ng the Mediterranean coast. The temperatures are comfortable in ter but summer temperatures are extremely high, particularly in the ıth. The rich soils deposited by floodwaters of the Nile can support a ɡe population, and the delta is one of the world's most fertile agricultural ions. Some 96% of the population live in the delta and Nile valley, where main crops are rice, cotton, sugar cane, maize, tomatoes and wheat. main industries are food processing and textiles. The economy has n boosted by the discovery of oil. Suez Canal shipping and tourism are important revenue earners.

Salvador

a 21,041 sq km (8123 sq miles); *population* 5,220,000; *capital* San Salvador; *r major cities* Santa Ana, San Miguel; *form of government* Republic; *religion* RC; *ency* Colón

Salvador is the smallest and most densely populated state in Central erica. It is bounded north and east by Honduras and has a Pacific coast ıe south. Two volcanic ranges run from east to west across the country. predominantly agricultural, and 32% of the land is used for crops such offee, cotton, maize, beans, rice and sorghum, and a slightly smaller a is used for grazing cattle, pigs, sheep and goats.

uatorial Guinea

a 28,051 sq km (10,830 sq miles); *population* 417,000; *capital* Malabo; *other r city* Bata; *form of government* Republic; *religion* RC; *currency* Franc CFA

atorial Guinea lies about 200 km (124 miles) north of the Equator on hot humid coast of West Africa. The country consists of a square-ped mainland area (Mbini), with its few small offshore islets, and the nds of Bioko and Pagalu. Bioko is a very fertile volcanic island and the tre of the country's cocoa production.

onia

45,100 sq km (17,413 sq miles); *population* 1,573,000; *capital* Tallinn; *other r cities* Tartu, Narva; *form of government* Republic; *religion* Eastern Orthodox, eranism; *currency* Rouble

onia lies to the northwest of the Russian Federation and is bounded to the north by the Gulf of Finland, to the west by the Baltic Sea and to south by Latvia. It is the smallest of the three former Soviet Ba Republics. Agriculture, especially dairy farming, is the chief occupati Almost 22% of Estonia is forested, and this provides material for sawm furniture, match and pulp industries. The country has rich, high-qua shale deposits, and phosphorus has been found near Tallinn.

Ethiopia

Area 1,221,900 sq km (471,776 sq miles); *population* 50,000,000; *capital* Addis Ababa (Adis Abeba); *other major cities* Asmara, Dire Dawa; *form of government* People's Republic; *religion* Ethiopian Orthodox, Sunni Islam; *currency* Ethiopian

Ethiopia, one of Africa's largest countries, stretches from the shores of Red Sea to the north of Kenya. Most of the country consists of highlar Because of the wide range of latitudes, Ethiopia has many clim variations between the high temperate plateau and the hot humid l lands. The country is very vulnerable to drought, but in some ar thunderstorms can erode soil from the slopes, reducing the area availa for crop planting. Coffee is the main source of rural income, and teff is main food grain. Droughts have brought much famine.

Fiji

Area 18,274 sq km (7056 sq miles); *population* 727,104; *capital* Suva; *form of government* Republic; *religions* Christianity, Hinduism; *currency* Fiji dollar

Fiji consists of some 320 islands and atolls, situated around the International Date Line and about 17° south of the Equator. Fiji has rainfall, high temperatures and plenty of sunshine all year round. The main islands, Viti Levu and Vanua Levu, are extinct volcanoes. The n cash crop is sugar cane. Tourism is now a major industry.

Finland

Area 338,127 sq km (130,551 sq miles); *population* 4,970,000; *capital* Helsinki (Helsingfors); *other major cities* Turku, Tampere; *form of government* Republic; *religion* Lutheranism; *currency* Markka

Finland lies in northern Europe, with the Russian Federation to the and the Gulf of Bothnia to the west. Most of it is low-lying except for north, which rises to over 1000 m (3281 ft) in Lappland. It is covere extensive forests and thousands of lakes. Winter is severe and summ short. It is largely self-sufficient in food and produces surpluses of c produce. Most crops are grown in the southwest. In the north, reindeer herded and forests yield much timber for export. Major industries timber products, wood pulp and paper, and machinery and shipbuilc

'ance

ɘa 551,500 sq km (212,934 sq miles); *population* 56,180,000; *capital* Paris; *other* ɟjor cities Bordeaux, Lyon, Marseille, Toulouse; *form of government* Republic; 'gion RC; *currency* Franc

ance is the largest country in western Europe and has a coastline on the glish Channel, the Mediterranean Sea and on the Atlantic Ocean. The vest parts of the country are the great basins of the north and southwest m which it rises to the Massif Central and the higher Alps, Jura and 'rénées. Climate ranges from moderate maritime in the northwest to editerranean in the south. Farming is possible in all parts of France. Its eyards produce some of the world's best wines. The main industrial ea of France is in the north and east.

abon

ɘa 267,667 sq km (103,346 sq miles); *population* 1,220,000; *capital* Libreville; 'er major city Port Gentile; *form of government* Republic; *religion* RC, Animism; 'rency Franc CFA

ıbon is a small country in west-central Africa, which straddles the uator. It has a low narrow coastal plain, and the rest of the country mprises a low plateau. Three-quarters of Gabon is covered with dense pical forest. The climate is hot, humid and typically equatorial, with little no seasonal variations. Until the 1960s timber was virtually Gabon's 'y resource. By the mid 1980s it was Africa's sixth largest oil producer. ıch of the earnings from this were squandered, however, and most ıbonese remain subsistence farmers.

ambia

a 11,295 sq km (4361 sq miles); *population* 875,000; *capital* Banjul; *form of* /ernment Republic; *religion* Sunni Islam; *currency* Dalasi

ımbia, the smallest country in Africa, pokes like a crooked finger into negal. The country is divided along its entire length by the River ımbia. Most Gambians grow enough millet and sorghum to feed emselves. Groundnuts are the main crop and the only export of any nificance. The river provides a thriving local fishing industry, and the ite sandy beaches on the coast are popular with foreign tourists.

eorgia

a 69,700 sq km (26,900 sq miles); *population* 5,976,000; *capital* Tbilisi; *other* jor cities Kutaisi, Rustavi, Batumi; *form of government* Republic; *religion* Russian hodox; *currency* Rouble

orgia is a republic in the southwest of the former USSR, occupying the central and western parts of the Caucasus. Almost 40% of the countr covered with forests. Agriculture is the main occupation, especially cultivation and fruit growing. It is rich in minerals and has many industr Georgia declared itself independent in 1991.

Germany

Area 356,910 sq km (137,803 sq miles); *population* 79,070,000; *capital* Berlin, B (Seat of government); *other major cities* Cologne, Frankfurt, Hamburg, Leipzig, Munich, Stuttgart; *form of government* Republic; *religions* Lutheranism, RC; *currency* Deutsche Mark

Germany is a large industrialized country in northern central Euro which comprises the former East and West German Republics, reuni in 1990. Its landscapes vary from flat coastal plains in the north, thro central plateaux to the Bavarian and Swabian Alps in the south. The m rivers, like the Rhine and Elbe, flow northwards. Generally, the country warm summers and cold winters. Agricultural products include wheat, barley, oats, potatoes and sugar beet. Principal industries are mechan and electrical engineering, chemicals, textiles and motor vehicles, loca in the large provincial cities and concentrated in the Ruhr and Rh valleys. The country depends heavily on imports.

Ghana

Area 238,533 sq km (92,098 sq miles); *population* 14,900,000; *capital* Accra; *oth major cities* Kumasi, Tamale, Sekondi-Takoradi; *form of government* Republic; *religions* Protestant, Animism, RC; *currency* Cedi

Ghana is located in West Africa between Côte d'Ivoire and Togo. It palm-fringed beaches of white sand along the Gulf of Guinea. The clim on the coast is equatorial, and towards the north there are steamy trop evergreen forests that give way in the far north to tropical savanna. landscape becomes harsh and barren near the border with Burkina. In south, cocoa, rubber, palm oil and coffee are grown. Ghana has impor mineral resources, such as manganese and bauxite.

Greece

Area 131,990 sq km (50,961 sq miles); *population* 10,140,000; *capital* Athens (Athinai); *other major cities* Patras, Piraeus, Thessaloníki; *form of government* Republic; *religion* Greek Orthodox; *currency* Drachma

Greece is a peninsular-shaped country, the most southeasterly extens of Western Europe. About 70% of the land is hilly, with harsh moun climates and poor soils. The Greek islands and coastal regions hav typical Mediterranean climate while winter in the northern mountain

vere. Agriculture is the chief activity, and large-scale farming is concen-
ted on the east coast. Fishing is important around the 2000 islands. urists visit the country for the sun and its spectacular ancient ruins.

'enada

a 344 sq km (133 sq miles); *population* 110,000; *capital* St. Georges; *form of ernment* Constitutional Monarchy; *religions* RC, Anglicanism, Methodism; *rency* East Caribbean dollar

enada is the most southerly of the Windward Island chain in the ribbean. It consists of the remains of extinct volcanoes and has an ractive wooded landscape. In the dry season its typical climate is very asant, with warm days and cool nights, but in the wet season it is hot y and night. Agriculture is the island's main industry, and tourism is an portant source of foreign revenue.

iatemala

a 108,889 sq km (42,042 sq miles); *population* 9,000,000; *capital* Guatemala ; *other major cities* Puerto Barrios, Quezaltenango; *form of government* public; *religion* RC; *currency* Quetzal;

atemala is situated where North America meets Central America. It is nountainous country with a ridge of volcanoes running parallel to the cific coast. It has a tropical climate. The Pacific slopes of the mountains exceptionally well watered and fertile, and it is here that most of the pulation are settled. Coffee growing on the lower slopes dominates the onomy. A small strip on the coast produces sugar, cotton and bananas.

iiana (French) *or* Guyane

a 90,000 sq km (34,749 sq miles); *population* 73,800; *capital* Cayenne; *form of ernment* French overseas department; *religion* RC; *currency* Franc

iana (French) or Guyane is situated on the northeast coast of South ierica. The climate is tropical with heavy rainfall. Guiana's economy ies almost completely on subsidies from France. It has little to export art from shrimps, and the small area of land that is cultivated produces , manioc and sugar cane.

iinea

a 245,857 sq km (94,925 sq miles); *population* 6,710,000; *capital* Conakry; *other or cities* Kankan, Labé; *form of government* Republic; *religion* :Sunni Islam; *rency* Guinea franc

inea, located on the coast at the "bulge" in Africa, is a lush, green, autiful country with a tropical climate. Guinea has great agricultural potential, and many of the coastal swamps and forested plains have be cleared for the cultivation of rice, cassava, yams, maize and vegetab Further inland, on the plateau of Fouta Djallon, dwarf cattle are raised, in the valleys bananas and pineapples are grown. Coffee and kola nuts important cash crops grown in the Guinea Highlands to the southwe

Guinea Bissau

Area 36,125 sq km (13,948 sq miles); *population* 966,000; *capital* Bissau; *form o government* Republic; *religion* Animism, Sunni Islam; *currency* Peso

Guinea Bissau, south of Senegal on the Atlantic coast of West Africa, country of stunning scenery and rises from a deeply indented and isla fringed coastline to a low inland plateau. The climate is tropical but it is of the poorest West African states. The main crops are groundnuts, su cane, plantains, coconuts and rice. Fishing is an important export indus

Guyana

Area 214,969 sq km (83,000 sq miles); *population* 990,000; *capital* Georgetown; *other major city* New Amsterdam; *form of government* Cooperative Republic; *religions* Hinduism, Protestantism, RC; *currency* Guyana dollar

Guyana, situated on the northeast coast of South America, is intersec by many rivers, and the coastal area comprises tidal marshes mangrove swamps. The jungle in the southwest has potential for production of minerals, hardwood and hydroelectric power, but 90% of population live in the coastal area, where the climate is moderated by breezes; here rice is grown, and vast plantations produce sugar.

Haiti

Area 27,750 sq km (10,714 sq miles); *population* 5,700,000; *capital* Port-au-Prin *other major cities* Les Cayes, Gonaïves, Jérémie; *form of government* Republic; *religions* RC, Voodooism; *currency* Gourde

Haiti occupies the western third of the large island of Hispaniola in Caribbean. It is a country of high mountain ranges separated by d valleys and plains. The climate is tropical but semi-arid conditions occur in the lee of the central mountains. Hurricanes and severe thun storms are a common occurrence. Only a third of the country is arable, agriculture is the chief occupation. Many farmers grow only enough to f their own families, and the export crops, coffee, sugar and sisal, are gr on large estates. Haiti remains the poorest country in the Americas.

Honduras

Area 112,088 sq km (43,277 sq miles); *population* 4,440,000; *capital* Tegucigalp *form of government* Republic; *religion* RC; *currency* Lempira

nduras is a fan-shaped country in Central America, which spreads out vards the Caribbean Sea. Four-fifths of the country is covered in untains, which are indented with river valleys running towards the very ort Pacific coast. There is little change in temperatures throughout the ar, and rainfall is heavy. The country is sparsely populated, and, hough agricultural, only about 25% of the land is cultivated. Bananas, ins, coffee and sugar are important crops, and these are grown mainly the coastal plains.

ng Kong

a 1045 sq km (403 sq miles); *population* 5,760,000; *form of government* Colony ler British administration until 1997 when China will take over.; *religions* dhism, Taoism, Christianity; *currency* Hong Kong dollar

ng Kong is located in the South China Sea and consists of Hong Kong nd, the peninsula of Kowloon, and about 1000 sq km (386 sq miles) of acent land known as the New Territories situated at the mouth of the arl River, southeast of Guangzhou (Canton). The climate is warm otropical with cool dry winters and hot humid summers. Hong Kong has natural resources. Its main assets are its magnificent natural harbour d its position close to the main trading routes of the Pacific. Hong Kong's in industries are textiles and clothing, which account for 38% of its nestic exports.

ngary

a 93,032 sq km (35,920 sq miles); *population* 10,590,000; *capital* Budapest; *er major cities* Debrecen, Miskolc, Pécs, Szeged; *form of government* Republic; *gions* RC, Calvinism, Lutheranism; *currency* Forint

ndlocked in the heartland of Europe, Hungary is dominated by the great in to the east of the River Danube, which runs north-south across the ntry. In the west lies the largest lake in Central Europe, Lake Balaton. nters are severe, but the summers are warm. Hungary experienced a dest boom in its economy in the 1970s and 1980s. Yields of cereals and have since soared, and large areas between the Danube and Tisza ers are now used to grow vegetables. Industries have been carefully oanded where adequate natural resources exist, and tourism is fast veloping.

land

a 103,000 sq km (39,768 sq miles); *population* 253,500; *capital* Reykjavík; *form overnment* Republic; *religion* Lutheranism; *currency* Icelandic króna

land is a large island situated in the North Atlantic Ocean, just south of the Arctic Circle. The island has over 100 volcanoes, at least one of wh erupts every five years. One-ninth of the country is covered with ice a snowfields, and there are about seven hundred hot springs, which are important source of central heating. The climate is cool temperate. O 1% of the land is cultivated. The island's economy is based on its se fishing industry, which accounts for 70% of exports.

India

Area 3,287,590 sq km (1,269,338 sq miles); *population* 843,930,000; *capital* New Delhi; *other major cities* Bangalore, Bombay, Calcutta, Delhi, Hyderabad, Madras *form of government* Federal Republic; *religion* Hinduism, Sunni Islam, Christianity *currency* Rupee

India is a vast country in South Asia, which is dominated in the extre north by the world's youngest and highest mountains, the Himalayas. their foot, a huge plain, drained by the Indus and Ganges rivers, is one the most fertile areas in the world and the most densely populated par India. Further south, the Deccan plateau extends to the southern tip of country. India generally has four seasons, the cool, the hot, the rainy, a the dry. Rainfall varies from 100 mm (3.94 inches) in the northwest des to 10,000 mm (394 inches) in Assam. About 70% of the population depe on agriculture for their living. Much rice, sugar cane, tea and wheat grown.

Indonesia

Area 1,904,569 sq km (735,354 sq miles); *population* 179,100,000; *capital* Jakart *other major cities* Badung, Medan, Semarang, Surabaya; *form of government* Republic; *religions* Sunni Islam, Christianity, Hinduism; *currency* Rupiah

Indonesia is made up of 13,667 islands that are scattered across the Ind and Pacific Oceans in a huge crescent. Its largest landmass is the provir of Kalimantan, which is part of the island of Borneo. Sumatra is the larg individual island. Java, however, is the dominant and most dens populated island. The climate is generally tropical monsoon. The cour has one hundred volcanoes, and earthquakes are frequent. Rice, ma and cassava are the main crops grown. Indonesia has the largest reser of tin in the world and is one of the world's leading rubber producers.

Iran

Area 1,648,000 sq km (636,293,sq miles); *population* 53,920,000; *capital* Tehran; *other major cities* Esfahan, Mashhad, Tabriz; *form of government* Islamic Republi *religion* Shia Islam; *currency* Rial

Iran lies across The Gulf from the Arabian peninsula and stretches from ıspian Sea to the Arabian Sea. It is a land dominated by mountains in the rth and west, with a huge expanse of desert in its centre. The climate is ainly hot and dry, although more temperate conditions are found on the ores of the Caspian Sea. Most of the population live in the north and st, where Tehran is situated. The only good agricultural land is on the ıspian coastal plains, and here rice is grown. Most of Iran's oil is in the uthwest on The Gulf. The main exports are petrochemicals, carpets and gs, textiles, raw cotton and leather goods.

aq

ea 438,317 sq km (169,234 sq miles); *population* 17,060,000; *capital* Baghdad; *er major cities* Al-Basrah, Al Mawsil; *form of government* Republic; *religion* Shia m, Sunni Islam; *currency* Iraqi dinar

q is located in southwest Asia, wedged between The Gulf and Syria. It almost landlocked except for its outlet to The Gulf at Shatt al Arab. Its great rivers, the Tigris and the Euphrates, flow from the northwest into e Gulf at this point. The climate is arid with very hot summers and cold nters. The high mountains on the border with Turkey are snow covered six months of the year, and desert in the southwest covers nearly half country. The only fertile land in Iraq is in the basins of the Tigris and phrates, where dates, wheat, barley, rice, tobacco and cotton are own.

land, Republic of

a 70,284 sq km (27,137 sq miles); *population* 3,540,000; *capital* Dublin (Baile a Cliath); *other major cities* Cork, Galway, Limerick, Waterford; *form of ernment* Republic; *religion* RC; *currency* Punt = 100 pighne

e Republic of Ireland is one of Europe's most westerly countries, ıated in the Atlantic Ocean and separated from Great Britain by the Irish a. It has an equable mild climate. The Republic extends over four-fifths he island of Ireland, and the west and southwest are mountainous. The ntral plain is largely limestone covered in boulder clay which provides od farmland and pasture. Despite the fertile land, the Republic of Ireland nains one of the poorest countries in western Europe. The rural oulation tend to migrate to the cities, mainly Dublin, which is the capital d the main industrial centre.

ael

a 20,770 sq km (8019 sq miles); *population* 4,820,000; *capital* Jerusalem ushalayim); *other major cities* Tel Aviv-Jaffa, Haifa; *form of government* ublic; *religion* Judaism, Sunni Islam, Christianity; *currency* Shekel

Israel occupies a long narrow stretch of land in the southeast of t Mediterranean. Its eastern boundary is formed by the River Jordan flowi into the Dead Sea. The south of the country is made up of a triangu wedge of the Negev Desert which ends at the Gulf of Aqaba. The clima in summer is hot and dry, in winter it is mild with some rain. Most of t population live on the coastal plain bordering the Mediterranean, whe Tel Aviv-Jaffa is the main commercial city. It is virtually self-sufficient foodstuffs and a major exporter of its produce. Main exports inclu finished diamonds, textiles, fruit, vegetables, chemicals, machinery a fertilizers.

Italy

Area 301,268 sq km (116,320 sq miles); *population* 57,600,000; *capital* Rome (Roma); *other major cities* Milan, Naples, Turin, Genoa, Palermo; *form of government* Republic; *religion* RC; *currency* Lira

Italy is a republic in southern Europe, which comprises a large penins and the two main islands of Sicily and Sardinia. The Alps form a natu boundary to the north. The Apennine Mountains form the backbone peninsular Italy. Between the Alps and the Apennines lies the Po Vall a great fertile lowland. Sicily and Sardinia are largely mountainous. It has four active volcanoes, including Etna and Vesuvius. It enjoys warm summers and mild winters. The north is the main industrial centre, a agriculture there is well mechanized. In the south, farms are small a traditional. Industries include motor vehicles, textiles, clothing, leat goods, glass, ceramics, and tourism.

Jamaica

Area 10,990 sq km (4243 sq miles); *population* 2,400,000; *capital* Kingston; *other major cities* Montego Bay, Spanish Town; *form of government* Constitutional Monarchy; *religion* Anglicanism, RC, other Protestantism; *currency* Jamaican dol

Jamaica is an island state in the Caribbean Sea about 150 km (93 mil south of Cuba. The centre of the island comprises a limestone plateau, a this is surrounded by narrow coastal flatlands and palm-fringed beach The climate is tropical with frequent hurricanes. The traditional cr grown are sugar cane, bananas, peppers, ginger, cocoa and coffee. T decline in the principal export products, bauxite and alumina, has resul in near economic stagnation. Tourism is an important industry.

Japan

Area 377,801 sq km (145,869 sq miles); *population* 123,260,000; *capital* Tokyo; *other major cities* Osaka, Nagoya, Sapporo, Kobe, Kyoto, Yokohama; *form of*

vernment Constitutional Monarchy; *religion* Shintoism, Buddhism, Christianity; rrency Yen

pan is located on the eastern margin of Asia and consists of four major ands, Honshu, Hokkaido, Kyushu and Shikoku, and many small islands. ie country is made up of six chains of steep, serrated mountains, which ntain about 60 active volcanoes. Earthquakes are frequent and wide-read. Summers are warm and humid, and winters mainly mild. Japan's riculture is highly advanced. Fishing is important. Japan is the second gest industrial economy in the world. It is very dependent on imported w materials.

rdan

ea 97,740 sq km (37,737 sq miles); *population* 3,170,000; *capital* Amman; *other jor cities* Irbid, Zarga; *form of government* Constitutional Monarchy; *religion* Sunni am; *currency* Jordan dinar

rdan is almost landlocked except for a short coastline on the Gulf of aba. It is bounded by Saudi Arabia, Syria, Iraq and Israel. Almost 80% the country is desert, and the rest comprises the East Bank Uplands and rdan Valley. In general, summers are hot and dry, and winters cool and t, with variations related to altitude. The east has a desert climate. Only e-fifth of the country is fertile, but it is self-sufficient in potatoes, onions d poultry meat. Amman is the capital and main industrial centre.

zakhstan

a 2,717,000 sq km (1,050,000 sq miles); *population* 15,654,000; *capital* Alma Ata maty); *other major city* Karaganda; *form of government* Republic; *religion* Sunni m; *currency* Rouble

zakhstan, the second largest republic of the former USSR, extends m the Caspian Sea to Mongolia. The west of the country is low-lying, the st hilly, and in the southeast mountainous. The climate is continental d very dry with great extremes of temperature. Much of the country is mi-desert. Crops can only be grown in the wetter northwest regions or ere irrigated. Extensive pastoral farming is carried out. The country is n in minerals. Kazakhstan declared itself independent in 1991.

nya

a 580,367 sq km (224,080 sq miles); *population* 24,080,000; *capital* Nairobi; *er major cities* Mombasa, Kisumu; *form of government* Republic; *religions* RC, testantism, other Christianity, Animism; *currency* Kenya shilling

cated in east Africa, Kenya straddles the Equator and extends from ke Victoria in the west to the Indian Ocean in the east. Highlands run north to south through central Kenya and are divided by the steep-sid Great Rift Valley. The coastal lowlands have a hot, humid climate, but the highlands it is cooler and rainfall heavier. In the east it is very arid. T fertile southwestern region accounts for almost all its economic produ tion. The main crops include wheat, maize, tea, coffee, sisal, sugar ca and cotton. Tourism is an important source of foreign revenue.

Kiribati

Area 726 sq km (280 sq miles); *population* 66,250; *capital* Tarawa; *form of government* Republic; *religions* RC, Protestantism; *currency* Australian dollar

Kiribati comprises three groups of coral atolls and one isolated volca island spread over a large expanse of the central Pacific. The climate maritime equatorial with a high rainfall. Most islanders are involved subsistence agriculture. The principal tree is the coconut. Soil is negligib and the only vegetable that can be grown is calladium. Tuna fishing is important industry. The country is heavily dependent on overseas aid

Korea, North

Area 120,538 sq km (46,540 sq miles); *population* 22,420,000; *capital* Pyongyang *other major cities* Chongjin, Nampo; *form of government* Socialist Republic; *religi* Chondoism, Buddhism; *currency* North Korean won

North Korea occupies just over half the Korean peninsula in east Asia is a mountainous country, three-quarters of which is forested highland scrubland. The climate is warm temperate, although winters can be c in the north. Most rain falls during the summer. Nearly 90% of its ara land is farmed by cooperatives, on which rice is the main crop grown. No Korea is quite well endowed with fuel and minerals including iron (Some 60% of the labour force are employed in industry, the most import of which are metallurgy, building, cement and chemicals.

Korea, South

Area 99,016 sq km (38,230 sq miles); *population* 42,800,000; *capital* Seoul (Soul *other major cities* Pusan, Taegu, Inch'on; *form of government* Republic; *religions* Buddhism, Christianity; *currency* South Korean won

South Korea occupies the southern half of the Korean peninsula. predominantly mountainous with the highest ranges running north to sc along the east coast. The west is lowland, which is extremely dens populated. The extreme south has a humid warm temperate climate, w farther north it is more continental. Cultivated land represents only 23% the country's total area, and the main crop is rice. The country ha flourishing manufacturing industry and is the world's leading supplie ɔs and footwear. Other important industries are electronic equipment, ctrical goods, steel, petrochemicals, motor vehicles and toys.

wait

a 17,818 sq km (6880 sq miles); *population* 2,040,000; *capital* Kuwait (Al ayt); *form of government* Constitutional Monarchy; *religion* Sunni Islam, Shia n; *currency* Kuwait dinar

vait is a tiny state on The Gulf, wedged between Iraq and Saudi Arabia. as a dry desert climate that is cool in winter but very hot and humid in nmer. There is little agriculture because of lack of water. Shrimp fishing ecoming important. Large reserves of petroleum and natural gas are mainstay of the economy. Apart from oil, industry includes boat-ding, food production, petrochemicals, and construction.

rgyzstan

a 198,500 sq km (76,600 sq miles); *population* 3,886,000; *capital* Bishkek; *form overnment* Republic; *religion* Sunni Islam; *currency* Rouble

gyzstan, a central Asian republic of the former USSR, declared itself ependent in 1991. It is located on the border with northwest China. ch of the country is occupied by the Tian Shan Mountains which rise to ctacular peaks. Most of the country is semi-arid or desert, but climate reatly influenced by altitude. Soils are poor except in the valleys, where eat and other grains can be grown. Grazing of sheep, horses and cattle arried out extensively. In the west the raising of silkworms is important. er industries include non-ferrous metallurgy, coal mining, tobacco, d processing, textiles and gold mining.

os

a 236,800 sq km (91,428 sq miles); *population* 4,050,000; *capital* Vientiane; *form overnment* People's Republic; *religion* Buddhism; *currency* Kip

s is a landlocked country in southeast Asia, which is ruggedly moun-ous apart from the Mekong River plains along its border with Thailand. Annam Mountains form a natural border with Vietnam. It has a tropical nsoon climate. Laos is one of the poorest countries in the world, and its elopment has been retarded by war, drought and floods. The principal ɔ is rice, grown on small peasant plots.

via

a 63,700 sq km (24,595 sq miles); *population* 2,681,000; *capital* Riga; *other or cities* Daugavpils, Jurmala, Liepaja; *form of government* Republic; *religion* eranism; *currency* Rouble

Latvia, a Baltic state that regained its independence in 1991 with the bre
up of the USSR, is sandwiched between Estonia and Lithuania. The c
agricultural occupations are cattle and dairy farming, and the main cr
grown are oats, barley, rye, potatoes and flax. Latvia's population is
70% urban, and its cities produce high-quality textiles, machinery, ele
cal appliances, paper, chemicals, furniture and foodstuffs. Latvia
extensive deposits of peat and gypsum.

Lebanon

Area 10,400 sq km (4015 sq miles); *population* 2,800,000; *capital* Beirut (Beyrou
other important cities Tripoli, Zahle; *form of government* Republic; *religions* Shia
Islam, Sunni Islam, Christianity; *currency* Lebanese pound

Lebanon is a mountainous country in the eastern Mediterranean. The
a fertile narrow coastal plain, and between the two main ranges lies
Beqa'a Valley. The climate is Mediterranean but rainfall can be torre
in winter and snow falls on high ground. Lebanon is an agricultural cou
and its main products include olives, grapes, citrus fruit, apples, co
tobacco and sugar beet. Industry is small scale.

Lesotho

Area 30,355 sq km (11,720 sq miles); *population* 1,720,000; *capital* Maseru; *for
government* Monarchy; *religions* RC, other Christianity; *currency* Loti

Lesotho is a small landlocked kingdom entirely surrounded by the Re
lic of South Africa. Snow-capped mountains and treeless uplands, c
spectacular gorges, cover two-thirds of the country. The climate is pl
ant with variable rainfall but frequent snow in the highlands. Due tc
mountainous terrain, only one-eighth of the land can be cultivated, an
main crop is maize. Wool, mohair and diamonds are exported, but r
foreign exchange comes from money sent home by Lesotho worke
South Africa. Tourism is beginning to flourish.

Liberia

Area 111,369 sq km (43,000 sq miles); *population* 2,440,000; *capital* Monrovia;
of government Republic; *religion* Animism, Sunni Islam, Christianity; *currency*
Liberian dollar

Liberia is located in West Africa between Sierra Leone and Côte d'Iv
It has a treacherous coast with rocky cliffs and lagoons enclosed by
bars. Inland the land rises to a densely forested plateau dissected by d
narrow valleys. Farther inland still, there are beautiful waterfalls, an
Nimba Mountains rise to over 1700 m (5577 ft). Agriculture employs th
quarters of the labour force and produces cassava and rice as subsist

ɔs, and rubber, coffee and cocoa for export. The Nimba Mountains are in iron ore, which accounts for 70% of export earnings.

ya

ɪ 1,759,540 sq km (679,358 sq miles); *population* 4,000,000; *capital* Tripoli abulus); *other major cities* Benghazi, Misurata; *form of government* Socialist ɔle's Republic; *religion* Sunni Islam; *currency* Libyan dinar

'a is a large north African country that stretches from the Mediterranean ınd in some parts beyond, the Tropic of Cancer. The Sahara Desert ers much of the country. The only green areas are the scrublands found e northwest and the forested hills near Benghazi. The coastal area has wet winters and hot dry summers, but the interior has had some of the ıest recorded temperatures of anywhere in the world. Only 14% of the ɔle work on the land. Many sheep, goats and cattle are reared, and e is an export trade in skins, hides and hairs. Libya is one of the world's est producers of oil and natural gas.

chtenstein

160 sq km (62 sq miles); *population* 28,181; *capital* Vaduz; *form of government* stitutional Monarchy; *religion* RC; *currency* Swiss franc

principality of Liechtenstein is a tiny central European mountainous e situated on the River Rhine between Austria and Switzerland. The ate is mild alpine. Once an agricultural country, it now has a great ety of light industries, such as textiles, high-quality metal goods, ision instruments, pharmaceuticals and ceramics. Tourism is also big ness, beautiful scenery and good skiing being the main attractions.

ıuania

65,200 sq km (25,174 sq miles); *population* 3,690,000; *capital* Vilnius; *other r cities* Kaunas, Klaipeda, Siauliai; *form of government* Republic; *religion* RC; *ncy* Rouble

ıania, lying to the northwest of the Russian Federation and Belorussia, e largest of the three former Soviet Baltic Republics. Before 1940 ıania was a mainly agricultural country but has since been consider- industrialized. Most of the land is lowland covered by forest and mp, and the main products are rye, barley, sugar beet, flax, meat, milk potatoes. Industry includes heavy engineering and shipbuilding.

embourg

2586 sq km (998 sq miles); *population* 378,400; *capital* Luxembourg; *form of rnment* Constitutional Monarchy; *religion* RC; *currency* Luxembourg franc

Luxembourg is a small country bounded by Belgium on the west, Fra on the south, and Germany on the east. In the north is a wooded plat and in the south a fertile lowland area of valleys and ridges. Nort winters are cold and raw, with snow covering the ground for almo month, but in the south winters are mild and summers cool. In the s crops grown include maize, roots, tubers and potatoes. Dairy farmir also important. It is in the south, also, that iron ore is mined as the b of the country's iron and steel industry.

Madagascar

Area 587,041 sq km (226,657 sq miles); *population* 11,440,000; *capital* Antananarivo; *other major cities* Fianarantsoa, Mahajanga, Toamasina; *form of government* Republic; *religions* Animism, RC, Protestantism; *currency* Malagasy franc

Madagascar is an island state situated off the southeast coast of Afric is the fourth largest island in the world, and the centre of it is made u high savanna-covered plateaux. In the east, forested mountains steeply to the coast, and in the southwest the land falls gradually thrc dry grassland and scrub. The staple food crop is rice, and 80% of population grow enough to feed themselves. Cassava is also grown some 58% of the land is pasture, and there are more cattle than pe The main export earners are coffee, vanilla, cloves and sugar.

Malawi

Area 118,484 sq km (45,747 sq miles); *population* 7,980,000; *capital* Lilongwe; *major cities* Blantyre, Mzuzu, Zomba; *form of government* Republic; *religions* Animism, RC, Presbyterianism; *currency* Kwacha

Malawi lies along the southern and western shores of the third largest in Africa, Lake Malawi. To the south of the lake the Shire river flows thr a valley, overlooked by wooded, towering mountains. The tropical cli has a dry season from May to October and a wet season for the remai months. Agriculture is the predominant occupation, and many Malaw live off their own crops. Plantation farming is used for exported crops c and tobacco. Hydroelectricity is now being used for industry, but im of manufactured goods remain high.

Malaysia

Area 329,749 sq km (127,316 sq miles); *population* 17,810,000; *capital* Kuala Lumpur; *other major cities* Ipoh, Georgetown, Johor Baharu; *form of governme* Federal Constitutional Monarchy; *religion* Sunni Islam; *currency* Malaysian ring

The Federation of Malaysia lies in southeast Asia, and comprises P r Malaysia and the states of Sabah and Sarawak on the island of ieo. The country is affected by a tropical monsoon climate. Peninsular aysia has always had thriving rubber-growing and tin-dredging indus-, and now oil palm growing is also important on the east coast. Sabah Sarawak have grown rich by exploiting their forests. There is also e offshore oil, and around the capital, Kuala Lumpur, new industries ı as electronics are expanding.

dives

298 sq km (115 sq miles); *population* 214,139; *capital* Malé; *form of govern-* Republic; *religion* Sunni Islam; *currency* Rufiyaa

Republic of Maldives lies in the Indian Ocean and comprises 1200 ying coral islands grouped into 12 atolls. The climate is hot and humid. islands are covered with coconut palms, and some millet, cassava, s and tropical fruit are grown. Rice, however, the staple diet of its ders, has to be imported. Fishing is an important occupation, and the f export is now canned or frozen tuna. Tourism is developing fast.

i

1,240,192 sq km (478,838 sq miles); *population* 9,090,000; *capital* Bamaku; *major cities* Segou, Mopti; *form of government* Republic; *religions* Sunni Islam, sm; *currency* Franc CFA

is a landlocked state in West Africa. The country mainly comprises and monotonous plains and plateaux. The Sahara, in the north of the try, is encroaching southwards, and the country is one of the poorest e world. In the south there is some rain, and plains are covered by sy savanna and a few scattered trees. The River Niger runs through outh of the country, and small steamboats use it for shipping. Only fifth of the land can be cultivated. Rice, cassava and millet are grown omestic consumption, and cotton for export.

a

316 sq km (122 sq miles); *population* 354,900; *capital* Valletta; *form of* *nment* Republic; *religion* RC; *currency* Maltese pound

ı, a small republic in the middle of the Mediterranean Sea, lies just ı of Sicily. It comprises three islands, Malta, Gozo and Comino, which ade up of low limestone plateaux with little surface water. The climate diterranean. Malta is virtually self-sufficient in agricultural products exports potatoes, vegetables, wine and cut flowers. Commercial uilding and repairing is one of the leading industries. Tourism has oomed.

Mauritania

Area 1,025,520 sq km (395,953 sq miles); *population* 1,970,000; *capital* Nouakc *form of government* Republic; *religion* Sunni Islam; *currency* Ouguiya

Mauritania is located on the west coast of Africa. About 47% of the cou is desert, the Sahara covering much of the north. The main agricul regions are in the Senegal river valley in the south. The rest of the cou is made up of the drought-stricken Sahel grasslands, from which traditionally nomadic herdsmen have moved to shanty towns in the sc Deposits of iron ore and copper provide the country's main exports, development of these and the fishing industry on the coast are the hope for a brighter future.

Mauritius

Area 2040 sq km (788 sq miles); *population* 1,081,669; *capital* Port Louis; *form government* Constitutional Monarchy; *religions* Hinduism, RC, Sunni Islam; *curr* Mauritius rupee

Mauritius is a beautiful volcanic island with tropical beaches, which li the Indian Ocean east of Madagascar. The climate is hot and humid. island has well-watered fertile soil, ideal for the sugar plantations cover 45% of the island. Although the export of sugar still dominate economy, diversification is being encouraged. The clothing and elect equipment industries are becoming increasingly important, and touris now the third largest source of foreign exchange.

Mexico

Area 1,958,201 sq km (756,061 sq miles); *population* 81,140,000; *capital* Méxic City; *other major cities* Guadalajara, Monterrey, Puebla de Zaragoza; *form of government* Federal Republic; *religion* RC; *currency* Mexican peso

Mexico is the most southerly country in North America. It is a lar volcanic mountain ranges and high plateaux, with coastal lowlands a the Pacific and the Gulf of Mexico. In the north there are arid and semi conditions, while in the south there is a humid tropical climate. Some of the labour force are involved in agriculture, growing maize, w kidney beans and rice for subsistence, and coffee, cotton, fruit vegetables for export. Mexico is the world's largest producer of silve has large reserves of oil and natural gas. Developing industries petrochemicals, textiles, motor vehicles and food processing.

Moldavia

Area 33,700 sq km (13,000 sq miles); *population* 4,052,000; *capital* Kishinev ; c ɔr *cities* Tiraspol, Bendery; *form of government* Republic; *religion* Russian odox; *currency* Rouble

davia was a Soviet republic from 1940 until 1991 when it became ependent of the former USSR. It is bounded to the west by Romania and ne north, east and south by Ukraine. It consists of a hilly plain of fertile s, and crops grown include wheat, corn, barley, tobacco, sugar beet, a beans and sunflowers. There are also extensive fruit orchards, yards and walnut groves. Beekeeping and silkworm breeding are espread throughout the country. Food processing is the main industry.

naco

195 hectares (48 acres); *population* 29,876; *capital* Monaco-Ville; *form of* ernment Constitutional Monarchy; *religion* RC; *currency* Franc

naco is a tiny principality on the Mediterranean, surrounded landwards France. It comprises a rocky peninsula and a narrow stretch of coast. old town of Monaco-Ville houses the royal palace and the cathedral. Monte Carlo district has its world-famous casino, and Fontvieille is an a reclaimed from the sea where now marinas and light industry are ted. Tourism is the main revenue earner.

ngolia

1,566,500 sq km (604,826 sq miles); *population* 2,095,000; *capital* Ulan Bator nbaatar); *other major cities* Darhan, Erdenet; *form of government* Republic; *on* Previously Buddhism but religion is now suppressed; *currency* Tugrik

ngolia is a landlocked country in northeast Asia, which is bounded to the h by the Russian Federation and by China to the south, west and east. t of Mongolia is mountainous. In the south there are grass-covered pes and the desert wastes of the Gobi. The climate is very extreme and For six months the temperatures are below freezing. Mongolia has a traditional nomadic pastoral economy for centuries, and cereals uding fodder crops are grown on a large scale on state farms. The ng of copper accounts for 40% of the country's exports.

rocco

446,550 sq km (172,413 sq miles); *population* 24,500,000; *capital* Rabat; *other* r *cities* Casablanca, Fez, Marrakech; *form of government* Constitutional archy; *religion* Sunni Islam; *currency* Dirham

occo, in northwest Africa, is a land of great contrasts, with the high ged Atlas Mountains in the north, the arid Sahara in the south, and its n Atlantic and Mediterranean coasts. The north has a pleasant literranean climate. Farther south, winters are warmer and summers even hotter. Morocco is largely a farming country, wheat, barley and m being the main food crops, and it is one of the world's chief exporte citrus fruit. Morocco's main wealth comes from phosphates. Indus include textiles, car assembly, cement and soap, and fishing. Touris also a major source of revenue.

Mozambique

Area 801,590 sq km (309,494 sq miles); *population* 14,900,000; *capital* Maputo *other major cities* Beira, Nampula; *form of government* Republic; *religions* Anim RC, Sunni Islam; *currency* Metical

Mozambique is a republic located in southeast Africa. The Zambezi separates the high plateaux in the north from the coastal lowlands ir south. The country has a humid tropical climate. Normally, condition: reasonably good for agriculture, but a drought in the early 1980s follc a few years later by severe flooding resulted in famine and more 100,000 deaths. A lot of industry was abandoned when the Portugues the country in 1975. There is little incentive to produce surplus agricu products for cash, and food rationing has now been introduced. A t market accounts for a sizable part of the economy.

Namibia

Area 824,292 sq km (318,259 sq miles); *population* 1,290,000; *capital* Windhoe *form of government* Republic; *religions* Lutheranism, RC, other Christianity; *cur* Rand

Namibia is situated on the Atlantic coast of southwest Africa. Ther three main regions in the country. Running down the entire At coastline is the Namib Desert, east of which is the Central Plate mountains, rugged outcrops, sandy valleys and poor grasslands. again and north is the Kalahari Desert. Namibia has a poor rainfal highest falling at Windhoek. Even here it amounts to only 200–250 m 10 inches) per year. It is essentially a stock-rearing country, with s and goats raised in the south, and cattle in the central and northern a Diamonds are mined just north of the River Orange, and the largest groove uranium mine in the world is located near Swakopmund. O Africa's richest fishing grounds lies off the coast of Namibia, and mac tuna and pilchards are an important export.

Nauru

Area 21 sq km (8 sq miles); *population* 8100; *capital* Yaren; *form of governme* Republic; *religions* Protestantism, RC; *currency* Australian dollar

Nauru, the world's smallest republic, is a coral island situated just so

Equator, halfway between Australia and Hawaii. The climate is tropical a high and irregular rainfall. The country is rich, due entirely to the high-lity phosphate rock in the central plateau, which is sold for fertilizer. vever, these deposits are likely to be exhausted by 1995, but the ernment is investing overseas.

pal

140,797 sq km (54,362 sq miles); *population* 18,000,000; *capital* Kathmandu; *of government* Constitutional Monarchy; *religion* Hinduism, Buddhism; *currency* alese rupee

al is a long narrow rectangular country, landlocked between China and a on the flanks of the eastern Himalayas. On its northern border is rest, the highest mountain in the world. The climate is subtropical in the h, and all regions are affected by the monsoon. Nepal is one of the d's least developed countries, with most of the population trying to ive as peasant farmers.

herlands, The

40,844 sq km (15,770 sq miles); *population* 14,890,000; *capital* Amsterdam; *of government* The Hague (Den Haag, 's-Gravenhage); *other major cities* hoven, Rotterdam; *form of government* Constitutional Monarchy; *religions* RC, h Reformed, Calvinism; *currency* Guilder

ated in northwest Europe, the Netherlands is bounded to the north and t by the North Sea. Over one-quarter of the country is below sea level, the Dutch have tackled some huge reclamation schemes including the elmeer. The Netherlands has mild winters and cool summers. Agricul- and horticulture are highly mechanized, with salad vegetables, fruit flowers grown under glass. Industries include chemicals, machinery, oleum refining, metallurgy and electrical engineering. The main port, erdam, is the largest in the world.

v Zealand

270,986 sq km (104,629 sq miles); *population* 3,390,000; *capital* Wellington; *major cities* Auckland, Christchurch, Dunedin, Hamilton; *form of government* stitutional Monarchy; *religions* Anglicanism, RC, Presbyterianism; *currency* New and dollar

Zealand, lying southeast of Australia in the South Pacific, comprises arge main islands. North Island is hilly, with isolated mountains and e volcanoes. On South Island the Southern Alps run north to south, the Canterbury Plains to their east. It enjoys very mild winters with lar rainfall. Two-thirds of New Zealand is suitable for agriculture and grazing, meat, wool and dairy goods being the main products. Fore supports the pulp and paper industry, and cheap hydroelectricity manufacturing industry, which now accounts for 30% of New Zeala exports.

Nicaragua

Area 130,000 sq km (50,193 sq miles); *population* 3,750,000; *capital* Managua; *of government* Republic; *religion* RC; *currency* Córdoba

Nicaragua is the largest of the countries situated on the isthmus of Ce America and lies between Honduras and Costa Rica. The east c contains forested lowland and is the wettest part of the country. western mountainous region, which contains the two huge lakes, Nic gua and Managua, is where most of the population live. The whole cou is subject to devastating earthquakes. Nicaragua is primarily an agr tural country. The main export crops are coffee, cotton and sugar ca enjoys very mild winters with regular rainfall.

Niger

Area 1,267,000 sq km (489,189 sq miles); *population* 7,450,000; *capital* Niame *form of government* Republic; *religion* Sunni Islam; *currency* Franc CFA

Niger is a landlocked republic in West Africa. Over half of the coun covered by the encroaching Sahara Desert in the north, and the sout in the drought-stricken Sahel. In the extreme southwest corner, the Niger flows through the country, and in the extreme southeast lies Chad, but the rest of the country is extremely short of water. subsistence farming and herding are the main occupations. Ura mined in the Aïr mountains is Niger's main export.

Nigeria

Area 923,768 sq km (356,667 sq miles); *population* 118,700,000; *capital* Abuja Federal Capital), Lagos (Capital until 1992); *other major cities* Ibadan, Kano, Ogbomsho; *form of government* Federal republic; *religions* Sunni Islam, Christi *currency* Naira

Nigeria is a large and populous country in West Africa, and from the of Guinea it extends north to the border with Niger. It has a va landscape and climate, from the hot and humid swampy coastal area tropical forest belts of the interior, to the arid mountains and savanna north. The two main rivers are the Niger and the Benue. The agricultural products are cocoa, rubber, groundnuts and cotton. cocoa, however, is of any significance for export. The country depen a fluctuating revenue from petroleum exports.

rway

323,895 sq km (125,056 sq miles); *population* 4,200,000; *capital* Oslo; *other* r cities Bergen, Trondheim, Stavanger; *form of government* Constitutional archy; *religion* Lutheranism; *currency* Norwegian krone

way occupies the western half of the Scandinavian peninsula in hern Europe, and is surrounded to the north, west and south by water. a country of spectacular scenery of fjords, cliffs, rugged uplands and sted valleys. The climate is temperate as a result of the warming effect e Gulf Stream, and although the winters are long and cold, the waters he west coast remain ice-free. Agriculture is chiefly concerned with ying and fodder crops. Fishing is an important industry, and the large rves of forest provide timber for export. Industry is now dominated by om the North Sea.

an

212,457 sq km (82,030 sq miles); *population* 2,000,000; *capital* Muscat qat); *form of government* Monarchy (sultanate); *religion* Ibadi Islam, Sunni ; *currency* Rial Omani

ated in the southeast of the Arabian peninsula, Oman is a small ntry in two parts. It comprises a small mountainous area overlooking Strait of Hormuz, which controls the entrance to The Gulf, and the main of the country, consisting of barren hills rising sharply behind a narrow stal plain. Oman has a desert climate. Only 0.1% of the land is vated, the main produce being dates. The economy is almost entirely endent on oil, which provides 90% of its exports.

istan

796,095 sq km (307,372 sq miles); *population* 105,400,000; *capital* Islamabad; *major cities* Faisalabad, Hyderabad, Karachi, Lahore; *form of government* ral Islamic Republic; *religion* Sunni Islam, Shia Islam; *currency* Pakistan rupee

stan lies just north of the Tropic of Cancer and has as its southern er the Arabian Sea. The valley of the Indus river splits the country into hland region in the west and a lowland region in the east. In the north some of the world's highest mountains. A weak form of tropical soon climate occurs over most of the country, and conditions in the and west are arid. Most agriculture is subsistence, with wheat and s the main crops. Cotton is the main cash crop. Industry concentrates od processing, textiles and consumer goods.

ama

77,082 sq km (29,761 sq miles); *population* 2,320,000; *capital* Panama City;

other major cities San Miguelito, Colón; *form of government* Republic; *religion* R
currency Balboa

Panama is located at the narrowest point in Central America, where 58 km (36 miles) of land separates the Caribbean Sea from the Pa Ocean, and the Panama Canal provides a major shipping route. climate is tropical, with high temperatures throughout the year. country is heavily forested, and very little is cultivated. Rice is the st food, and hardwoods a main export. The economy is heavily depen on the Canal as a major foreign currency earner.

Papua New Guinea

Area 462,840 sq km (178,703 sq miles); *population* 3,800,000; *capital* Port More *form of government* Constitutional Monarchy; *religion* Protestantism, RC; *curren* Kina

Papua New Guinea, in the southwest Pacific, comprises the eastern of the island of New Guinea, together with hundreds of islands, of w New Britain, Bougainville and New Ireland are the largest. The country a mountainous interior surrounded by broad swampy plains. The clin is tropical, with high temperatures and heavy rainfall. Subsistence farr is the main economic activity. Timber is cut for export. Minerals suc copper, gold, silver and oil form the mainstay of the economy.

Paraguay

Area 406,752 sq km (157,047 sq miles); *population* 4,160,000; *capital* Asunción *other major city* Ciudad Alfredo Stroessner; *form of government* Republic; *religi* RC; *currency* Guaraní

Paraguay, landlocked in central South America, is bordered by Bo Brazil and Argentina. The climate is tropical, with abundant rain and a s dry season. The River Paraguay splits the country into the Chaco, a semi-arid plain of huge meat-exporting cattle ranches on the west, a partly forested undulating fertile plateau on the east where almost 95 the population live. Crops grown on the fertile plains include cass sugar cane, maize, cotton and soya beans. The world's largest hydroe tric dam has been built at Itaipú, and cheap power from this has stimu industry.

Peru

Area 1,285,216 sq km (496,235 sq miles); *population* 22,330,000; *capital* Lima; *other major cities* Arequipa, Callao, Cuzco, Trujillo; *form of government* Republ *religion* RC; *currency* Sol

Peru is located just south of the Equator, on the Pacific coast of S erica. The country has three distinct regions from west to east: the sert coast, the wet and cool high sierra of the Andes, and the hot and nid tropical jungle of the Amazon Basin. Most large-scale agriculture is he oases and fertile, irrigated river valleys that cut across the coastal sert. Sugar and cotton are the main exports. The fishing industry was e the largest in the world, but recently the shoals have become leted. Peru's main source of wealth is oil, but present reserves are aring exhaustion.

ilippines

a 300,000 sq km (115,830 sq miles); *population* 60,500,000; *capital* Manila; *er major cities* Cebu, Davao, Quezon City; *form of government* Republic; *jions* RC, Aglipayan, Sunni Islam; *currency* Philippine peso

e Philippines comprise a group of mountainous islands, in the western cific, which are scattered over a great area. Earthquakes are common. e climate is humid, with high temperatures and heavy rainfall. Typhoons frequent. Rice and maize are the main subsistence crops, and onuts, sugar cane, pineapples and bananas are grown for export. oper is a major export, and industries include textiles, food processing, emicals and electrical engineering.

land

a 312,677 sq km (120,725 sq miles); *population* 37,930,000; *capital* Warsaw rszawa); *other major cities* Gdansk, Kraków, Lódz, Wroclow; *form of govern-t* Republic; *religion* RC; *currency* Zloty

and, situated on the North European Plain, consists mainly of lowlands has long severe winters and short warm summers. Agriculture is dominantly small-scale. The main crops are potatoes, wheat, barley, ar beet and fodder crops. The industrial sector of the economy is large-le. Poland has big deposits of coal and reserves of natural gas, copper silver. Vast forests stretching inland from the coast supply the paper furniture industries.

rtugal

92,389 sq km (35,671 sq miles); *population* 10,300,000; *capital* Lisbon oa); *other major cities* Braga, Coimbra, Oporto, Setúbal; *form of government* ublic; *religion* RC; *currency* Escudo

tugal, in the southwest corner of Europe, makes up about 15% of the ian peninsula. The most mountainous areas lie to the north of the us river, while south of it lies the Alentajo, an area of wheat fields and plantations, which continues to the hinterland of the Algarve, with beautiful groves of almond, fig and olive trees. Agriculture employs o quarter of the labour force. Manufacturing industry includes textiles a clothing for export, and footwear, food processing and cork produc Tourism, particularly in the south, is the main foreign currency earne

Puerto Rico

Area 8897 sq km (3435 sq miles); *population* 3,196,520; *capital* San Juan; *form c government* Self-governing Commonwealth (USA); *Relgion* RC, Protestantism; *currency* US dollar

Puerto Rico, the most easterly island of the Greater Antilles in Caribbean, is a self-governing commonwealth in association with United States. The climate is tropical, modified slightly by cooling s breezes. The main mountains on Puerto Rico are the Cordillera Cent Dairy farming is the most important agricultural activity. Tax relief a cheap labour encourage American businesses to be based in Puerto Ri Products include textiles, clothing, electrical and electronic goods, plas and chemicals. Tourism is another developing industry.

Qatar

Area 11,000 sq km (4247 sq miles); *population* 371,863; *capital* Doha (Ad Dawha *form of government* Monarchy; *religion* Wahhabi Sunni Islam; *currency* Qatari riy

Qatar is a small emirate that lies halfway along the coast of The Gu consists of a low barren peninsula and a few small islands. The climat hot and uncomfortably humid in summer, and the winters are mild with r in the north. The herding of sheep, goats and some cattle is carried out, a the country is famous for its high-quality camels. The discovery a exploitation of oil have resulted in a high standard of living. In orde diversify the economy, new industries have been developed.

Romania

Area 237,500 sq km (91,699 sq miles); *population* 23,000,000; *capital* Bucharest (Bucuresti); *other major cities* Brasov, Constanta, Timisoara; *form of governmen* Republic; *religions* Romanian Orthodox, RC; *currency* Leu

Apart from a small extension towards the Black Sea, Romania is an alm circular country located in southeast Europe. The Carpathian Mounta run through Romania, enclosed by a ring of rich agricultural plains a Transylvania within the Carpathian arc. Romania has cold snowy win and hot summers. Agriculture has been neglected in favour of industry, major crops include maize, sugar beet, wheat, potatoes and grapes wine. Industry is state-owned and includes mining, metallurgy, mech cal engineering and chemicals.

ıssian Federation, The

·a 17,075,400 sq km (6,592,800 sq miles); *population* 142,117,000; *capital* scow (Moskva); *other major cities* St Petersburg (formerly Leningrad), Nizhniy vgorod, Novosibirsk; *form of government* Republic; *religions* Russian Orthodox, nni Islam, Shia Islam, RC; *currency* Rouble

e Russian Federation, which is the largest country in the world, extends m eastern Europe through the Ural Mountains east to the Pacific Ocean. e Caucasus Mountains form its boundary in the south. The environment ıges from the vast frozen wastes of Siberia in the north to subtropical serts in the south. Agriculture is organized into either state or collective ms, which mainly produce sugar beet, cotton, potatoes and vegetables. e country has extensive reserves of coal, oil, gas, iron ore and nganese. Major industries include iron and steel, cement, transport uipment, engineering, armaments, electronic equipment and chemi- s. The Russian Federation declared itself independent in 1991.

vanda

·a 26,338 sq km (10,169 sq miles); *population* 6,710,000; *capital* Kigali; *form of* ·*ernment* Republic; *religions* RC, Animism; *currency* Rwanda franc

·anda is a small mountainous republic in the heart of central Africa, ich lies just 2° south of the Equator. Active volcanoes are found in the th. The climate is highland tropical, with temperatures decreasing with tude. The soils are not fertile, and subsistence agriculture dominates economy. Staple food crops are sweet potatoes, cassava, dry beans, ghum and potatoes. The main cash crops for export are coffee, tea and ethrum.

n Marino

a 61 sq km (24 sq miles); *population* 22,746; *capital* San Marino; *form of* *ernment* Republic; *religion* RC; *currency* Lira

n Marino is a tiny landlocked state in central Italy, lying in the eastern thills of the Apennines. It has wooded mountains and pasture land with ild Mediterranean climate. The majority of the population work on the d or in forestry. Some 3.5 million tourists visit the country each year, and ch of the country's revenue comes from the sale of stamps, postcards, venirs and duty-free liquor.

o Tomé and Príncipe

a 964 sq km (372 sq miles); *population* 115,600; *capital* São Tomé; *form of* *ernment* Republic; *religion* RC; *currency* Dobra

) Tomé and Príncipe consists of two volcanic islands that lie off the west coast of Africa. The coastal areas are hot and humid, with heavy rair from October to May. Some 70% of the work force work on the land, ma in state-owned cocoa plantations.

Saudi Arabia

Area 2,149,690 sq km (829,995 sq miles); *population* 12,000,000; *capital* Riyadh Riyah); *other major cities* Mecca, Jedda, Medina, Ta'if; *form of government* Monarchy; *religions* Sunni Islam, Shia Islam; *currency* Rial

Saudi Arabia occupies over 70% of the Arabian Peninsula. Over 95% the country is desert, and the largest expanse of sand in the world, Rub Khali, is found in the southeast of the country. In the west, a narrow, hu coastal plain along the Red Sea is backed by steep mountains. The clim is hot, with very little rain. The main products are dates, tomatoes, wa melons and wheat. The country's prosperity, however, is based alm entirely on the exploitation of its vast reserves of oil and natural gas.

Senegal

Area 196,722 sq km (75,954 sq miles); *population* 7,170,000; *capital* Dakar; *othe major cities* Kaolack, Thies, St Louis; *form of government* Republic; *religions* Sur Islam, RC; *currency* Franc CFA

Senegal is a former French colony in West Africa that extends from most western point in Africa, Cape Verde, to the border with Mali. Sene is mostly low-lying savanna apart from the Fouta Djallon mountains in south. The climate is tropical. Almost 80% of the labour force wor agriculture, growing groundnuts and cotton for export, and millet, ma rice and sorghum as subsistence crops.

Seychelles

Area 280 sq km (108 sq miles); *population* 67,378; *capital* Victoria; *form of government* Republic; *religion* RC; *currency* Seychelles rupee

The Seychelles are a group of volcanic and coral islands that lie in western Indian Ocean about 1200 km (746 miles) from the coast of E Africa. The climate is tropical maritime, with heavy rain. The staple foc coconut, imported rice and fish. Tourism accounts for about 90% of country's foreign exchange earnings and employs one-third of the lab force.

Sierra Leone

Area 71,740 sq km (27,699 sq miles); *population* 4,140,000; *capital* Freetown; *fo of government* Republic; *religion* Animism, Sunni Islam, Christianity; *currency* Le

Sierra Leone, on the Atlantic coast of West Africa, consists of w ampy forested coastal plains that rise to a mountainous plateau in the t. The climate is tropical. The main food of Sierra Leoneans is rice, and is grown in the swamplands at the coast. On the plateau,much forest been cleared for growing groundnuts. Most of the country's revenue nes from mining. Diamonds are panned from the rivers, and there are osits of iron ore, bauxite, rutile and some gold.

gapore

a 618 sq km (239 sq miles); *population* 2,690,000; *capital* Singapore; *form of ernment* Republic; *religions* Buddhism, Sunni Islam, Christianity; *currency* apore dollar

gapore, one of the world's smallest yet most successful countries, nprises 60 islands that are located at the foot of the Malay peninsula in theast Asia. The main island, Singapore Island, is very low-lying, and climate is hot and wet throughout the year. Only 3% of the land area sed for agriculture, and most food is imported. It is self-sufficient in fish. gapore has the largest oil-refining centre in Asia. The country has a rishing manufacturing industry for which it relies heavily on imports. rism is an important source of foreign revenue.

vakia

a 49,032 sq km (19,931 sq miles); *population* 5,013,000; *capital* Bratislava; *other or city* Kovice; *form of government* Republic; *religion* RC; *currency* Koruna

vakia was constituted on 1 January 1993. Landlocked in central ope, the northern half of the republic is occupied by the Tatra Mouns, which have vast forests and pastures used for intensive sheep zing, and are rich in high-grade minerals. The southern part is a plain ned by the River Danube and its tributaries, with farms, vineyards, ards and pastures for stock.

venia

20,251 sq km (7817 sq miles); *population* 1,891,900; *capital* Ljubljana; *other r cities* Maribor, Celje; *form of government* Republic; *religion* RC; *currency* ene Tolar

venia made a unilateral declaration of independence from former oslavia on 25 June 1991. Most of Slovenia is situated in the spectacu-Karst Plateau and in the scenic Julian Alps. Although farming and stock raising are the chief occupations, Slovenia is very industrialized urbanized. Iron, steel and aluminium are produced, and mineral urces include oil, coal and mercury. Tourism is an important industry. northeast of the republic is famous for its wine production.

Solomon Islands

Area 28,896 sq km (11,157 sq m); *population* 308,796; *capital* Honiara; *form of government* Constitutional Monarchy; *religions* Anglicanism, RC, other Christian *currency* Solomon Island dollar

The Solomon Islands lie in an area between 5° and 12° south of Equator to the east of Papua New Guinea, in the Pacific Ocean. The na consists of six large mountainous islands covered with forests innumerable smaller ones. The climate is hot and wet, and typhoons frequent. The main food crops grown are coconut, cassava, sw potatoes, yams, taros and bananas. The forests are worked commerci and a fishing industry is developing.

Somalia

Area 637,657 sq km (246,199 sq miles); *population* 6,260,000; *capital* Mogadish *other major cities* Hargeisa, Baidoa, Burao, Kismaayo; *form of government* Republic; *religion* Sunni Islam; *currency* Somali shilling

Somalia is shaped like a large number seven and lies on the hor Africa's east coast. The country is arid, and most of it is low plateaux scrub vegetation. Most of the population live in the mountains and valleys, and there are a few towns on the coast. Main exports are animals, meat, hides and skins. A few large-scale banana plantation found by the rivers. Years of drought have left Somalia heavily depen on foreign aid.

South Africa

Area 1,221,037 sq km (471,442 sq miles); *population* 30,190,000; *capital* Preto (Administrative), Cape Town (Legislative); *other major cities* Johannesburg, Du Port Elizabeth, Bloemfontein; *form of government* Republic; *religions* Dutch Reformed, Independent African, other Christianity, Hinduism; *currency* Rand

South Africa lies at the southern tip of the African continent and has a coastline on both the Atlantic and Indian Oceans. The country occup huge saucer-shaped plateau, surrounded by a belt of land that dro steps to the sea. In general the climate is healthy, with plenty of suns and relatively low rainfall. Of the total land area, 58% is used as na pasture. The main crops grown are maize, sorghum, wheat, groun and sugar cane. It is South Africa's extraordinary mineral wealth overshadows all its other natural resources. These include gold, copper, iron ore, manganese and chrome ore.

Spain

Area 504,782 sq km (194,896 sq miles); *population* 39,540,000; *capital* Madrid;

r major cities Barcelona, Seville, Zaragosa, Malaga, Bilbao; *form of government* stitutional Monarchy; *religion* RC; *currency* Peseta

ain occupies the greater part of the Iberian peninsula, sealed off from rest of Europe by the Pyrénées. Much of the country is a vast plateau, Meseta Central, cut across by valleys and gorges. Its longest shoreline ne one that borders the Mediterranean Sea. It has a climate with mild ist winters and hot dry summers. Spain's principal agricultural products cereals, vegetables and potatoes, and large areas are under vines for wine industry. Industry represents 72% of the country's export value, production includes textiles, paper, cement, steel and chemicals. irism is a major revenue earner.

Lanka

a 65,610 sq km (25,332 sq miles); *population* 16,810,000; *capital* Colombo; *other or cities* Dehiwela-Mt. Lavinia, Moratuwa, Jaffna; *form of government* Republic; *ions* Buddhism, Hinduism, Christianity, Sunni Islam; *currency* Sri Lankan rupee

Lanka is a teardrop-shaped island lying south of the Indian peninsula. climate is equatorial, but it is affected by both the northeast and thwest monsoons. Agriculture engages 47% of the work force, and the n crops are rice, tea, rubber and coconuts. Amongst the chief minerals ed and exported are precious and semiprecious stones. The main istries are food, tobacco, textiles, clothing, chemicals and plastics.

Christopher (St Kitts) and Nevis

a 261 sq km (101 sq miles); *population* 43,410; *capital* Basseterre; *form of ernment* Constitutional Monarchy; *religions* Anglicanism, Methodism; *currency* : Caribbean dollar

islands of St Christopher (popularly known as St Kitts) and Nevis lie ne Leeward group in the eastern Caribbean. St Kitts consists of three nct volcanoes linked by a sandy isthmus to other volcanic remains in south. Sugar is the chief export crop, but market gardening and stock are being expanded on the steeper slopes above the cane fields. is, 3 km (2 miles) south, is an extinct volcano. Farming is declining e, and tourism is now the main source of income.

Lucia

622 sq km (240 sq miles); *population* 146,600; *capital* Castries; *form of ernment* Constitutional Monarchy; *religion* RC; *currency* East Caribbean dollar

ucia is one of the Windward Islands in the eastern Caribbean, formed xtinct volcanoes. The climate is wet tropical, with a dry season from uary to April. The economy depends on the production of bananas and, to a lesser extent, coconuts. Production, however, is often affected hurricanes, drought and disease. Tourism is becoming an import industry, and Castries, the capital, is a popular calling point for cru liners.

St Vincent and the Grenadines

Area 388 sq km (150 sq miles); *population* 113,950; *capital* Kingstown; *form of government* Constitutional Monarchy; *religions* Anglicanism, Methodism, RC; *currency* East Caribbean dollar

St Vincent is a volcanic island of the Lesser Antilles, in the east Caribbean, separated from Grenada by a chain of some 600 small isla known as the Grenadines, the northern islands of which form the other p of the country. The climate is tropical, with very heavy rain in mountains. The volcano, Soufrière (1234 m/4049 ft), is active and its eruption was in 1979. Farming is the main occupation on the isla Bananas for the United Kingdom are the main export, and it is the wor leading producer of arrowroot starch.

Sudan

Area 2,505,813 sq km (967,494 sq miles); *population* 25,560,000; *capital* Kharto (El Khartum); *other major cities* Omdurman, Khartoum North, Port Sudan; *form c government* Republic; *religions* Sunni Islam, Animism, Christianity; *currency* Sudanese pound

Sudan, the largest country in Africa, covers much of the upper Nile ba The climate is tropical, and temperatures are high throughout the y Rainfall increases in amount from north to south, the northern areas b virtually desert. Sudan is an agricultural country, subsistence farm accounting for 80% of production. Cotton is farmed commercially accounts for about two-thirds of Sudan's exports. Sudan is the wo greatest source of gum arabic, used in medicines and inks.

Suriname

Area 163,265 sq km (63,037 sq miles); *population* 416,839; *capital* Paramaribo; *form of government* Republic; *religions* Hinduism, RC, Sunni Islam; *currency* Suriname guilder

Suriname, in northeast South America, comprises a swampy coastal p a forested central plateau, and southern mountains. The climat tropical, with heavy rainfall. Rice and sugar are farmed on the coa plains, but the mining of bauxite is what the economy depends on. makes up 80% of exports. Suriname has resources of oil and timber these are so far underexploited.

›waziland

›a 1736 sq km (6704 sq miles); *population* 681,059; *capital* Mbabane; *other major* ›es Big Bend, Manzini, Mhlume; *form of government* Monarchy; *religion* ›ristianity, Animism; *currency* emalangeni

›vaziland is a landlocked hilly enclave almost entirely within the borders the Republic of South Africa. The mountains in the west of the country e to almost 2000 m (6562 ft), then descend in steps of savanna towards ›y country in the east. The climate is subtropical, moderated by altitude. ›anges, pineapples and sugar cane are the main crops, and asbestos is ›ned. Swaziland attracts a lot of tourists from South Africa.

›veden

›a 449,964 sq km (173,731 sq miles); *population* 8,500,000; *capital* Stockholm; ›*er major cities* Göteborg, Malmö, Uppsala, Orebro; *form of government* ›nstitutional Monarchy; *religion* Lutheranism; *currency* Krona

›veden is a large country in northern Europe, which makes up half of the ›andinavian peninsula. The south is generally flat, the north mountain-›s. Summers are warm but short, and winters are long and cold. Dairy ›ming is the predominant agricultural activity. Only 7% of Sweden is ›ltivated. About 57% of the country is covered in forest, and the sawmill, ›od pulp and paper industries are all of great importance. Sweden is one the world's leading producers of iron ore. Other principal industries are ›gineering and electrical goods, motor vehicles and furniture making.

›vitzerland

›a 41,293 sq km (15,943 sq miles); *population* 6,700,000; *capital* Berne (Bern); ›*er major cities* Zürich, Basle, Geneva, Lausanne; *form of government* Federal ›ublic; *religions* RC, Protestantism; *currency* Swiss franc

›vitzerland is a landlocked country in central Europe. The Alps occupy the ›uthern half of the country, forming two main east-west chains divided by › rivers Rhine and Rhône. Summers are generally warm and winters ›d, and both are affected by altitude. Northern Switzerland is the ›ustrial part of the country and where its most important cities are ›ated. It is also in this region that the famous cheeses, clocks, watches ›d chocolates are produced. Switzerland has huge earnings from inter-›tional finance and tourism.

›ria

›a 185,180 sq km (71,498 sq miles); *population*: 11,300,000; *capital* Damascus ›nashq); *other major cities* Aleppo, Homs, Lattakia, Hama; *religion* Sunni Islam; ›*rency* Syrian pound

Syria is a country in southwest Asia that borders on the Mediterranean S
in the west. Much of the country is mountainous desert behind a narrc
fertile coastal plain that has hot dry summers and mild wet winters. Abc
50% of the work force get their living from agriculture. Sheep, goats a
cattle are raised, and cotton, barley, wheat, tobacco, fruit and vegetab
are grown. Reserves of oil are small but enough to make the country se
sufficient and to provide three-quarters of the nation's export earnings

Taiwan

Area 36,179 sq km (13,969 sq miles); *population* 20,300,000; *capital* Taipei; *other major cities* Kaohsiung, Taichung, Tainan; *form of government* Republic; *religions* Taoism, Buddhism, Christianity; *currency* New Taiwan dollar

Taiwan is a large mountainous island that lies about 160 km (99 miles) the southeast coast of mainland China. The climate is warm and humid most of the year. The soils are fertile, and a wide range of crops, includi tea, rice, sugar cane and bananas, is grown. Taiwan is a major interr tional trading nation. Exports include machinery, electronics, textil footwear, toys and sporting goods.

Tajikistan

Area 143,100 sq km (55,250 sq miles); *population* 5,100,000; *capital* Dushanbe; *form of Government* Republic; *religion* Shia Islam; *currency* Rouble

Tajikistan, a republic of southern central former USSR, declared its independent in 1991. More than half the country lies over 3000 m (98 ft). Most of the country is desert or semi-desert, and pastoral farming cattle, sheep, horses and goats is important. The lowland areas irrigated so that cotton, mulberry trees, fruit, wheat and vegetables can grown. The republic is rich in deposits of coal, lead, zinc, oil and uraniu which are now being exploited.

Tanzania

Area 945,087 sq km (364,898 sq miles); *population* 24,800,000; *capital* Dodoma; *other major cities* Dar es Salaam, Zanzibar, Mwanza, Tanga; *form of government* Republic; *religions* Sunni Islam, RC, Anglicanism, Hinduism; *currency* Tanzanian shilling

Tanzania lies on the east coast of central Africa, and comprises a la mainland area as well as the islands of Pemba and Zanzibar. T mainland consists mostly of plateaux, broken by mountainous areas, a the Great Rift Valley. The coast is hot and humid, the central plateau dr and the mountains semi-temperate. Some 80% of Tanzanians mak subsistence living from the land. Cash crops include cotton and coff he islands are more successful agriculturally and have important coconut nd clove plantations.

hailand

ea 513,115 sq km (198,114 sq miles); *population* 55,900,00; *capital* Bangkok rung Thep); *other major cities* Chiengmai, Hat Yai, Songkhla; *form of government* onstitutional Monarchy; *religions* Buddhism, Sunni Islam; *currency* Baht

hailand, a kingdom located in southeast Asia, is a tropical country of ountains and jungles, rainforests and green fertile plains. It has a ibtropical climate with heavy monsoon rains. The central plain of hailand contains vast expanses of paddy fields, which produce enough ce to rank Thailand as the world's leading exporter. The narrow southern eninsula is very wet, and it is here that rubber is produced. Thailand is the orld's third largest exporter of rubber.

ogo

ea 56,785 sq km (21,925 sq miles); *population* 3,400,000; *capital* Lomé; *form of vernment* Republic; *religions* Animism, RC, Sunni Islam; *currency* Franc CFA

ogo is a tiny West African country with a narrow coastal plain on the Gulf Guinea and the heavily forested Togo Highlands inland. Over 80% of the opulation are involved in agriculture, with yams and millet as the principal ops. Coffee, cocoa and cotton are grown for cash. Minerals, especially osphates, are now the main export earners.

onga

ea 750 sq km (290 sq miles); *population* 95,200; *capital* Nuku'alofa; *form of vernment* Constitutional Monarchy; *religions* Methodism, RC; *currency* Pa'anga

onga is situated about 20° south of the Equator and just west of the ernational Date Line in the Pacific Ocean. It comprises over 170 islands, ly about one-fifth of which are inhabited. The climate is warm, with heavy infall. Yams, cassava and taro are grown as subsistence crops, and fish om the sea supplements the diet. Bananas and coconuts are grown for port. The main industry is coconut processing.

inidad and Tobago

ea 5130 sq km (1981 sq miles); *population* 1,240,000; *capital* Port-of-Spain; *form government* Republic; *religions* RC, Hinduism, Anglicanism, Sunni Islam; *rrency* Trinidad and Tobago dollar

inidad and Tobago, situated off northeastern Venezuela, are the most utherly of the islands of the Lesser Antilles. Trinidad consists of a ountainous region in the north and undulating plains in the south. Tobago is more mountainous. The climate is tropical. Trinidad is one of the olde oil-producing countries in the world. Output is small but provides 90% Trinidad's exports. Sugar, coffee and cocoa are grown for export, b imports of food now account for 10% of total imports. Tobago depen mainly on tourism to make a living.

Tunisia

Area 163,610 sq km (63,170 sq miles); *population* 7,750,000; *capital* Tunis; *other major cities* Sfax, Bizerta, Djerba; *form of government* Republic; *religion* Sunni Islam; *currency* Tunisian dinar

Tunisia is a North African country consisting of hills, plains and valleys the northern central mountains and the Sahara Desert in the sou Climate ranges from warm temperate in the north to desert in the sou Some 40% of the population are engaged in agriculture. The mainstay Tunisia's modern economy, however, is oil from the Sahara, phosphat and tourism on the Mediterranean coast.

Turkey

Area 779,452 sq km (300,946 sq miles); *population* 50,670,000; *capital* Ankara; *other major cities* Istanbul, Izmir, Adana, Bursa; *form of government* Republic; *religion* Sunni Islam; *currency* Turkish lira

With land on the continents of Europe and Asia, Turkey forms a brid between the two. It guards the sea passage between the Mediterrane Sea and the Black Sea. Its landscapes vary from fertile lowlands European Turkey to high coastal mountains and central plains in Asi Anatolia. The climate ranges from Mediterranean on the coasts to h summers and bitterly cold winters in the central plains. Agriculture e ploys over half the work force. Major crops are wheat, rice, tobacco a cotton. Manufacturing industry includes iron and steel, textiles, mo vehicles and the production of carpets for which the country is famo Tourism is a fast-developing industry.

Turkmenistan

Area 488,100 sq km (186,400 sq miles); *population* 3,600,000; *capital* Ashkhabad *form of government* Republic; *religion* Sunni Islam; *currency* Rouble

Turkmenistan, a central Asian republic of the former USSR, declared its a republic in 1991. Much of the west and central areas are covered by sandy Kara Kum Desert, while the east is a plateau. The climate extremely dry, and most of the population live in oasis settlements near rivers, where agriculture is intensive. There are rich mineral depos especially natural gas. Silk, oil and sulphur are also produced.

ıvalu

ea 26 sq km (10 sq miles); *population* 8229; *capital* Funafuti; *form of government* nstitutional Monarchy; *religion* Protestantism; *currency* Australian dollar

ıvalu is located just north of Fiji, in the South Pacific, and consists of nine ral atolls. The climate is tropical. Coconut palms are the main crop, and it and vegetables are grown for local consumption. Sea fishing is tremely good although largely unexploited. Most export revenue comes m the sale of elaborate postage stamps to philatelists.

ganda

ea 235,880 sq km (91,073 sq miles); *population* 17,000,000; *capital* Kampala; *er major cities* Jinja, Masaka, Mbale; *form of government* Republic; *religions* RC, otestantism, Animism, Sunni Islam; *currency* Uganda shilling

jandu is a landlocked country in east central Africa, and for the most part s a richly fertile land, well watered, with a kindly climate. The lowlands ound Lake Victoria, once forested, have now mostly been cleared for ltivation. Agriculture employs over three-quarters of the labour force, d the main crops grown for subsistence are plantains, cassava and eet potatoes. Coffee is the main cash crop and accounts for 90% of the untry's exports.

kraine

a 603,700 sq km (233,100 sq miles); *population* 51,700,000; *capital* Kiev; *other jor cities* Dnepropetrovsk, Donetsk, Kharkov, Odessa; *form of government* public; *religions* Russian Orthodox, RC; *currency* Rouble

raine, formerly a Soviet republic, declared itself independent in 1991. It nsists largely of fertile steppes. The climate is continental, although this greatly modified by the proximity of the Black Sea. It is one of the chief eat-producing regions of Europe. Other major crops include corn, sugar et, flax, tobacco, soya, hops and potatoes. There are rich reserves of al and raw materials for industry. The central and eastern regions form e of the world's densest industrial concentrations. Manufacturing indus-s include ferrous metallurgy, machine building, chemicals, food process-, and gas and oil refining.

ited Arab Emirates

a 83,600 sq km (32,278 sq miles); *population* 1,600,000; *capital* Abu Dhabi; *er major cities* Dubai, Sharjh, Ras al Khaymah; *form of government* Monarchy irates); *religion* Sunni Islam; *currency* Dirham

e United Arab Emirates is a federation of seven oil-rich sheikdoms ated on The Gulf. The land is mainly flat infertile sandy desert. The summers are hot and humid, with temperatures reaching 49°C, but fr October to May the weather is warm and sunny with pleasant, c evenings. Abu Dhabi and Dubai are the main industrial centres, and, us the wealth from the oil industry, they are now diversifying industry building aluminium smelters, cement factories and steel-rolling mills.

United Kingdom

Area 244,100 sq km (94,247 sq miles); *population* 57,240,000; *capital* London; *o major cities* Birmingham, Manchester, Glasgow, Liverpool; *form of government* Constitutional Monarchy; *religion* Anglicanism, RC, Presbyterianism, Methodism; *currency* Pound sterling

Situated in northwest Europe, the United Kingdom comprises the islan Great Britain and the northeast of Ireland, plus many smaller islar especially off the west coast of Scotland. The south and east is low-ly and fertile, while the rest is hilly, with large areas of rugged mountain northern Scotland. The climate is cool temperate, with mild conditions an even annual rainfall. Mixed farming is highly mechanized. Fishin important off the east coast. It is primarily an industrial country, althou the recent recession has led to the decline of some of the older industr such as coal, textiles and heavy engineering.

United States of America

Area 9,372,614 sq km (3,618,766 sq miles); *population* 249,630,000; *capital* Washington D.C.; *other major cities* New York, Chicago, Detroit, Houston, Los Angeles, Philadelphia, San Diego, San Francisco; *form of government* Federal Republic; *religion* Protestantism, RC, Judaism, Eastern Orthodox; *currency* US dollar

The United States of America stretches across central North Amer from the Atlantic Ocean to the Pacific Ocean. It consists of fifty sta including outlying Alaska and Hawaii. The climate varies from p conditions to the subtropical. Although agricultural production is hig employs only 1.5% of the population because of advanced technolo The United States is a world leader in oil production. The main indus are iron and steel, chemicals, motor vehicles, aircraft, telecommunicat equipment, computers, electronics and textiles. It is the richest and m powerful nation in the world.

Uruguay

Area 177,414 sq km (68,500 sq miles); *population* 3,100,000; *capital* Montevide *form of government* Republic; *religions* RC, Protestantism; *currency* Uruguayan nuevo peso

uguay, a small country lying on the east coast of South America, nsists of low plains and plateaux. About 90% of the land is suitable for riculture but only 10% is cultivated, the remainder being used to graze st herds of cattle and sheep. Uruguay has only one major city, in which lf the population live. The country has no mineral resources, oil or gas, t has built hydroelectric power stations.

zbekistan

a 449,500 sq km (173,546 sq miles); *population* 20,300,000; *capital* Tashkent; *er major city* Samarkand; *form of government* Republic; *religion* Sunni Islam; *rency* Rouble

bekistan, a central Asian republic of the former USSR, declared itself lependent in 1991. It has varied landscapes: mountainous Tian Shan, oil-rich Kyzlkum Desert, the stony Usturt Plateau, and the irrigated and tile Fergana and lower Amudar'ya river regions. Uzbekistan is a major tton producer, and Karakul lambs are reared for wool and meat.

nuatu

a 12,189 sq km (4706 sq miles); *population* 142,630; *capital* Vila; *form of ernment* Republic; *religion* Protestantism, Animism; *currency* Vatu

nuatu, located in the western Pacific, comprises about eighty islands, me of which are mountainous and include active volcanoes. Vanuatu s a tropical climate that is moderated by the southeast trade winds from y to October. The majority of the labour force are engaged in subsistce farming, and the main exports include copra, fish and cocoa.

tican City State

a 44 hectares (108.7 acres); *population* 1000; *capital* Vatican City (Città del icano); *form of government* Papal Commission; *religion* RC; *currency* Vatican lira

tican City State, in the heart of Rome, is the world's smallest independt state and headquarters of the Roman Catholic Church. It has its own ice, newspaper, coinage, stamps and radio station. Its main tourist actions are the frescoes of the Sistine Chapel, painted by Michelangelo. e Pope exercises sovereignty and has absolute legislative, executive d judicial powers.

nezuela

a 912,050 sq km (352,143 sq miles); *population* 9,250,000; *capital*: Caracas; *er major cities* Maracaibo, Valencia, Barquisimeto; *form of government* Federal public; *religion* RC; *currency* Bolívar

Venezuela forms the northernmost crest of South America. In the nor west a spur of the Andes runs southwest to northeast. The River Orinc cuts the country in two, and north of the river run the undulating plai known as the Llanos. South of the river are the Guiana Highlands. T climate ranges from warm temperate to tropical. In the Llanos area, cat are herded across the plains. Sugar cane and coffee are grown for expc but petroleum and gas account for 95% of export earnings. The oil fie lie in the northwest, near Lake Maracaibo.

Vietnam

Area 331,689 sq km (128,065 sq miles); *population* 65,000,000; *capital* Hanoi; *oth major cities* Ho Chi Minh City, Haiphong; *form of government* Socialist Republic; *religion* Buddhism, Taoism, RC; *currency* Dong

Vietnam is a long narrow country in southeast Asia, which runs down t coast of the South China Sea. It has a central hilly area that links broa plains centred on the Red and Mekong rivers. The climate is humid, w tropical conditions in the south and subtropical in the north. The far nc can be very cold when polar air blows over Asia. Agriculture employs ov three-quarters of the labour force. The main crop is rice. Rubber, tea a coffee are grown for export. Vietnam, however, remains underdevelop and is still recovering from the ravages of many wars this century.

Western Samoa

Area 2831 sq km (1093 sq miles); *population* 163,000; *capital* Apia; *form of government* Constitutional Monarchy; *religion* Protestantism; *currency* Tala

Western Samoa, lying in the Polynesian sector of the Pacific Oce consists of seven small islands and two larger volcanic islands. T climate is tropical, with high temperatures and very heavy rainfall. Subs ence agriculture is the main activity, and copra, cocoa and bananas are main exports. Many tourists visit the grave of the Scottish writer Rob Louis Stevenson, who died here and whose home is now the official ho of the king.

Yemen

Area 195,000 sq km (75,290 sq miles); *population* 12,000,000; *capital* Sana'a; *commercial capital* Aden; *form of government* Republic; *religion* Zaidism, Shia Isl Sunni Islam; *currency* Riyal and dinar

Yemen is bounded by Saudi Arabia in the north, Oman in the east, the C of Aden in the south, and the Red Sea in the west. Most of the cour comprises rugged mountains and trackless desert lands. It is alm entirely dependent on agriculture even though a very small percentag rtile. The main crops are coffee, cotton, millet, sorghum and fruit. Fishing an important industry. Other industry is on a very small scale.

ugoslavia

ea 127,886 sq km (49,377 sq miles); *population* 11,807,098; *capital* Belgrade eograd); *other major cities* Nis, Skopje, Titograd; *form of government* Federal epublic; *religions* Eastern Orthodox; *currency* Dinar

ugoslavia today refers only to the republics of Serbia, Montenegro and acedonia, the other republics having gained independence in 1991–92. acedonia may follow suit. The economy is largely agricultural, but ports include chemicals, machinery, textiles and clothing.

aïre

ea 2,345,409 sq km (905,562 sq miles); *population* 34,140,000; *capital* Kinshasa; *ner major cities* Lubumbashi, Mbuji-Mayi, Kananga; *form of government* Republic; *igion* RC, Protestantism, Animism; *currency* Zaïre

tuated in west central Africa, Zaïre is a vast country with a very short astline on the Atlantic Ocean. Mountain ranges and plateaux surround e Zaïre Basin, drained by the river Zaïre and its main tributaries. The mate is equatorial, and rainforests, containing valuable hardwoods, ver about half the country. Agriculture employs 75% of the population, t less than 3% of the country can be cultivated. Grazing land is limited the infestation of the tsetse fly. Cassava is the main subsistence crop, d coffee, tea, cocoa, rubber and palms are grown for export. Minerals, ainly copper, cobalt, zinc and diamonds, account for 60% of exports.

ambia

ea 752,614 sq km (290,584 sq miles); *population* 8,500,000; *capital* Lusaka; *other ijor cities* Kitwe, Ndola, Mufulira; *form of government* Republic; *religion* Christian-, Animism; *currency* Kwacha

mbia, situated in central Africa, is made up of high plateaux, large rivers, d lakes. The climate is tropical, modified somewhat by altitude. The untry has a wide range of wildlife, and there are large game parks on the angwa and Kafue rivers. Agriculture is underdeveloped, and most odstuffs have to be imported. Zambia's economy relies heavily on the ning of copper, lead, zinc and cobalt.

mbabwe

ea 390,580 sq km (150,803 sq miles); *population* 9,370,000; *capital* Harare; *other ijor cities* Bulawayo, Mutare, Gweru; *form of government* Republic; *religion* imism, Anglicanism, RC; *currency* Zimbabwe dollar

nbabwe, landlocked, in southern Africa, is a country with spectacular physical features and is teeming with wildlife. It is bordered in the north the Zambezi river, which flows over the mile-wide Victoria Falls befo entering Lake Kariba. In the south, the River Limpopo marks its border w South Africa. A great plateau between 1200 m (3937 ft) and 1500 m (49 ft) high occupies the central area. Massive granite outcrops, called *kopje* also dot the landscape. The climate is tropical in the lowlands a subtropical in the higher land. About 75% of the labour force are employ in agriculture. Tobacco, sugar cane, cotton, wheat and maize are export and form the basis of processing industries. Tourism is a major grow industry.

Principal Mountains of the World

ame (location)	Height (m)	(ft)
verest (Asia)	8848	29,028
odwin-Austen or K2 (Asia)	8611	28,250
angchenjunga (Asia)	8586	28,170
akalu (Asia)	8463	27,766
haulagiri (Asia)	8167	26,795
anga Parbat (Asia)	8125	26,657
nnapurna (Asia)	8091	26,545
osainthan (Asia)	8012	26,286
anda Devi (Asia)	7816	25,643
amet (Asia)	7756	25,446
amcha Barwa (Asia)	7756	25,446
urla Mandhata (Asia)	7728	25,355
ongur (Asia)	7720	25,325
ich Mir (Asia)	7691	25,230
nya Kanka (Asia)	7556	24,790
la Kangri (Asia)	7555	24,784
uztagh Ata (Asia)	7546	24,757
mmunizma (Asia)	7495	24,590
bedy (Asia)	7439	24,406
omo Lhar (Asia)	7313	23,992
nina (Asia)	7134	23,405
ongagua (S Amer)	6960	22,834
os del Salado (S Amer)	6908	22,664
pungato (S Amer)	6801	22,310
ascarán (S Amer)	6769	22,205
llailaco (S Amer)	6723	22,057
ilas (Asia)	6714	22,027
ngri Khan (Asia)	6695	21,965
jama (S Amer)	6542	21,463
imborazo (S Amer)	6310	20,702
Kinley (N Amer)	6194	20,320
gan (N Amer)	5951	19,524
topaxi (S Amer)	5896	19,344
imanjaro (Africa)	5895	19,340

Name (location)	Height (m)	(ft)
Huila (S Amer)	5750	18,865
Citlaltepi (C Amer)	5699	18,697
Demavend (Asia)	5664	18,582
Elbrus (Asia)	5642	18,510
St Elias (N Amer)	5489	18,008
Popocatepetl (C Amer)	5452	17,887
Foraker (N Amer)	5304	17,400
Ixtaccihuati (C Amer)	5286	17,342
Dykh Tau (Europe)	5203	17,070
Kenya (Africa)	5200	17,058
Ararat (Asia)	5165	16,945
Vinson Massif (Antarctica)	5140	16,863
Kazbek (Europe)	5047	16,558
Jaya (Asia)	5030	16,502
Klyucheveyskava (Asia)	4750	15,584
Mont Blanc (Europe)	4808	15,774
Vancouver (N Amer)	4786	15,700
Trikora (Asia)	4750	15,584
Monte Rosa (Europe)	4634	15,203
Ras Dashen (Africa)	4620	15,158
Belukha (Asia)	4506	14,783
Markham (Antarctica)	4350	14,271
Meru (Africa)	4566	14,979
Karisimbi (Africa)	4508	14,787
Weisshorn (Europe)	4505	14,780
Matterhorn/Mont Cervin (Europe)	4477	14,690
Whitney (N Amer)	4418	14,495
Elbert (N Amer)	4399	14,431
Massive Mount (N Amer)	4397	14,424
Rainier or Tacoma (N Amer)	4392	14,410
Longs (N Amer)	4345	14,255
Elgon (Africa)	4321	14,176
Pikes Peak (N Amer)	4301	14,110
Finsteraarhorn (Europe)	4274	14,022

Principal Mountains of the World (contd)

Name (location)	Height (m)	(ft)	Name (location)	Height (m)	(
Wrangell (N Amer)	4269	14,005	Assiniboine (N Amer)	3618	11,87
Mauna Kea (N Amer)	4205	13,796	Hood (N Amer)	3428	11,2
Gannet (N Amer)	4202	13,785	Pico de Aneto (Europe)	3404	11,1
Mauna Loa (N Amer)	4169	13,677	Etna (Europe)	3323	10,9
Jungfrau (Europe)	4158	13,642	St Helens (N Amer)	2950	967
Kings (N Amer)	4124	13,528	Pulog (Asia)	2934	96
Kinabalu (Asia)	4102	13,455	Tahat (Africa)	2918	957
Cameroon (Africa)	4095	13,435	Shishaldin (N Amer)	2862	93
Fridtjof Nansen (Antarctica)	4068	13,346	Roraima (S Amer)	2810	92
Tacaná (C Amer)	4064	13,333	Ruapehu (Oceania)	2797	917
Waddington (N Amer)	4042	13,262	Katherine (N Amer)	2637	86
Yu Shan (Asia)	3997	13,113	Doi Inthanon (Asia)	2594	85
Truchas (C Amer)	3994	13,102	Galdhöpiggen (Europe)	2469	81
Wheeler (N Amer)	3981	13,058	Parnassus (Europe)	2457	80
Robson (N Amer)	3954	12,972	Olympus (N Amer)	2425	79
Granite (N Amer)	3902	12,799	Kosciusko (Oceania)	2230	73
Borah (N Amer)	3858	12,655	Harney (N Amer)	2208	72
Monte Viso (Europe)	3847	12,621	Mitchell (N Amer)	2038	66
Kerinci (Asia)	3805	12,483	Clingmans Dome (N Amer)	2025	66
Grossglockner (Europe)	3797	12,460	Washington (N Amer)	1917	62
Erebus (Antarctica)	3794	12,447	Rogers (N Amer)	1807	59
Fujiyama (Asia)	3776	12,388	Marcy (N Amer)	1629	53
Cook (Oceania)	3753	12,313	Cirque (N Amer)	1573	51
Adams (N Amer)	3752	12,307	Pelée (C Amer)	1463	48
Teyde or Tenerife (Africa)	3718	12,198	Ben Nevis (Europe)	1344	44
Mahameru (Asia)	3676	12,060	Vesuvius (Europe)	1281	42

Principal Rivers of the World

ne (location)	Length (km)	(miles)
(Africa)	6695	4160
azon (S Amer)	6516	4050
gtze (Asia)	6380	3965
sissippi-Missouri (N Amer)	6019	3740
Irtysh (Asia)	5570	3460
isel-Angara (Asia)	5553	3450
ang Ho (Asia)	5464	3395
e (Africa)	4667	2900
ong (Asia)	4426	2750
ur (Asia)	4416	2744
a (Asia)	4400	2730
kenzie (N Amer)	4250	2640
er (Africa)	4032	2505
aná (S Amer)	4000	2485
souri (N Amer)	3969	2466
sissippi (N Amer)	3779	2348
ray-Darling (Oceania)	3750	2330
a (Europe)	3686	2290
eira (S Amer)	3203	1990
awrence (N Amer)	3203	1990
on (N Amer)	3187	1980
s (Asia)	3180	1975
Darya (Asia)	3079	1913
ing (Oceania)	3057	1900
veen (Asia)	3060	1901
Grande (N Amer)	3034	1885
Francisco (S Amer)	2897	1800
ube (Europe)	2850	1770
maputra (Asia)	2840	1765
hrates (Asia)	2815	1750
-Tocantins (S Amer)	2752	1710
ma (Asia)	2600	1600
ges (Asia)	2525	1568
nsas (N Amer)	2350	1460
rado (N Amer)	2330	1450

Name (location)	Length (km)	(miles)
Xi Jiang (Asia)	2300	1437
Dnepr (Europe)	2285	1420
Negro (S Amer)	2254	1400
Aldan (Asia)	2242	1393
Irrawaddy (Asia)	2150	1335
Ohio (N Amer)	2102	1306
Orange (Africa)	2090	1299
Kama (Europe)	2028	1260
Xingú (S Amer)	2012	1250
Columbia (N Amer)	1950	1210
Juruá (S Amer)	1932	1200
Peace (N Amer)	1923	1195
Tigris (Asia)	1900	1180
Don (Europe)	1870	1165
Pechora (Europe)	1814	1127
Araguaya (S Amer)	1771	1100
Snake (N Amer)	1670	1038
Red (N Amer)	1639	1018
Churchill (N Amer)	1610	1000
Marañón (S Amer)	1610	1000
Pilcomayo (S Amer)	1610	1000
Ucayali (S Amer)	1610	1000
Uruguay (S Amer)	1610	1000
Magdalena (S Amer)	1529	950
Oka (Europe)	1481	920
Canadian (N Amer)	1459	906
Godavari (Asia)	1465	910
Parnaíba (S Amer)	1449	900
Dnestr (Europe)	1411	877
Brazos (N Amer)	1401	870
Fraser (N Amer)	1370	850
Salado (S Amer)	1368	850
Rhine (Europe)	1320	825
Narmada (Asia)	1288	800
Tobol (Asia)	1288	800

Principal Rivers of the World (contd)

Name (location)	Length (km)	(miles)	Name (location)	Length (km)	(m
Athabaska (N Amer)	1231	765	Loire (Europe)	1012	
Pecos (N Amer)	1183	735	Tagus (Europe)	1007	
Green (N Amer)	1175	730	Tisza (Europe)	997	
Elbe (Europe)	1160	720	North Platte (N Amer)	995	
Ottawa (N Amer)	1121	696	Ouachita (N Amer)	974	
White (N Amer)	1111	690	Sava (Europe)	940	
Cumberland (N Amer)	1106	687	Neman (Europe)	937	
Vistula (Europe)	1090	677	Oder (Europe)	910	
Yellowstone (N Amer)	1080	671	Cimarron (N Amer)	805	
Donets (Europe)	1079	670	Gila (N Amer)	805	
Tennesse (N Amer)	1050	652	Gambia (Africa)	483	

Continents of the World

	Highest Point (m)	(ft)	Area (sq km)	(sq m
Asia	8848	29,028	43,608,000	16,833
Africa	5895	19,340	30,335,000	11,710
North & Central America	6194	20,320	25,349,000	9,785
South America	6960	22,834	17,611,000	6,798
Antarctica	5140	16,863	14,000,000	5,400
Europe	5642	18,510	10,498,000	4,052
Oceania	4205	13,796	8,900,000	3,400

Oceans of the World

	Maximum Depth (m)	(ft)	Area (sq km)	(sq m
Pacific	11,033	36,198	165,384,000	63,838
Atlantic	8381	27,496	82,217,000	31,736
Indian	8047	26,401	73,481,000	28,364
Arctic	5450	17,880	14,056,000	5,426

Principal Waterfalls of the World

e (location)	Height (m)	(ft)
el (S Amer)	979	3212
mite (N Amer)	740	2,425
naãm (S Amer)	610	2,000
erland (Oceania)	581	1904
omombie (Oceania)	519	1700
on (N Amer)	492	1612
r Yosemite (N Amer)	436	1430
rnie (Europe)	422	1384
la (Africa)	412	1350
akau (N Amer)	366	1200
bach (Europe)	300	984
melbach (Europe)	290	950
e Cascade (N Amer)	278	910
foss (Europe)	271	889
Edward VIII (S Amer)	256	840
ppa (Asia)	253	830
efos (Europe)	250	820
eur (S Amer)	226	741
nbo (Africa)	222	726
dalsfos (Europe)	199	650
sunyane (Africa)	192	630
veil (N Amer)	189	620
omah (N Amer)	189	620
gfoss (Europe)	182	597
da (N Amer)	181	594
(Europe)	180	590
gedalsfoss (Europe)	160	525
a (S Amer)	153	500
abies (Africa)	147	480
ndama (S Amer)	131	427

Name (location)	Height (m)	(ft)
Guaíra (S Amer)	114	374
Illilouette (N Amer)	113	370
Victoria (Africa)	108	355
Kegon-no-tali (Asia)	101	330
Lower Yosemite (N Amer)	98	320
Cauvery (Asia)	98	320
Vernal (N Amer)	97	317
Virginia (N Amer)	96	315
Lower Yellowstone (N Amer)	94	308
Churchill (N Amer)	92	302
Reichenbach (Europe)	91	300
Sluiskin (N Amer)	91	300
Lower Gastein (Europe)	86	280
Paulo Alfonso (S Amer)	84	275
Snoqualmie (N Amer)	82	268
Seven (N Amer)	81	266
Montmorency (N Amer)	77	251
Handegg (Europe)	76	250
Taughannock (N Amer)	66	215
Iguassú (S Amer)	64	210
Shoshone (N Amer)	64	210
Upper Gastein (Europe)	63	207
Comet (N Amer)	61	200
Narada (N Amer)	52	168
Niagara (N Amer)	51	167
Tower (N Amer)	41	132
Stora Sjöfallet (Europe)	40	131
Kabalega (Africa)	40	130
Upper Yellowstone (N Amer)	34	109

Cartography designed and produced by Euromap Ltd, Pangbourne, Berkshire.

This edition published 1993 by Bloomsbury Books, an imprint of The Godfrey Cave Group, 42 Bloomsbury Street, London, WC1B 3QJ.

ISBN 1 85471 109 1

Printed and bound by New Interlitho, Milan, Italy.